...LACE
...ADOKAWA CORPORATION, Tokyo.
...th KADOKAWA CORPORATION, Tokyo.

...duced or transmitted in any form without
... holders. This is a work of fiction. Names,
characters, places, and incidents are the products of the author's imagination
or are used fictitiously. Any resemblance to actual events, locales, or persons,
living or dead, is entirely coincidental.

Seven Seas books may be purchased in bulk for promotional, educational, or
business use. Please contact your local bookseller or the Macmillan Corporate
and Premium Sales Department at 1-800-221-7945, extension 5442, or by
e-mail at MacmillanSpecialMarkets@macmillan.com.

Seven Seas and the Seven Seas logo are trademarks of
Seven Seas Entertainment, LLC. All rights reserved.

ISBN: 978-1-626928-10-7

Printed in Canada

First Printing: October 2018

10 9 8 7 6 5 4 3 2 1

COVER DESIGN
Nicky Lim

PROOFREADER
Brett Hallahan

ASSISTANT EDITOR
Jenn Grunigen

PRODUCTION ASSISTANT
CK Russell

PRODUCTION MANAGER
Lissa Pattillo

EDITOR-IN-CHIEF
Adam Arnold

PUBLISHER
Jason DeAngelis

FOLLOW US ONLINE: *www.sevenseasentertainment.com*

READING DIRECTIONS

This book reads from *right to left*, Japanese style.
If this is your first time reading manga, you start
reading from the top right panel on each page and
take it from there. If you get lost, just follow the
numbered diagram here. It may seem backwards at
first, but you'll get the hang of it! Have fun!!

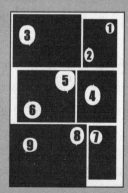

Afterword

ZOWLS

I hope you enjoyed the third volume of *Nirvana.* Yachiyo has grown a little after exchanging blows with her rival, but now she has hit another hurdle in this volume.

How will she face the unimaginable darkness that looms ahead? I hope you enjoy the heated twists of the next volume, as well.

By the way, Yachiyo got a hole in her stomach at the end of this volume. I hope she is okay. Her creators also get stomachaches often, so we are a bit worried.

I truly hope that you continue to support Yachiyo as she tries her best.

See you next time!

Here's some patil soft serve.
Wow!!
I thought I'd never get a chance to eat it!
This is like a dream...!
Thank you for the--!

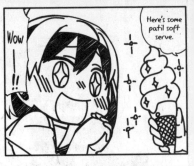

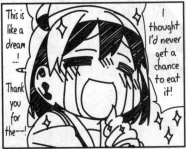

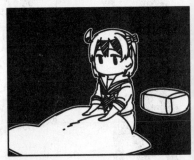

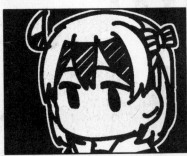

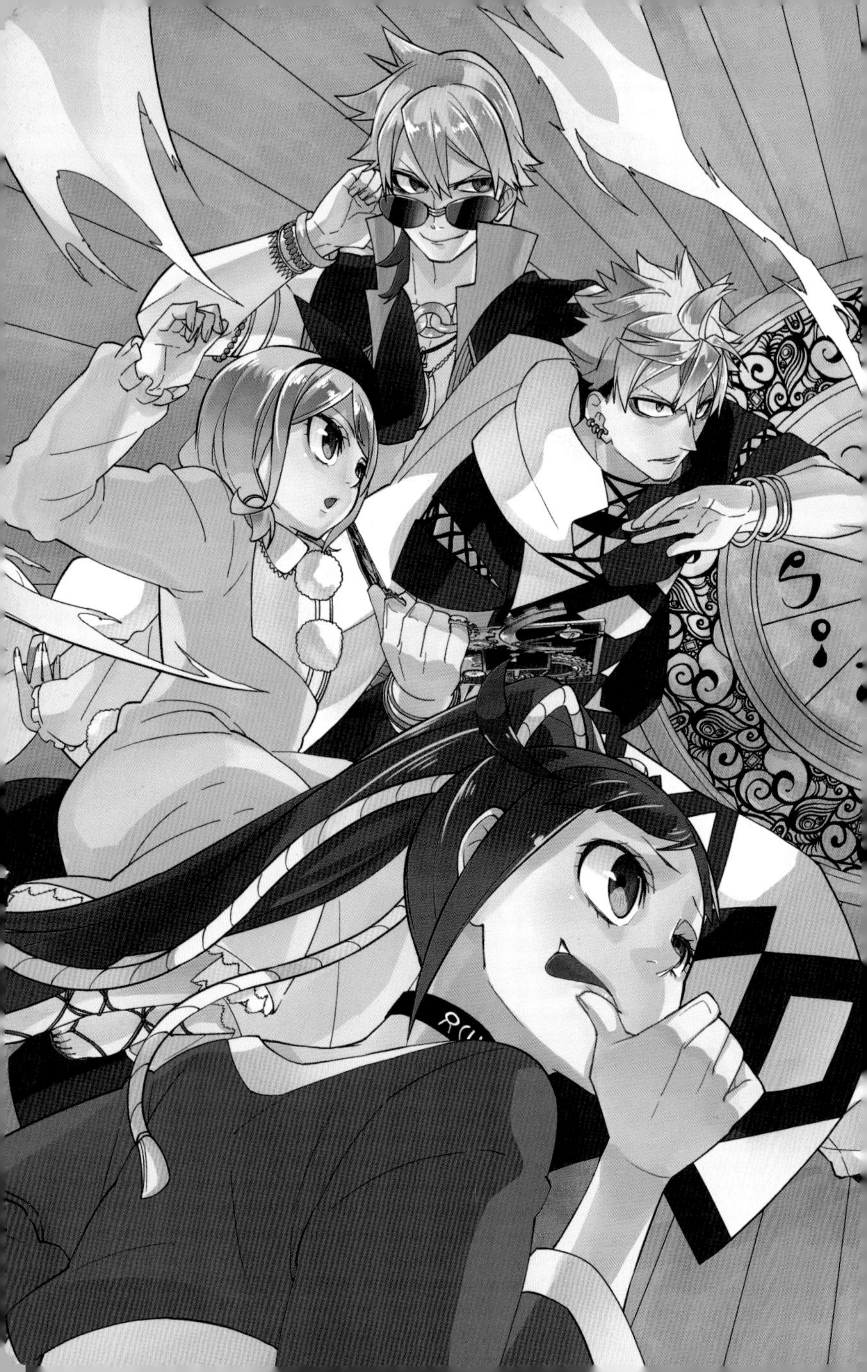

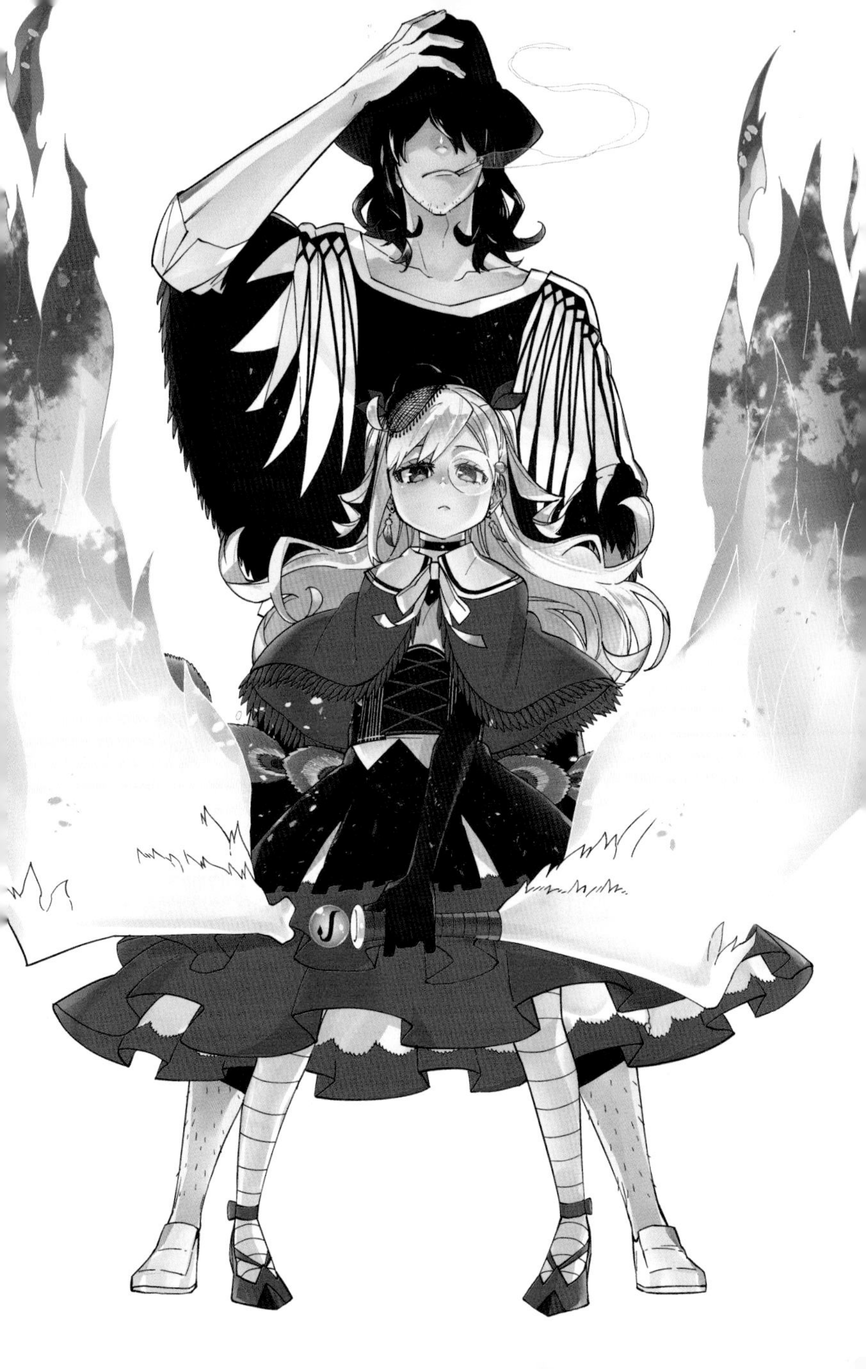

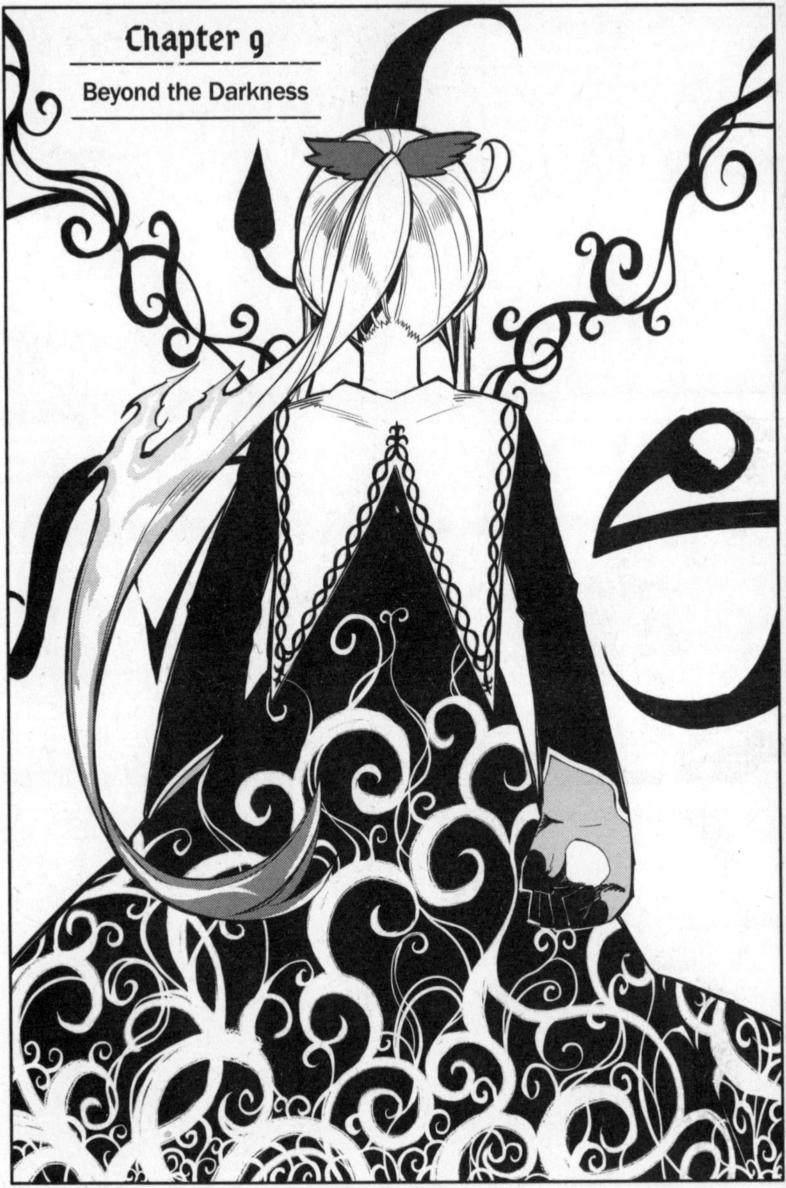
Chapter 9
Beyond the Darkness

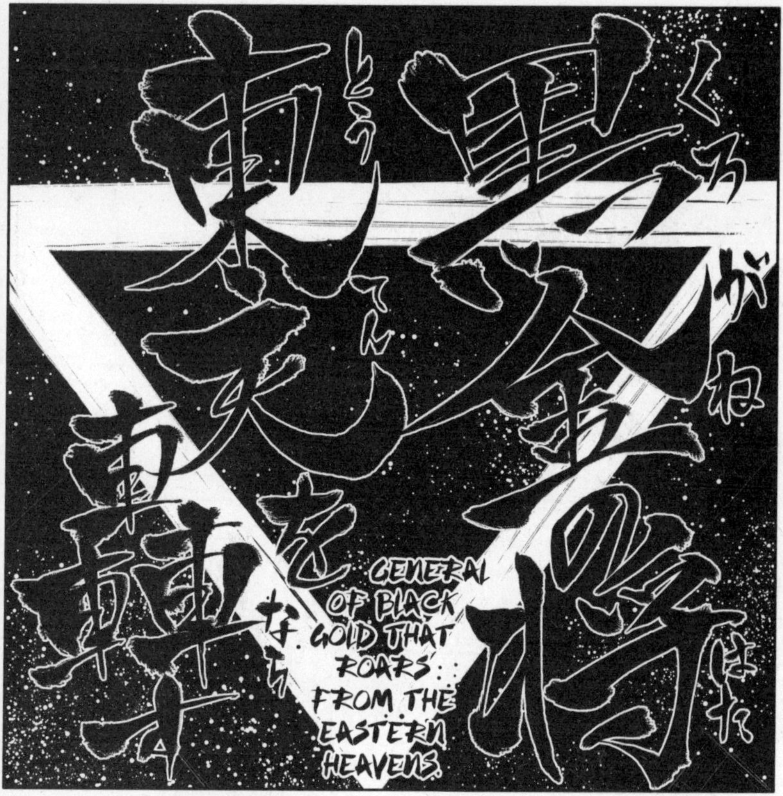
黒金の将
東天を轟
GENERAL OF BLACK GOLD THAT ROARS FROM THE EASTERN HEAVENS.

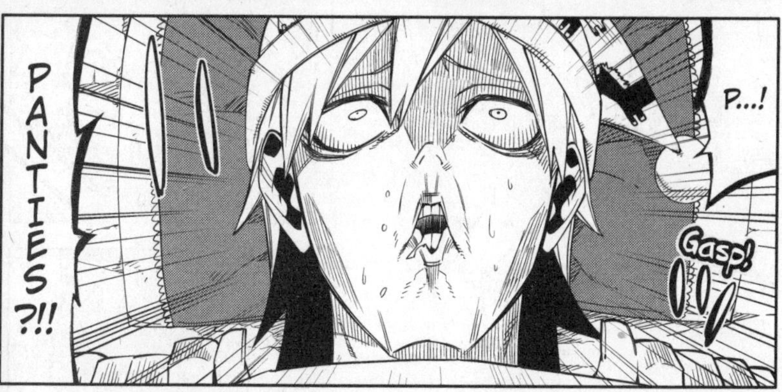
P...!
Gasp!
PANTIES?!!

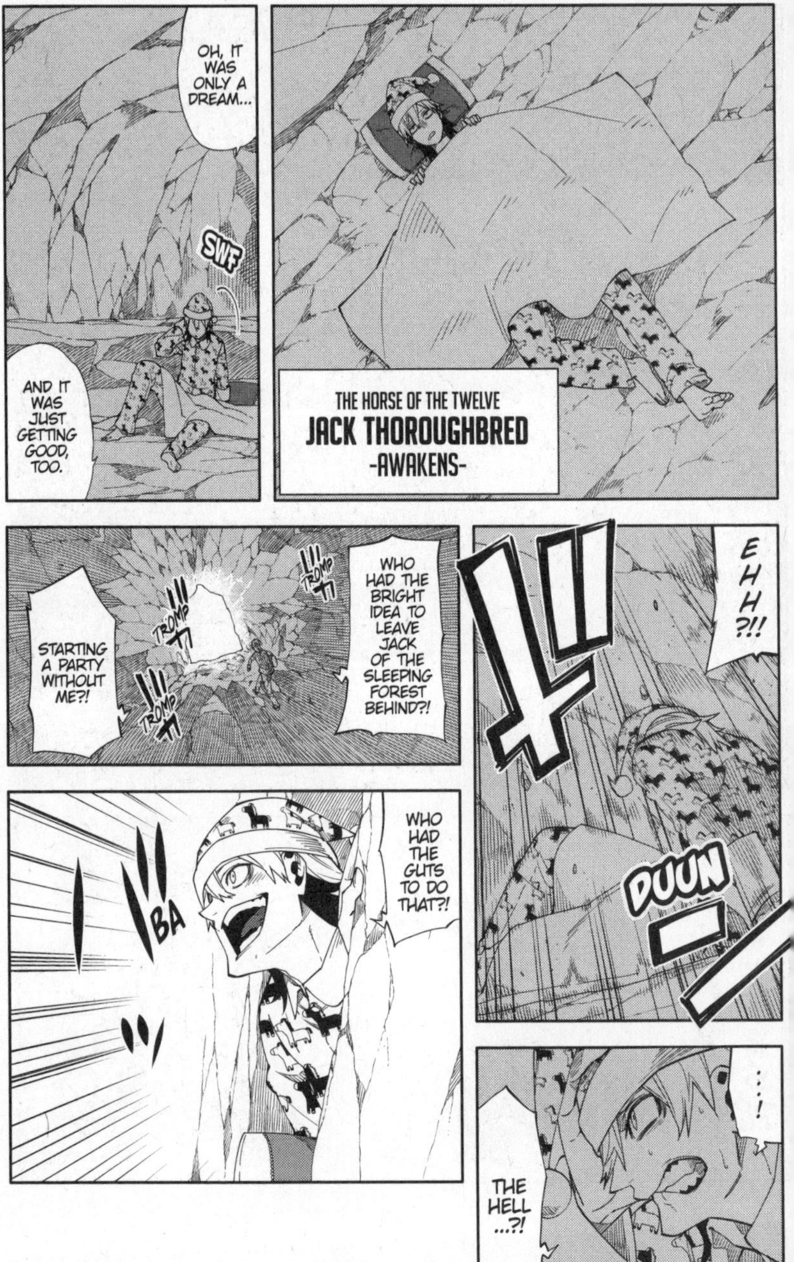
THE HORSE OF THE TWELVE
JACK THOROUGHBRED
-AWAKENS-
OH, IT WAS ONLY A DREAM...
SWF
AND IT WAS JUST GETTING GOOD, TOO.
EHH?!!
!!
DUUN
...!
THE HELL ...?!
WHO HAD THE BRIGHT IDEA TO LEAVE JACK OF THE SLEEPING FOREST BEHIND?!
TROMP
TROMP
STARTING A PARTY WITHOUT ME?!
TROMP
WHO HAD THE GUTS TO DO THAT?!
BA

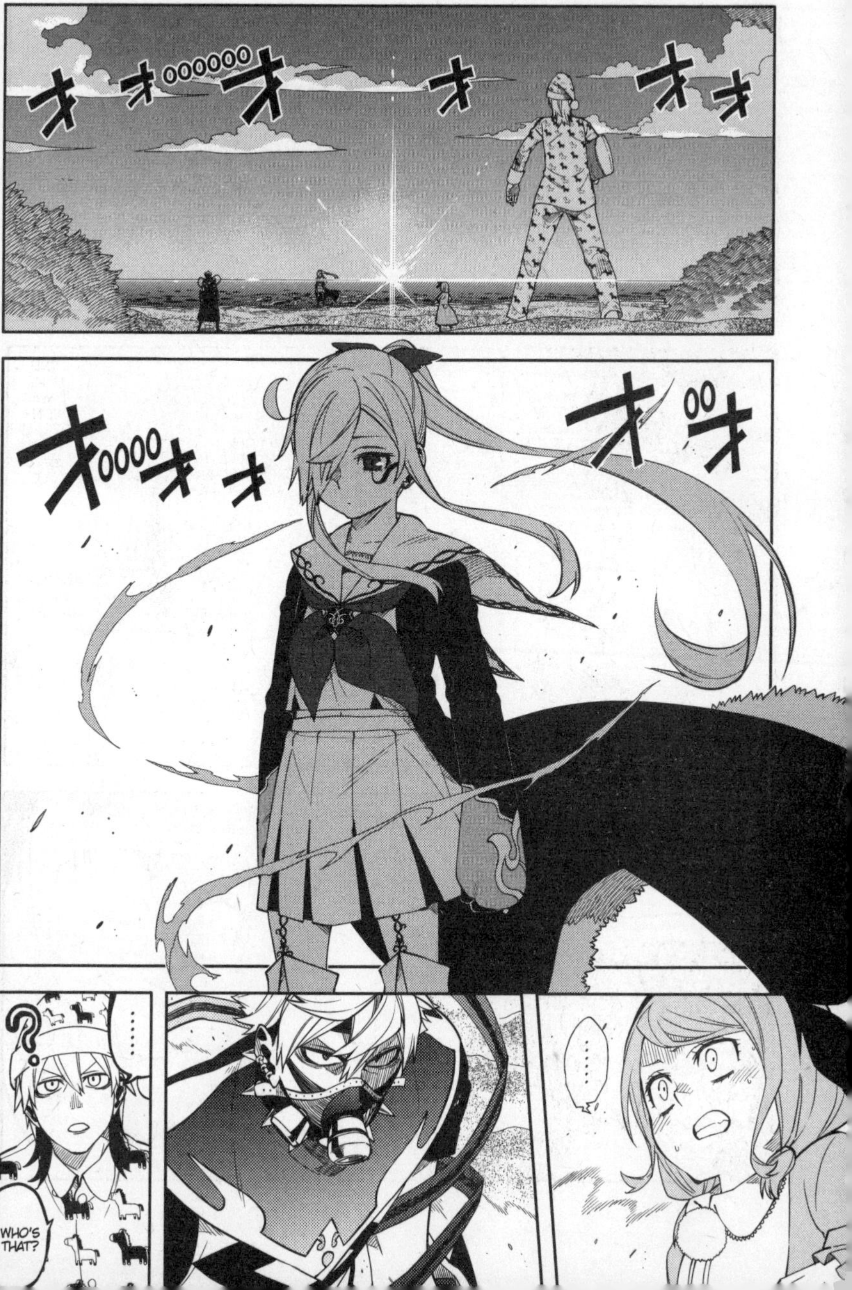
オォOOOOOOオォ
オォ
オOOオ
オOOOOォォ
......
......
?
WHO'S THAT?

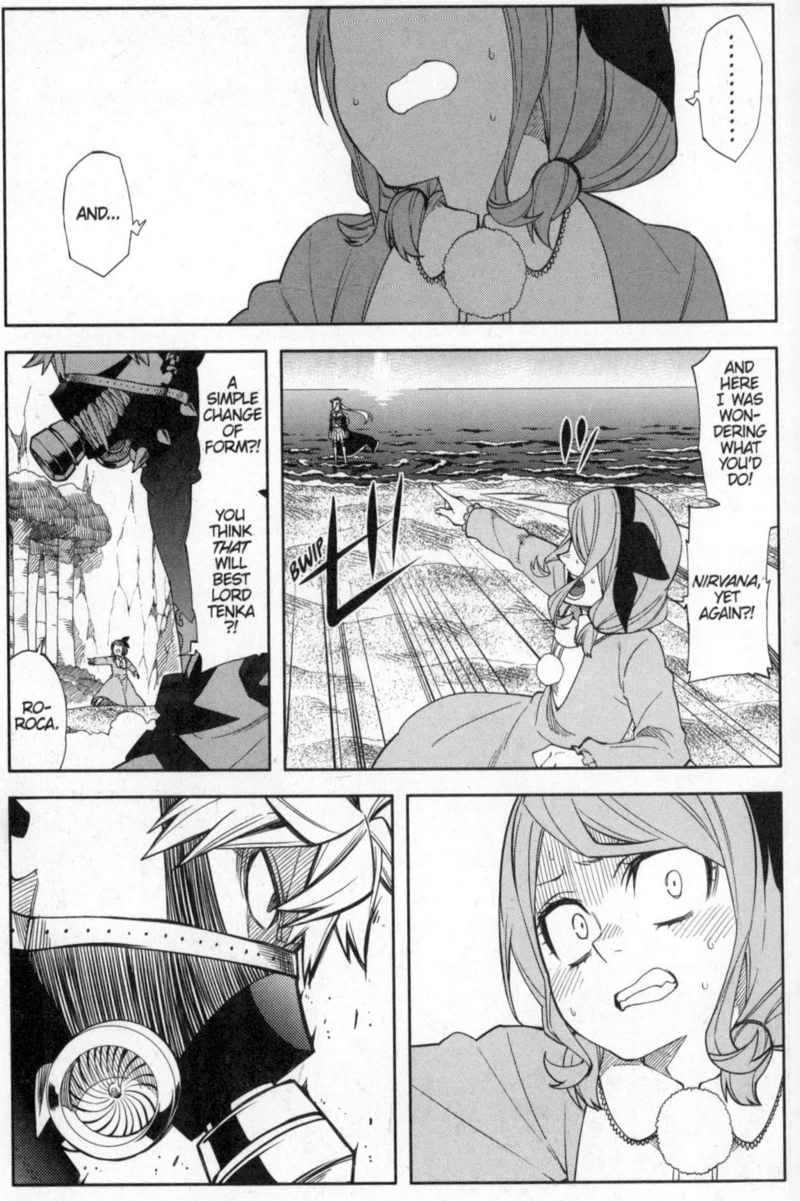
......
AND...
AND HERE I WAS WONDERING WHAT YOU'D DO!
NIRVANA, YET AGAIN?!
BWIP
A SIMPLE CHANGE OF FORM?!
YOU THINK *THAT* WILL BEST LORD TENKA?!
RO-ROCA.

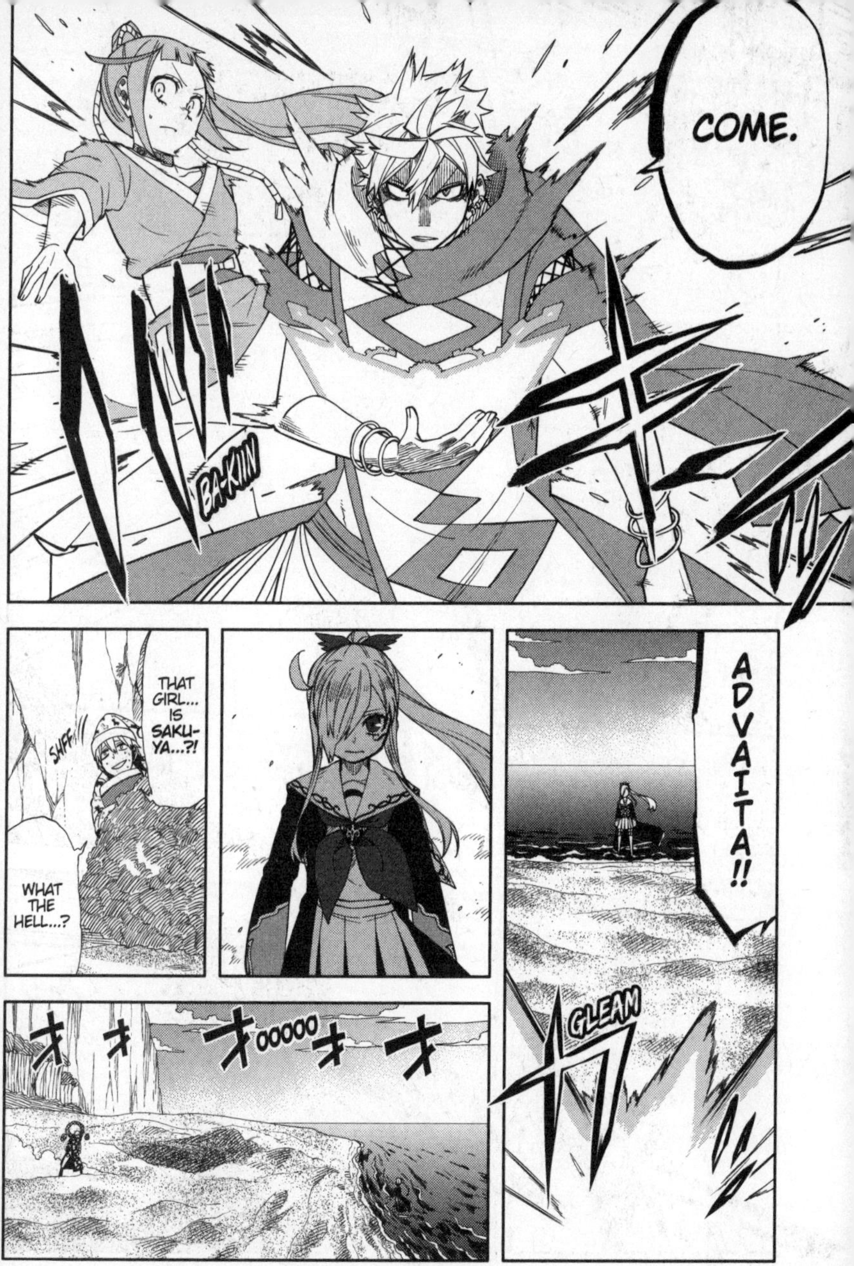
COME.
BA-KIIN
ADVAITA!!
GLEAM
THAT GIRL... IS SAKU-YA...?!
SHFF
WHAT THE HELL...?
オオオooooo オオ

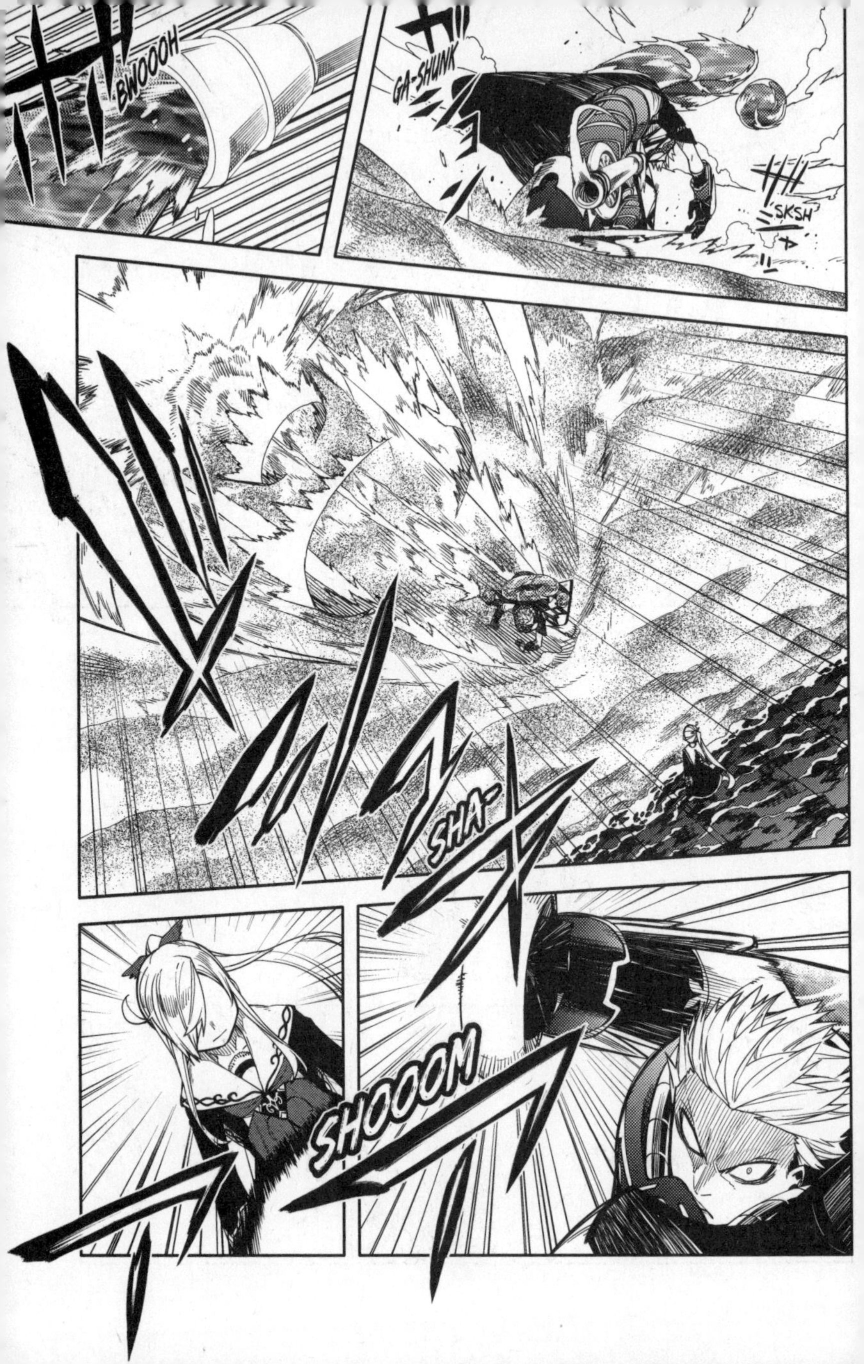
GA-SHUNK
SKSH
BWOOOH
SHA-
SHOOOM

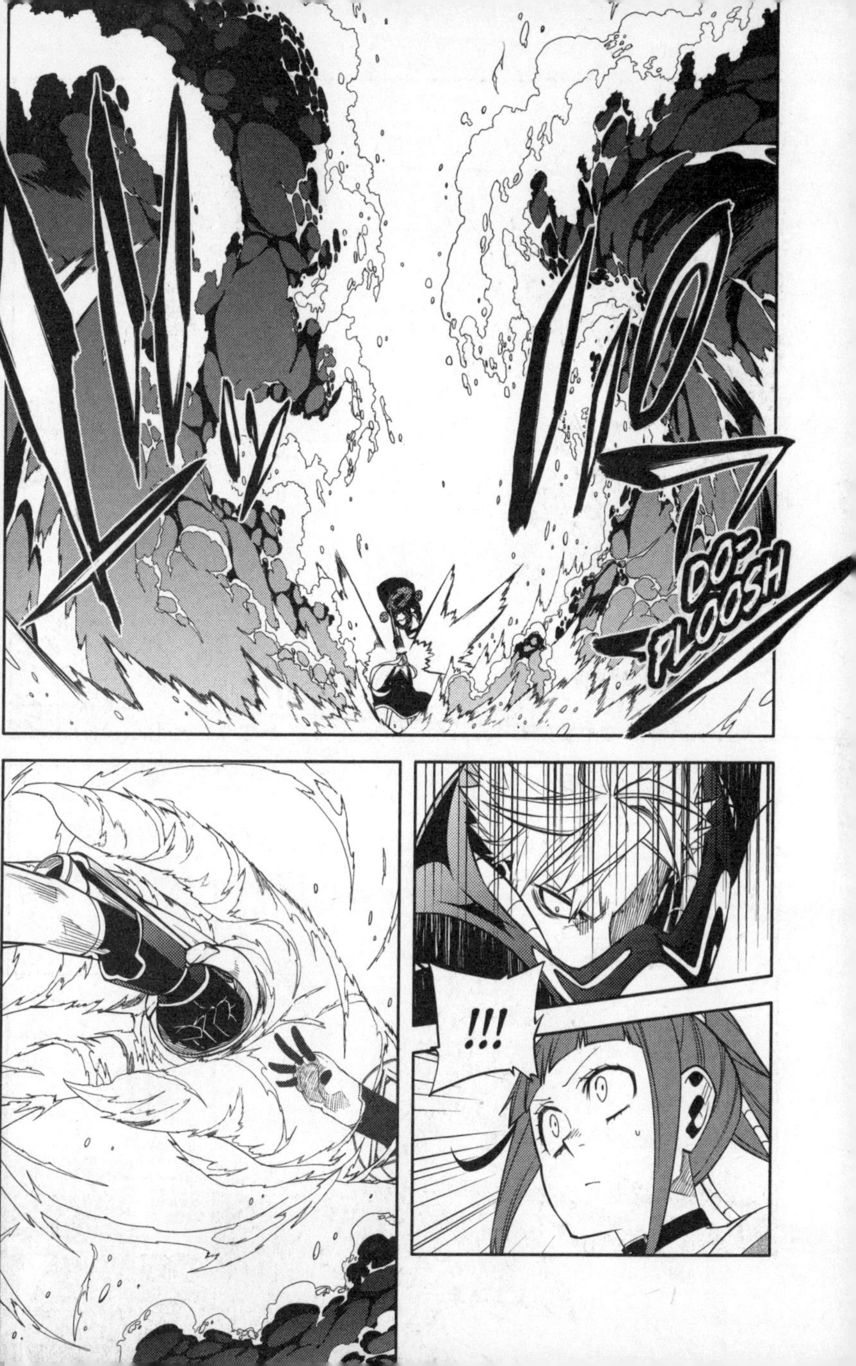
DO-PLOOSH
!!!

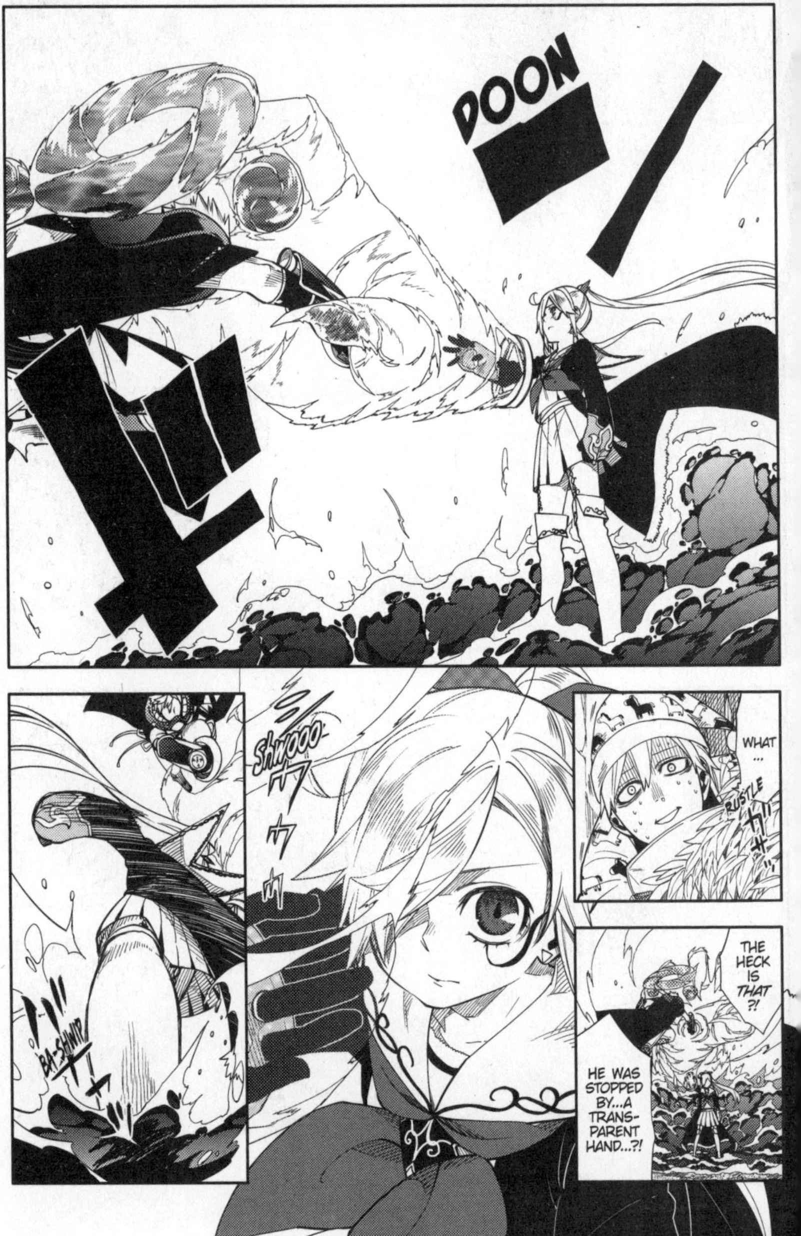
DOON
WHAT...
RUSTLE
THE HECK IS *THAT*?!
HE WAS STOPPED BY...A TRANS-PARENT HAND...?!
SHWOOO
BA-SHWIP

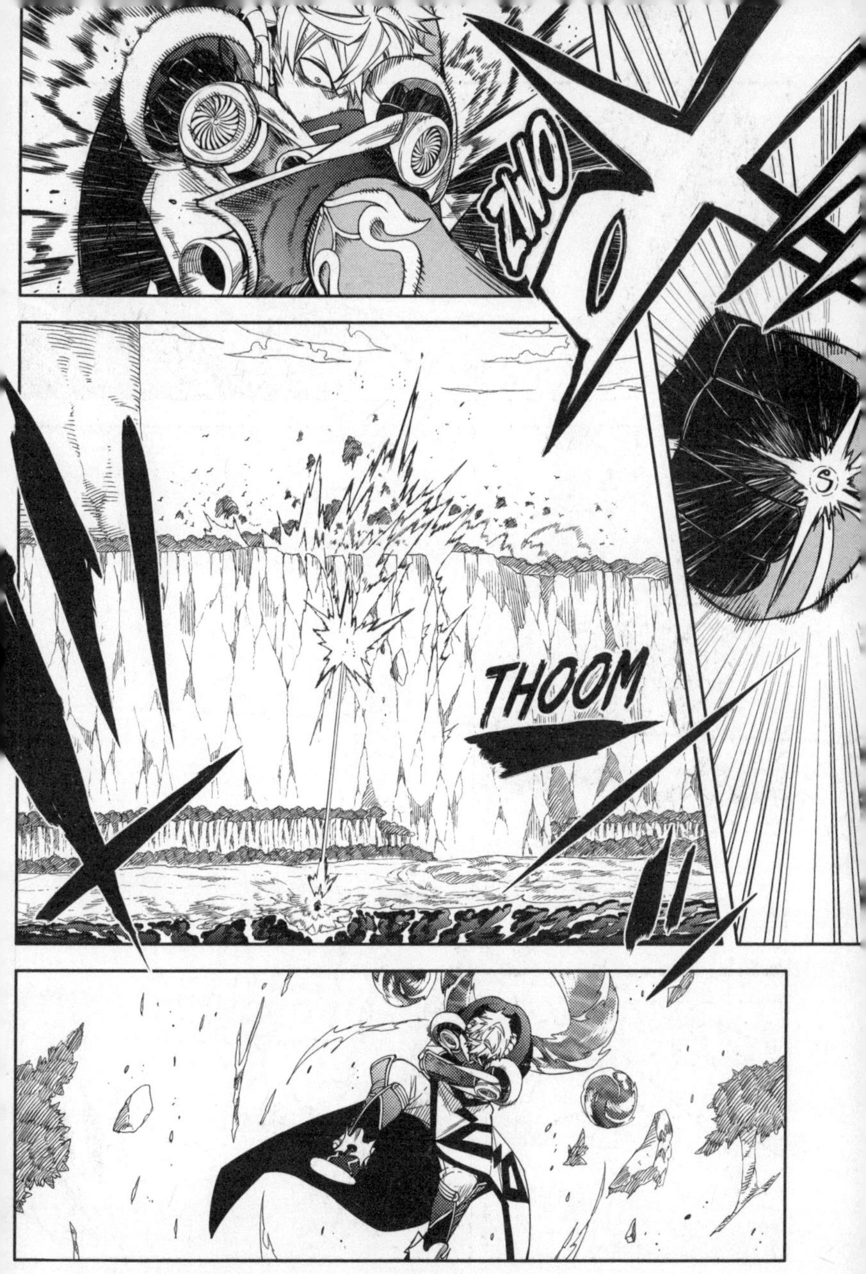
ZWO
THOOM

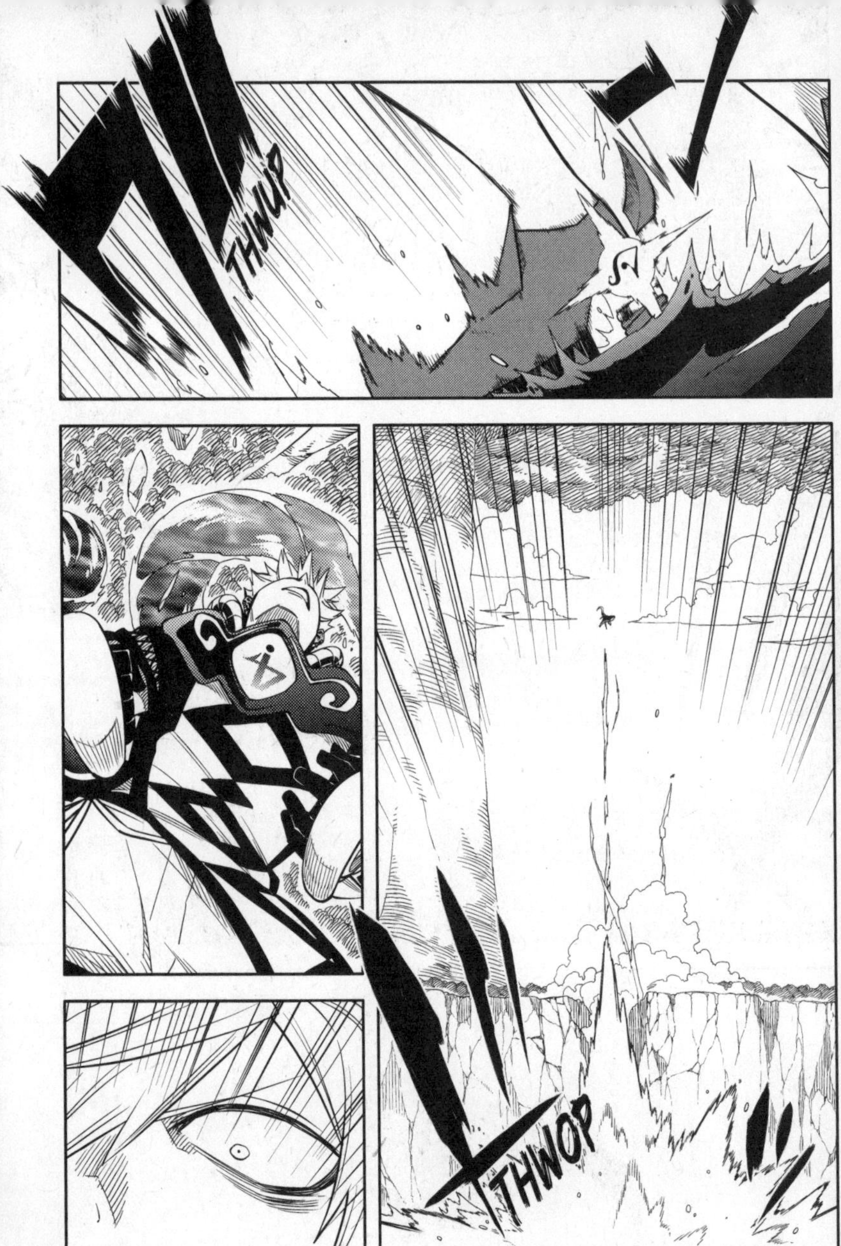
THWUP
THWOP

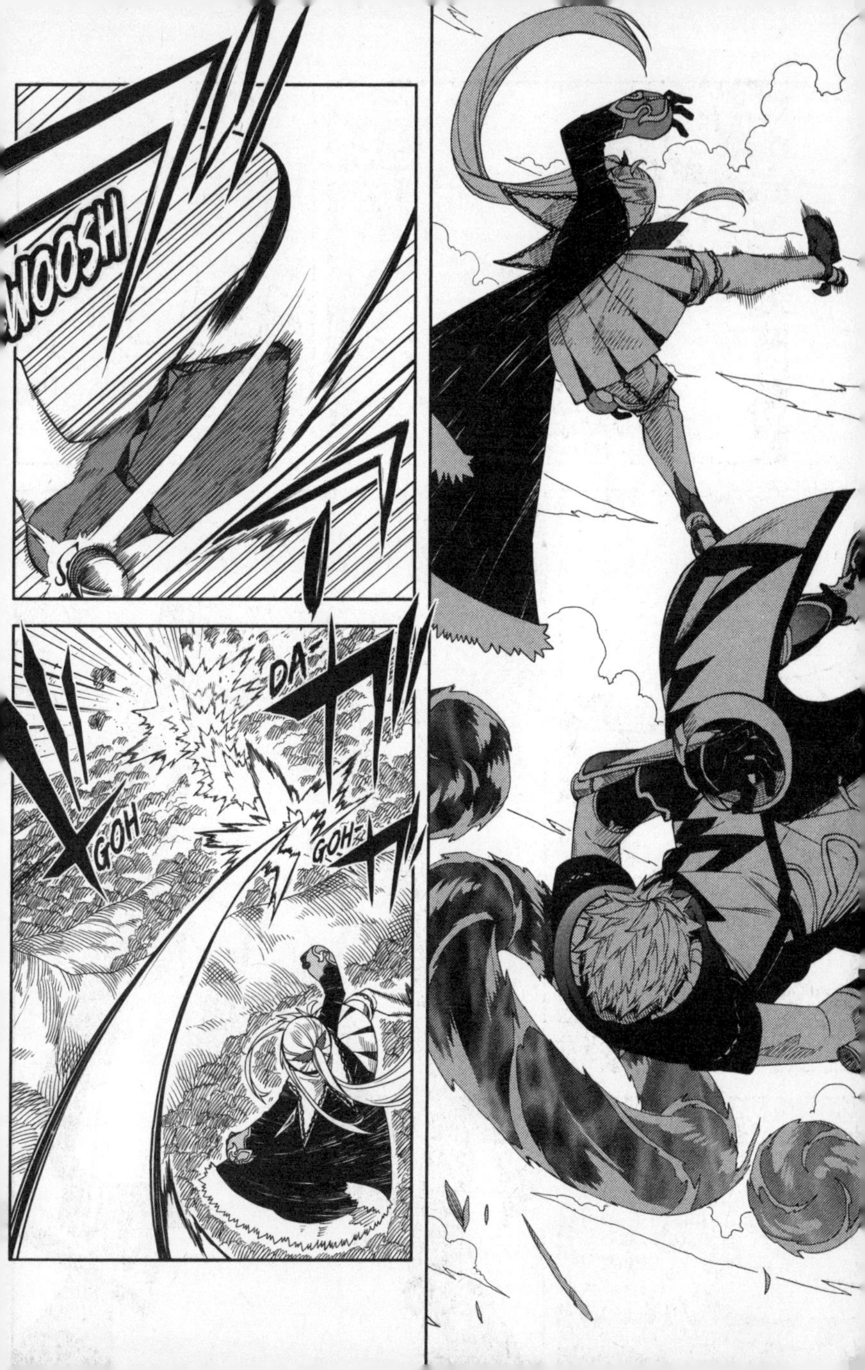
WOOSH
DA–
GOH–
GOH

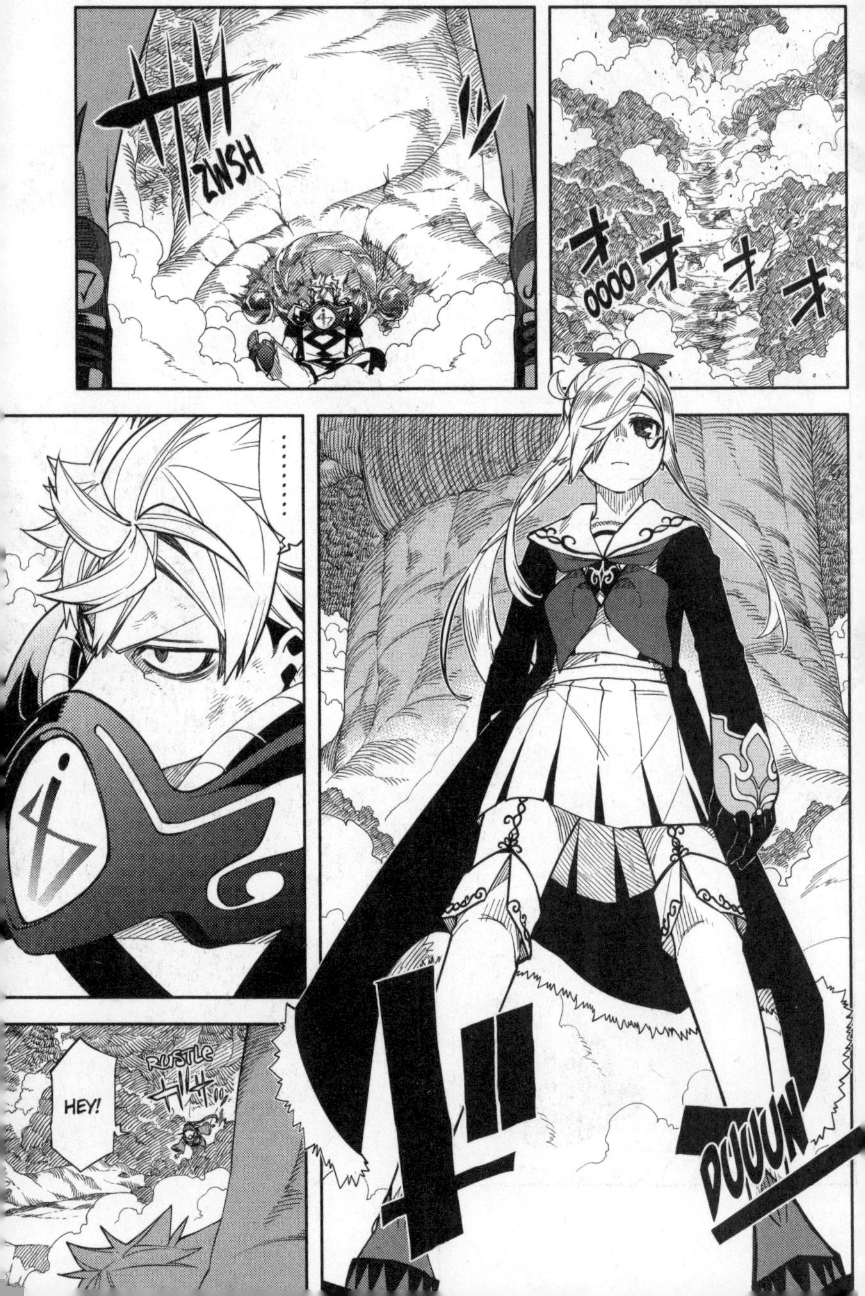
OOOO
ZWSH
DOOUN
......
RUSTLE
HEY!

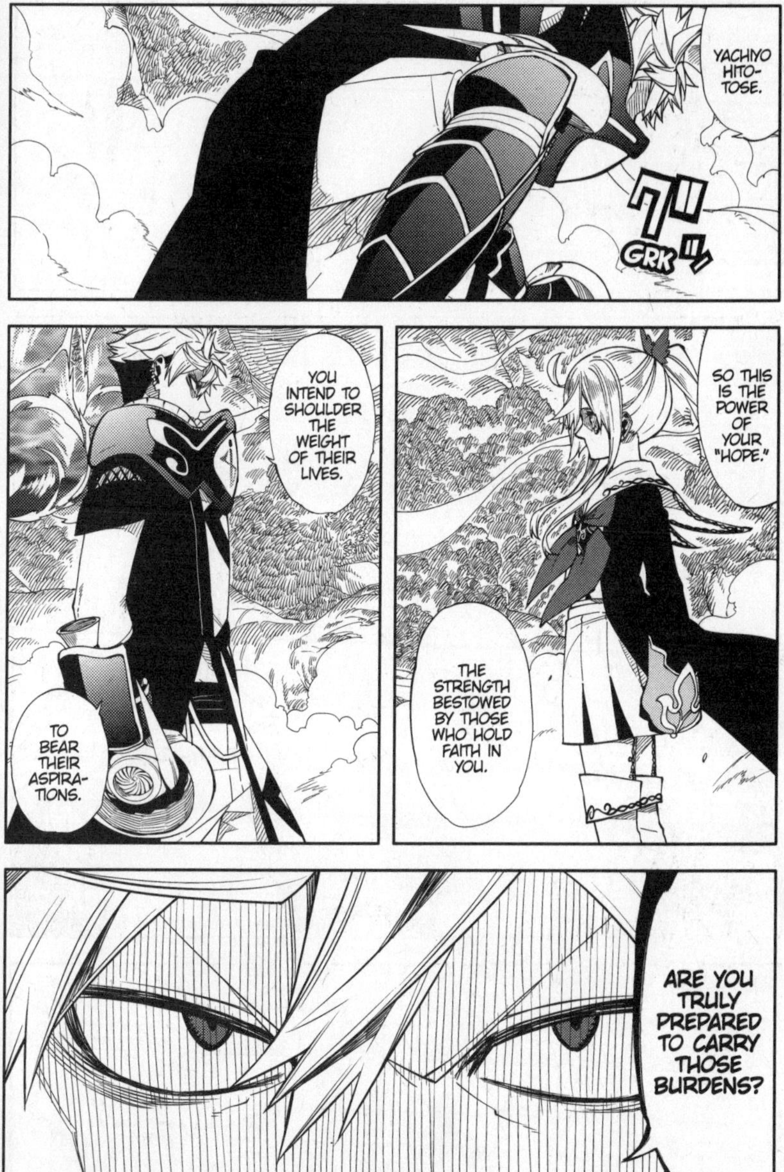
YACHIYO HITOTOSE.
GRK
SO THIS IS THE POWER OF YOUR "HOPE."
THE STRENGTH BESTOWED BY THOSE WHO HOLD FAITH IN YOU.
YOU INTEND TO SHOULDER THE WEIGHT OF THEIR LIVES.
TO BEAR THEIR ASPIRATIONS.
ARE YOU TRULY PREPARED TO CARRY THOSE BURDENS?

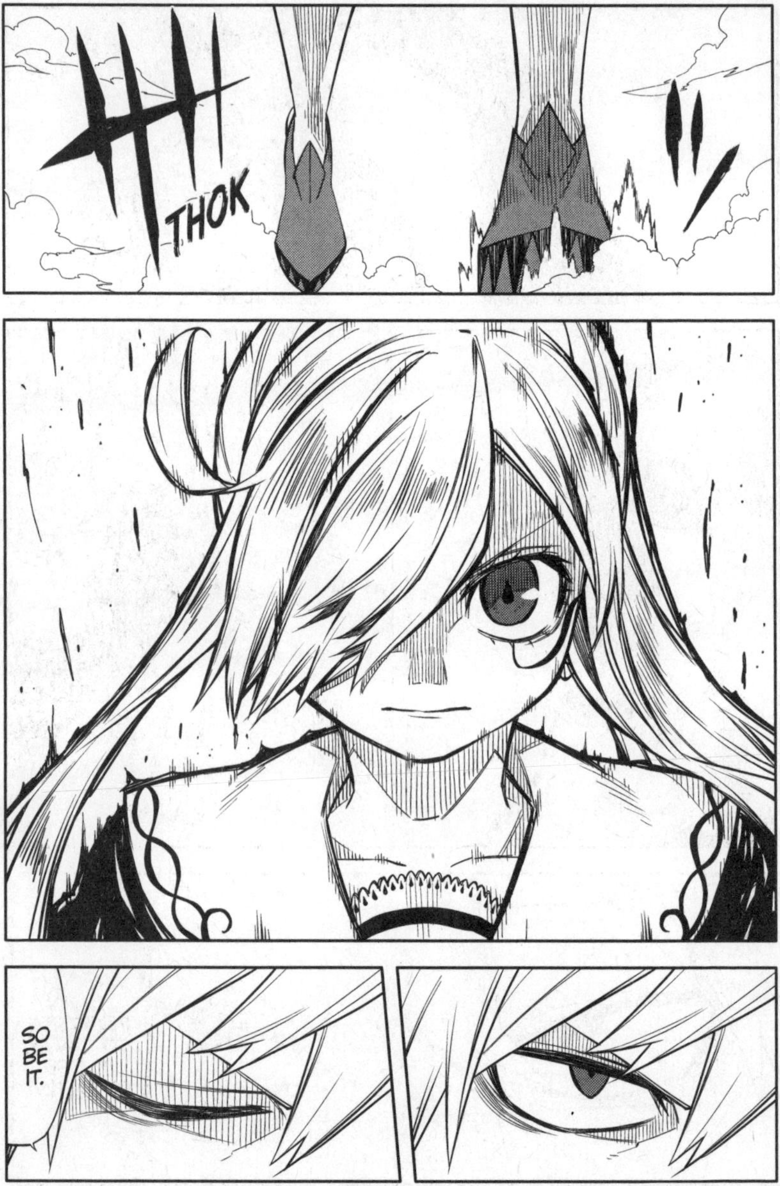
THOK
SO BE IT.

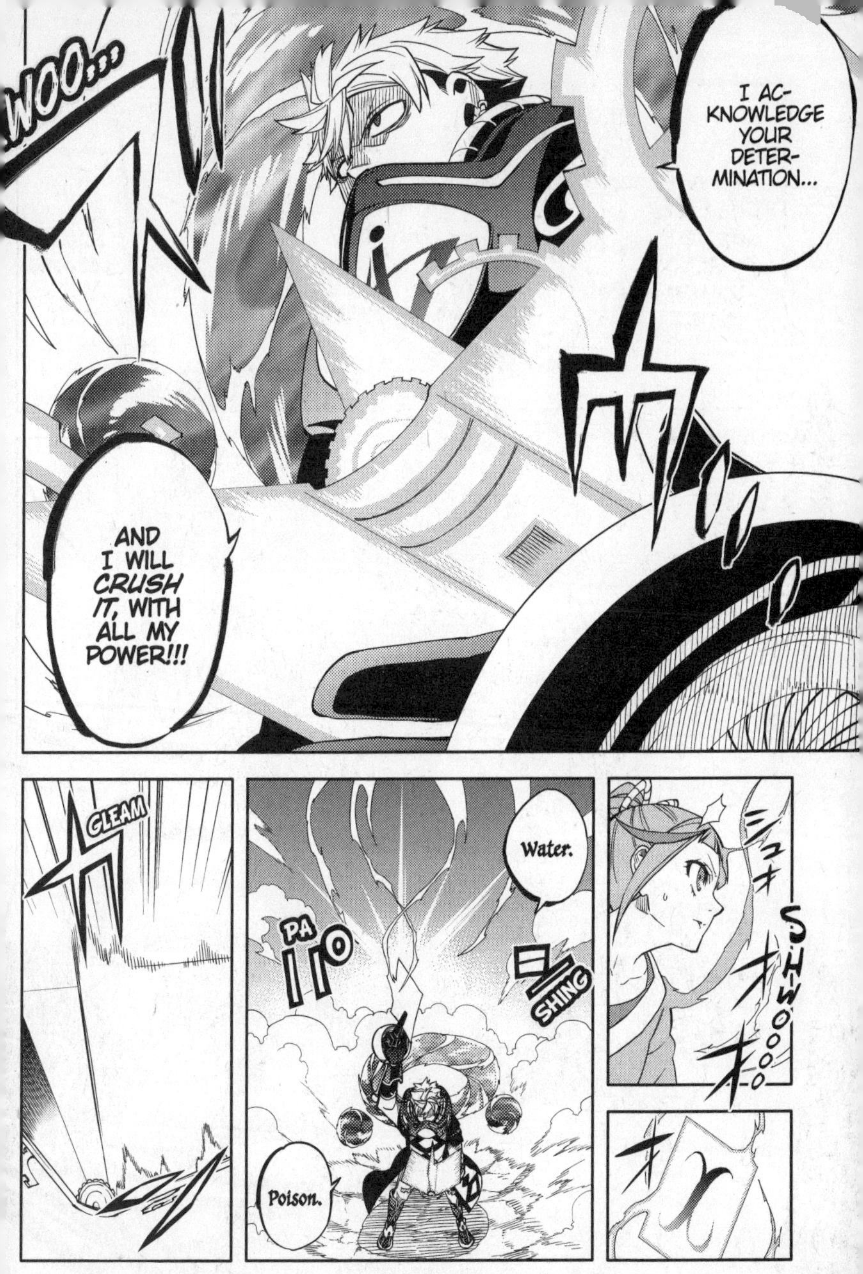
I AC-
KNOWLEDGE
YOUR
DETER-
MINATION...
WOO...
AND I WILL CRUSH IT, WITH ALL MY POWER!!!
SHWOOOOO
Water.
PA
SHING
Poison.
GLEAM

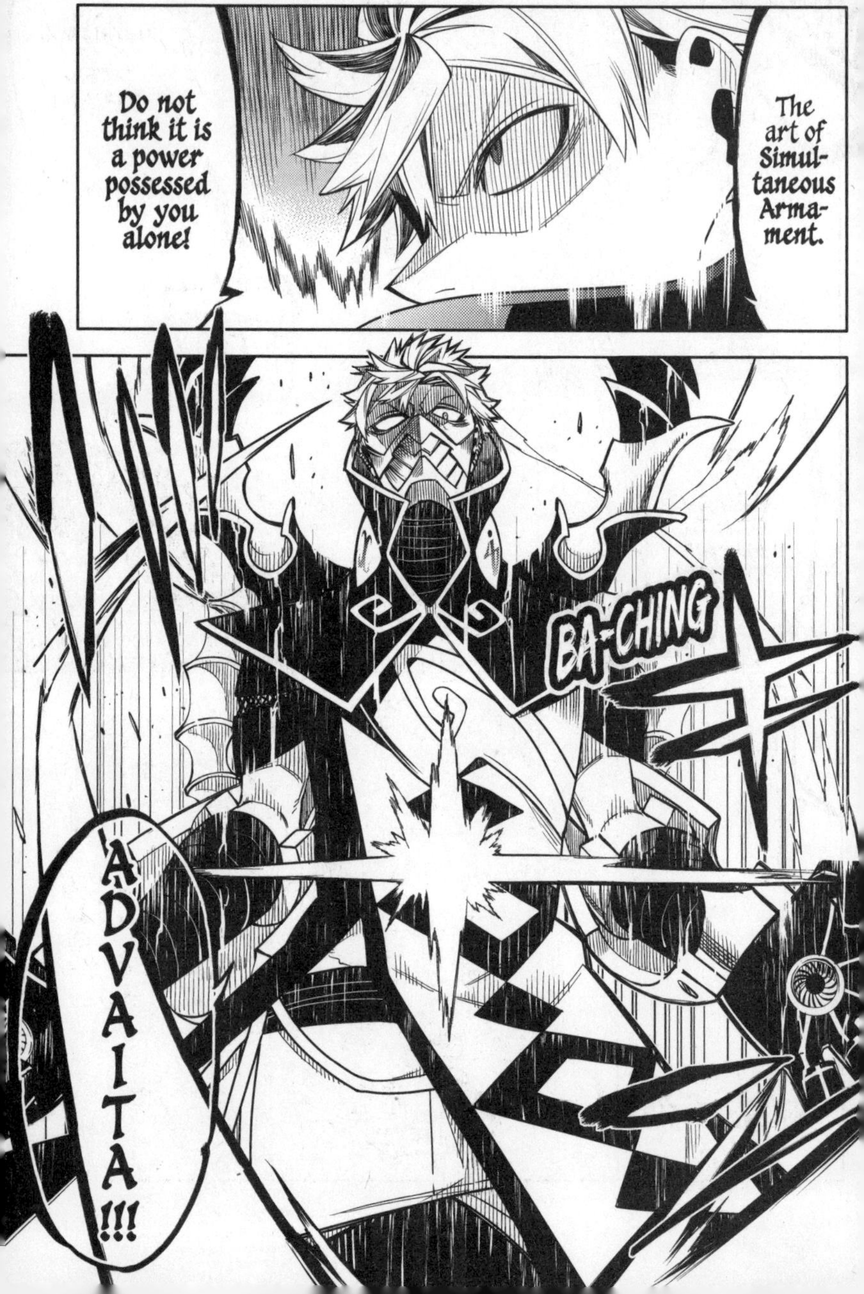
The art of Simultaneous Armament.
Do not think it is a power possessed by you alone!
BA-CHING
ADVAITA!!!

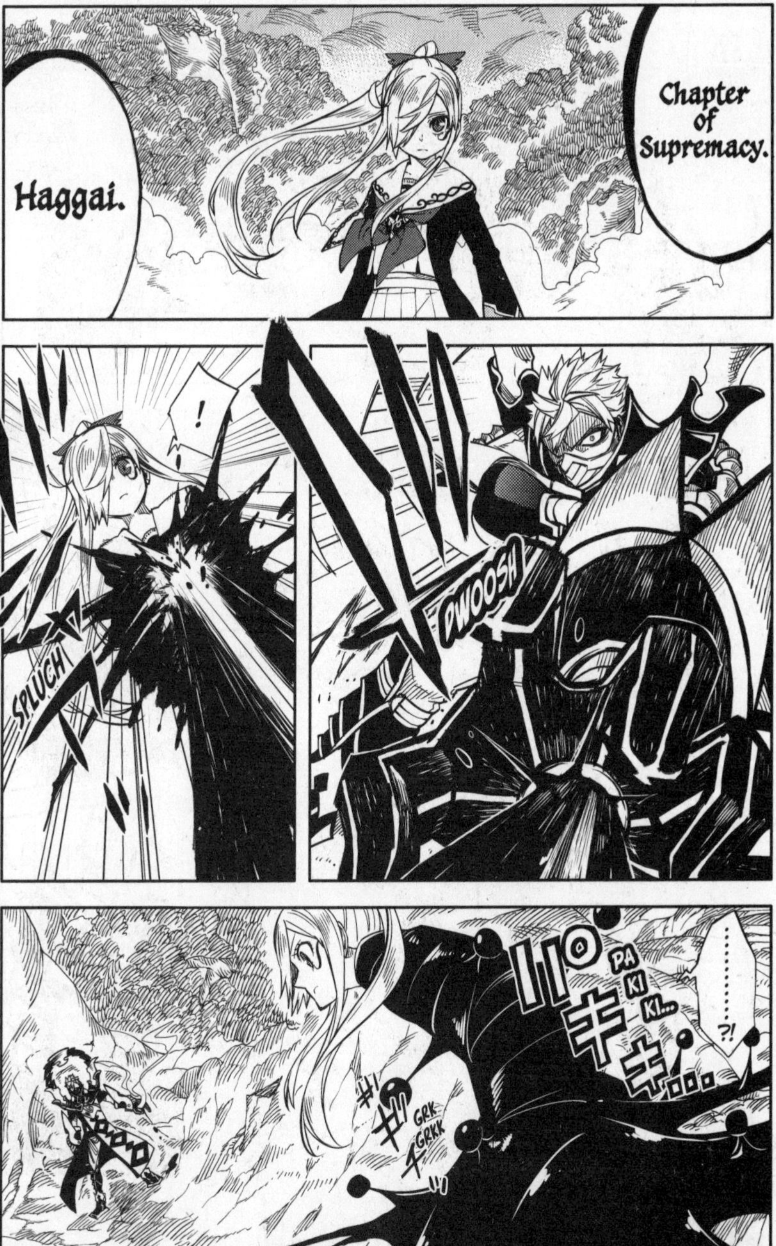
Chapter of Supremacy.
Haggai.
DWOOSH
!
SPLUCH
......?!
PA KI KI...
GRK GRKK

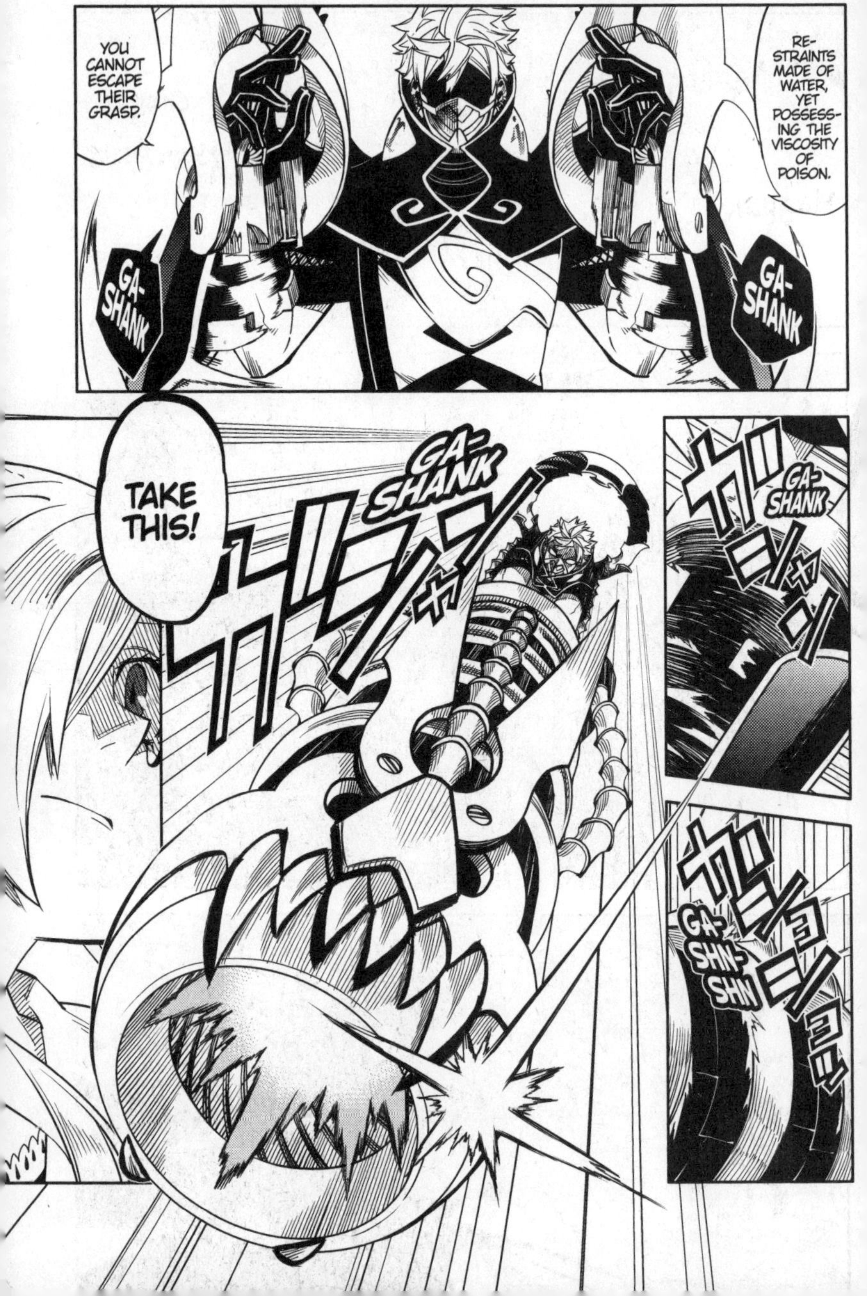
RE-STRAINTS MADE OF WATER, YET POSSESSING THE VISCOSITY OF POISON.
YOU CANNOT ESCAPE THEIR GRASP.
GA-SHANK
GA-SHANK
GA-SHANK
GA-SHN-SHN
TAKE THIS!
GA-SHANK

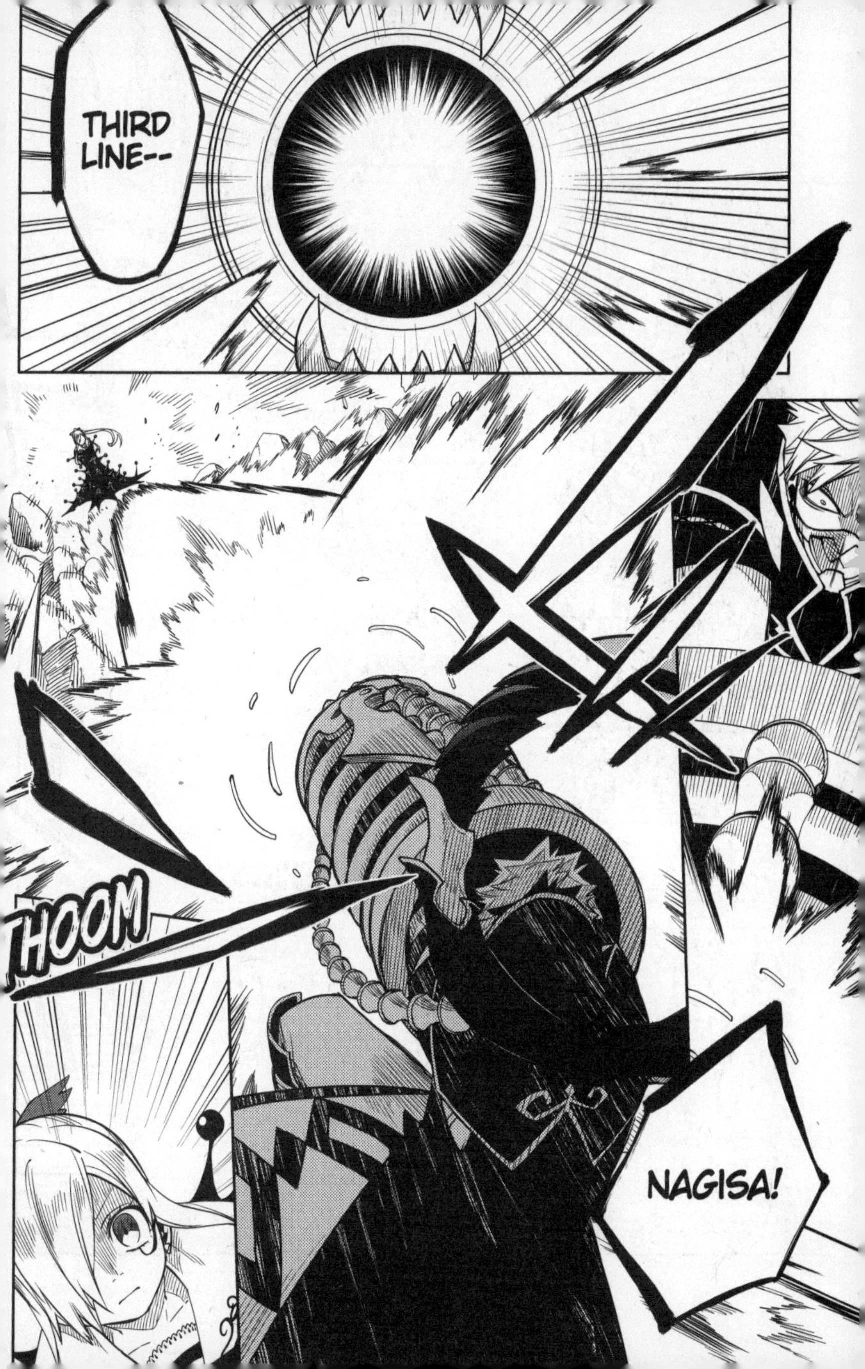
THIRD LINE--
THOOM
NAGISA!

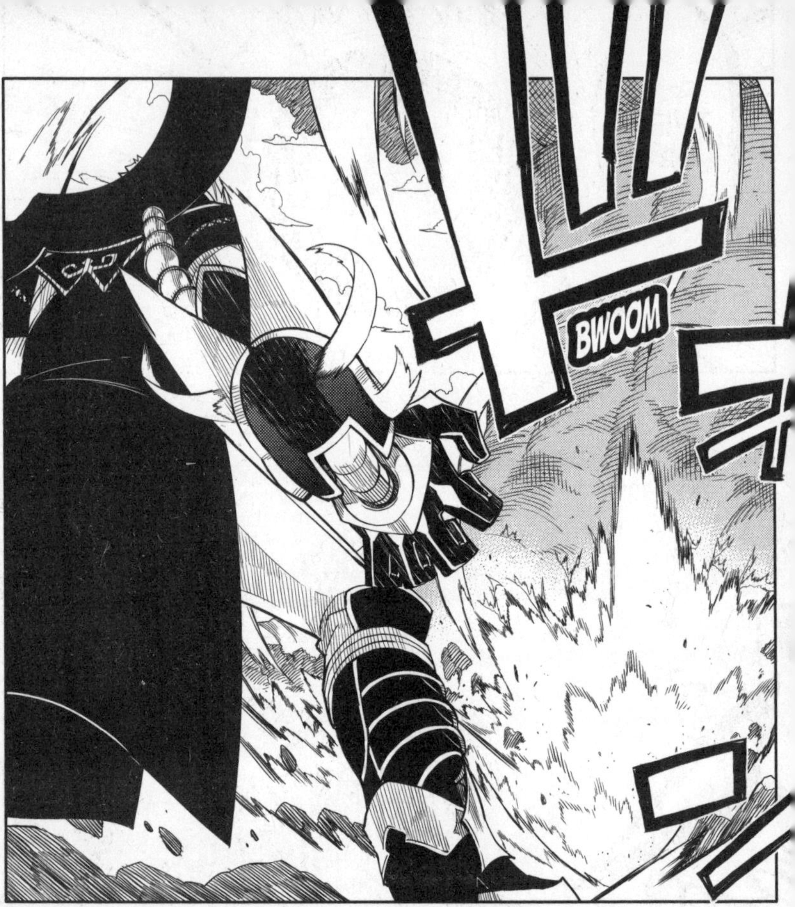
BWOOM

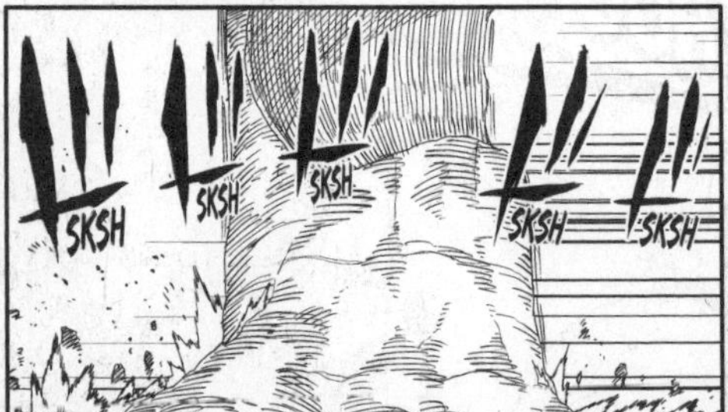
SKSH
SKSH
SKSH
SKSH
SKSH

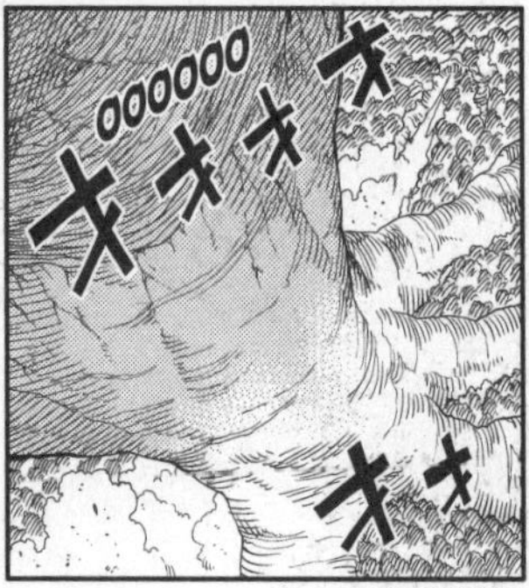
OOOOOO

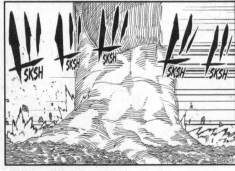

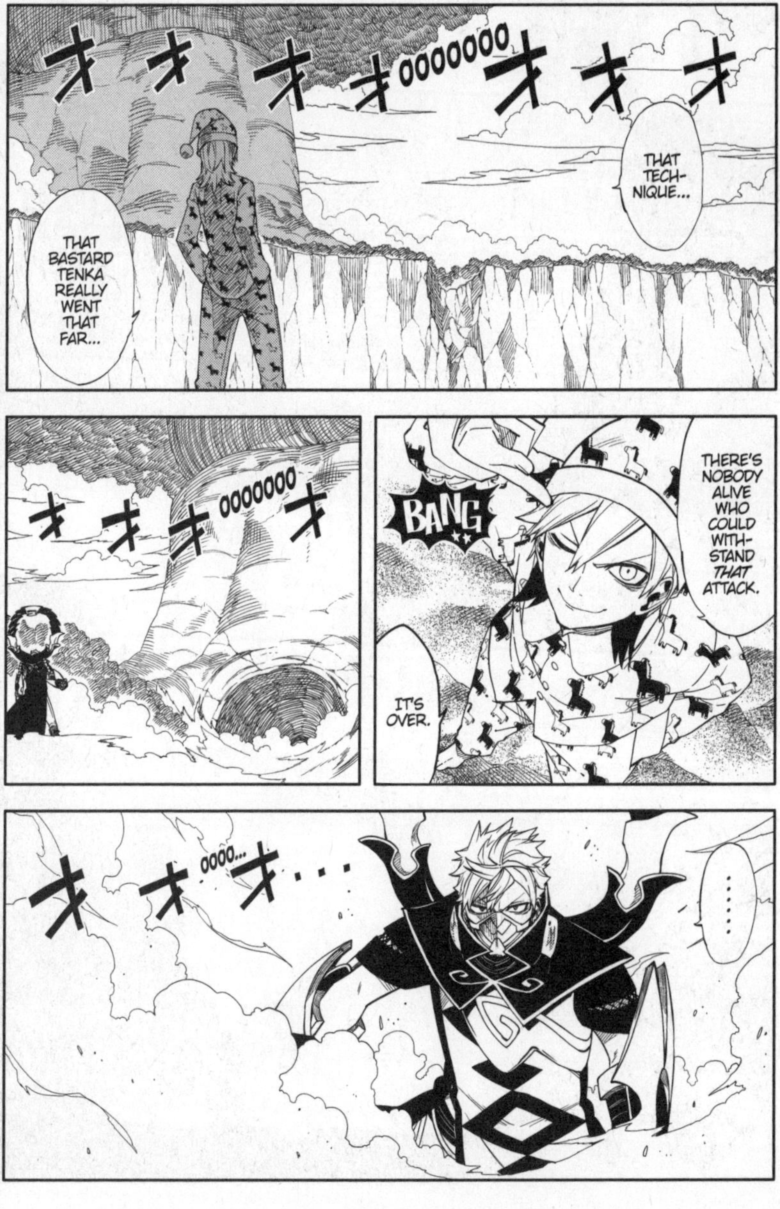
オオオオOOOOOOOオオオ
THAT TECH-NIQUE...
THAT BASTARD TENKA REALLY WENT THAT FAR...
THERE'S NOBODY ALIVE WHO COULD WITH-STAND *THAT* ATTACK.
BANG
IT'S OVER.
オオオOOOOOOOオ
オオOOOO...オ...
......

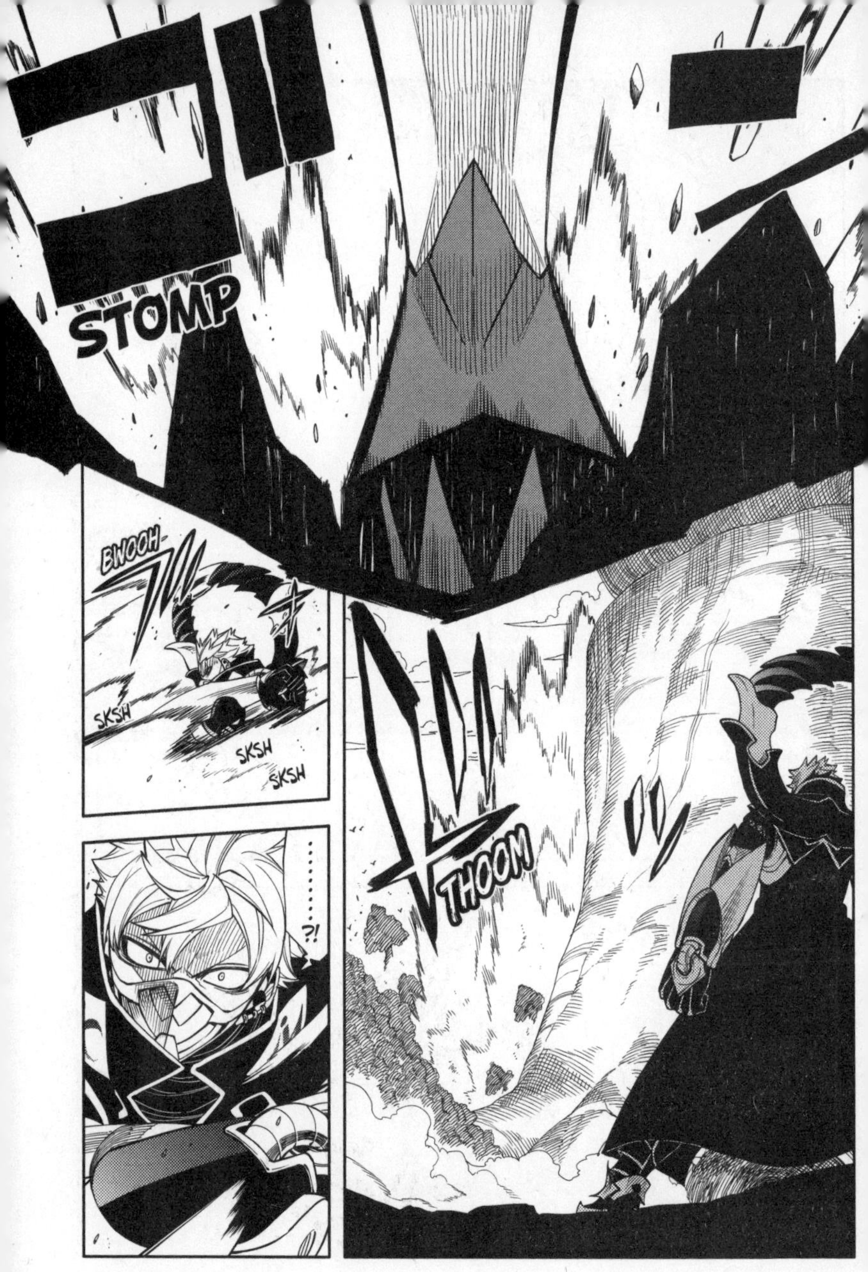
STOMP
THOOM
BWOOH
SKSH
SKSH
SKSH
......
?!

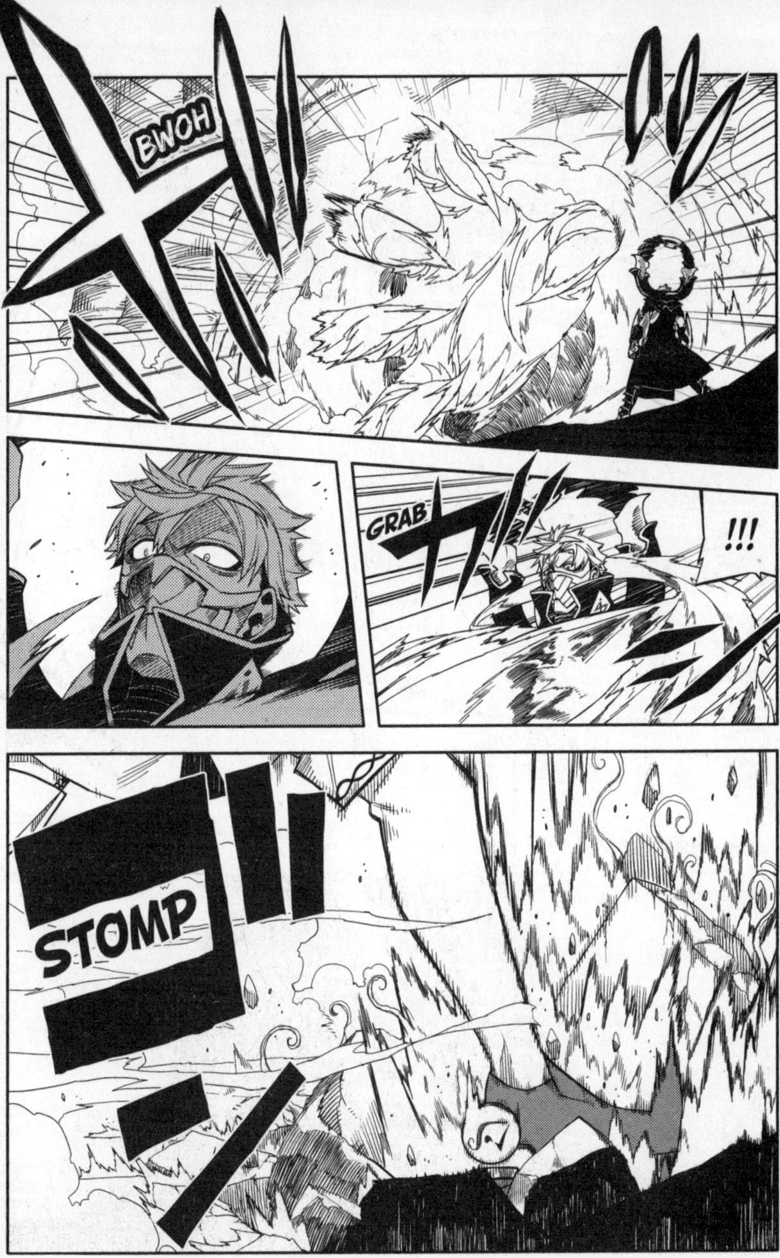
BWOH
!!!
GRAB
STOMP

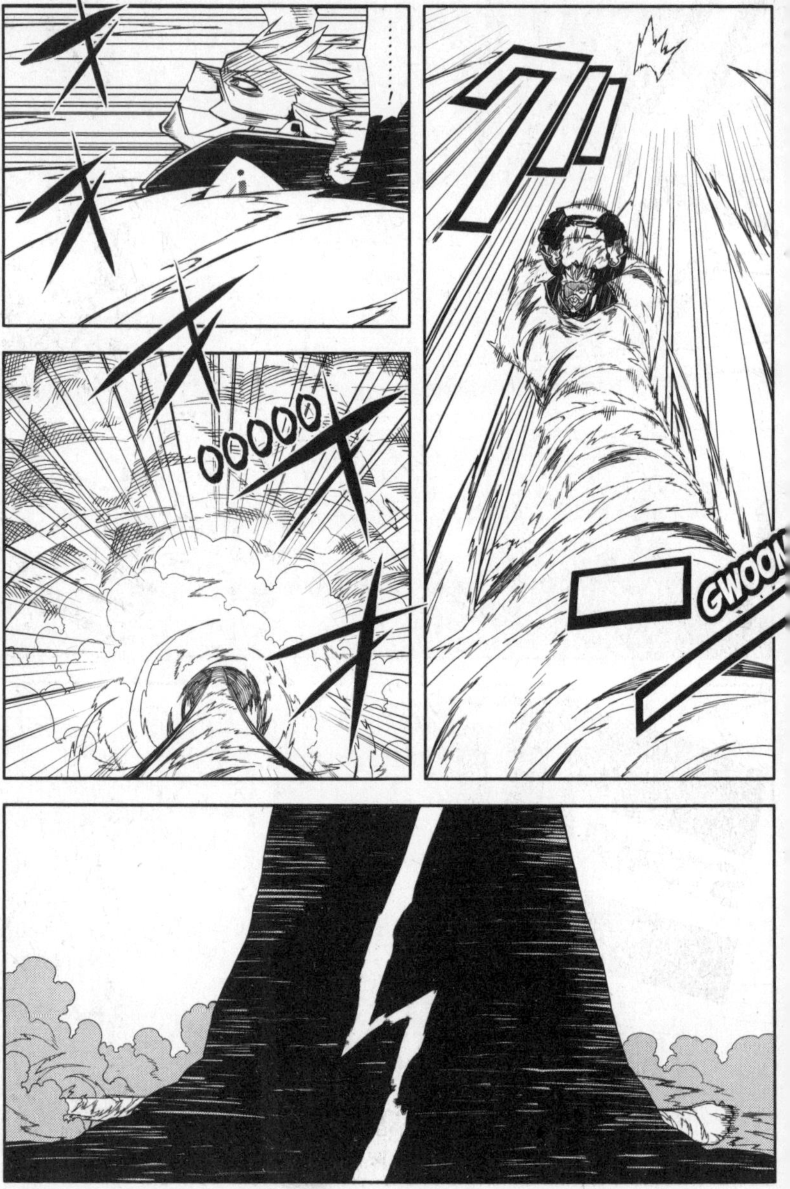
GWOOM
......!
OOOOO

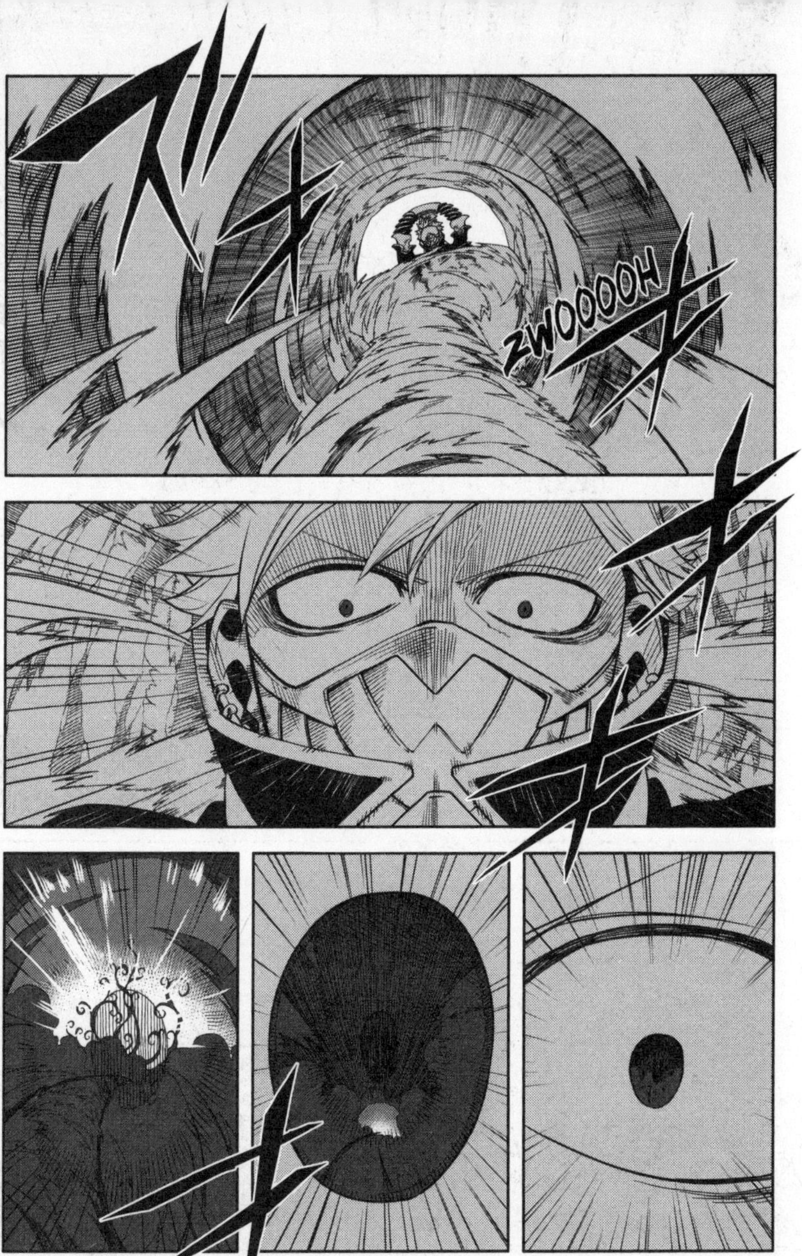
ZWOOOOH

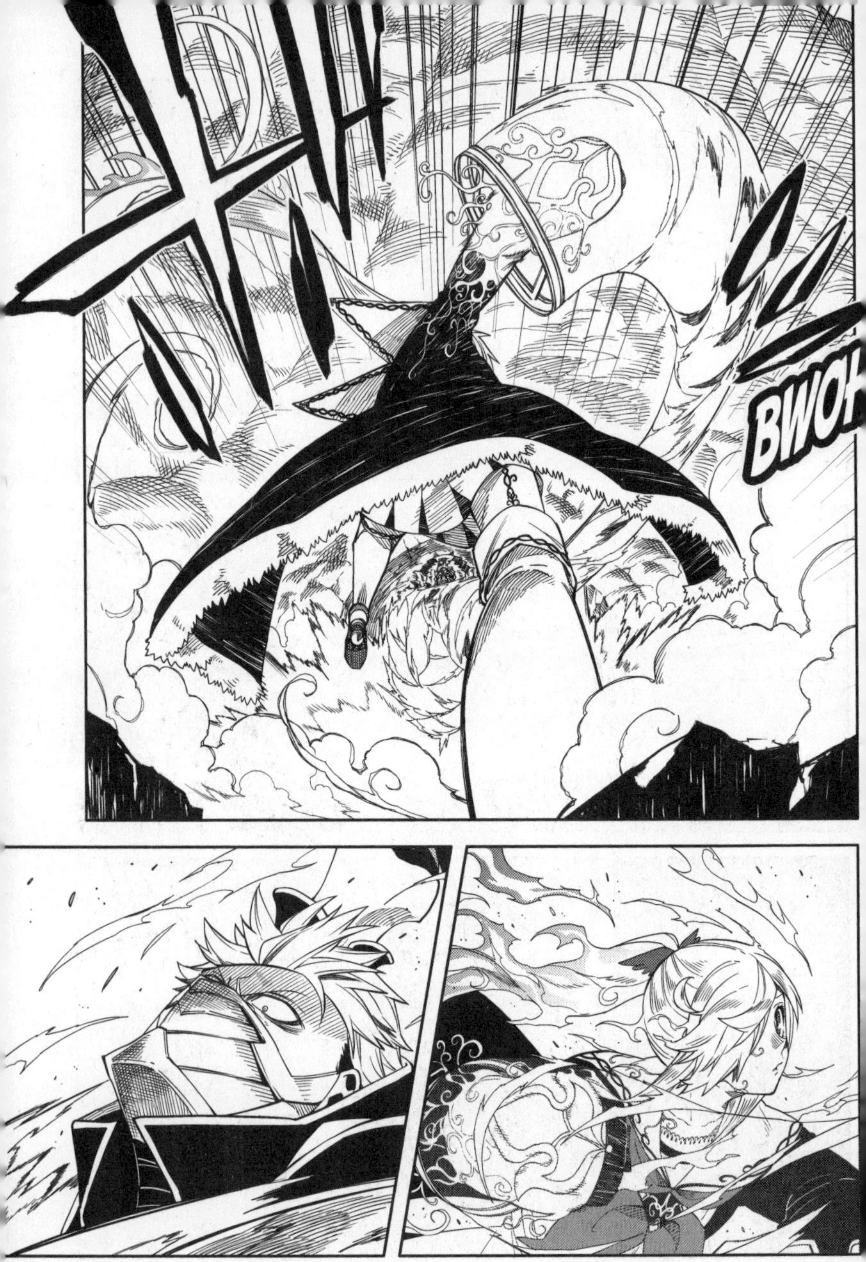
BWOH

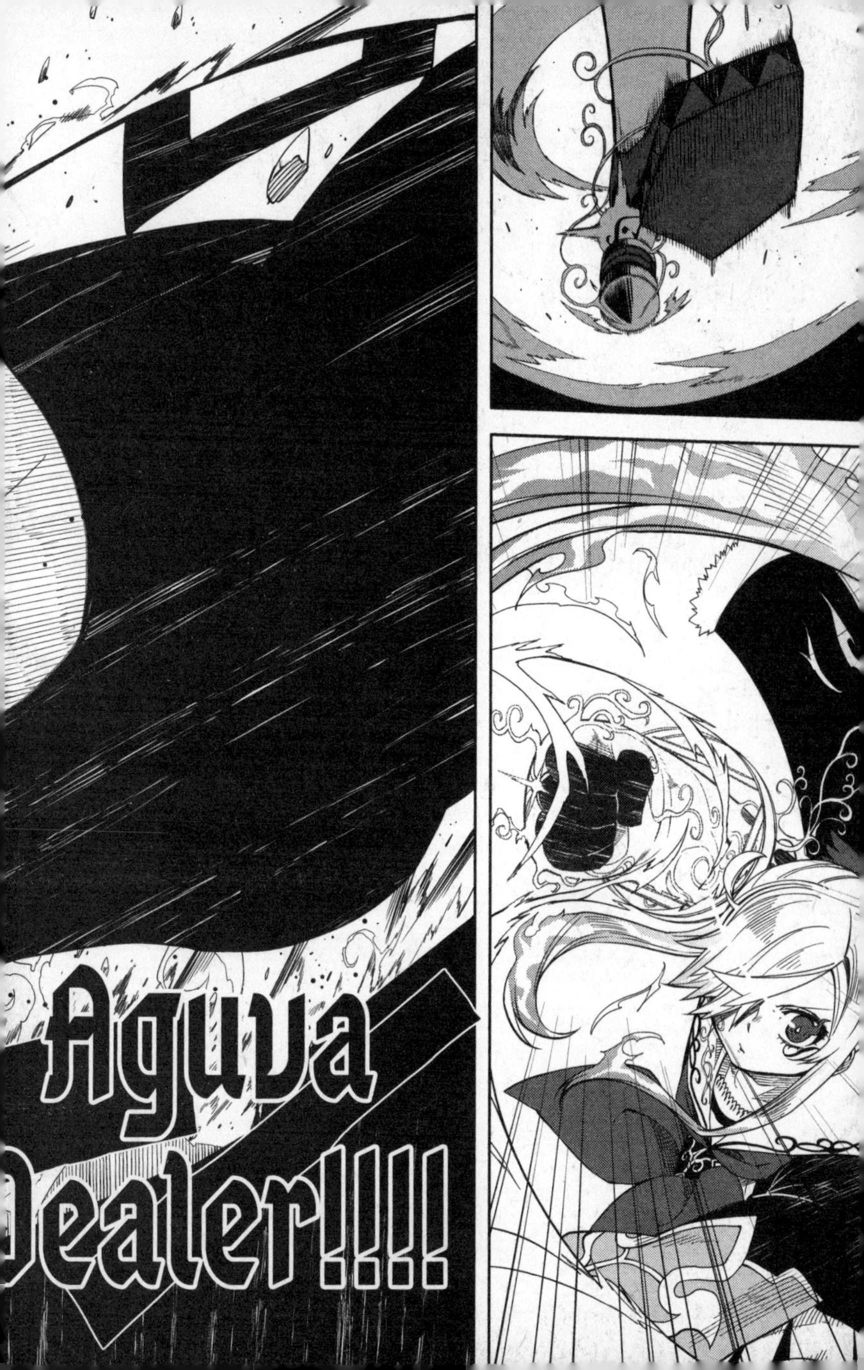
Agua
Dealer!!!!

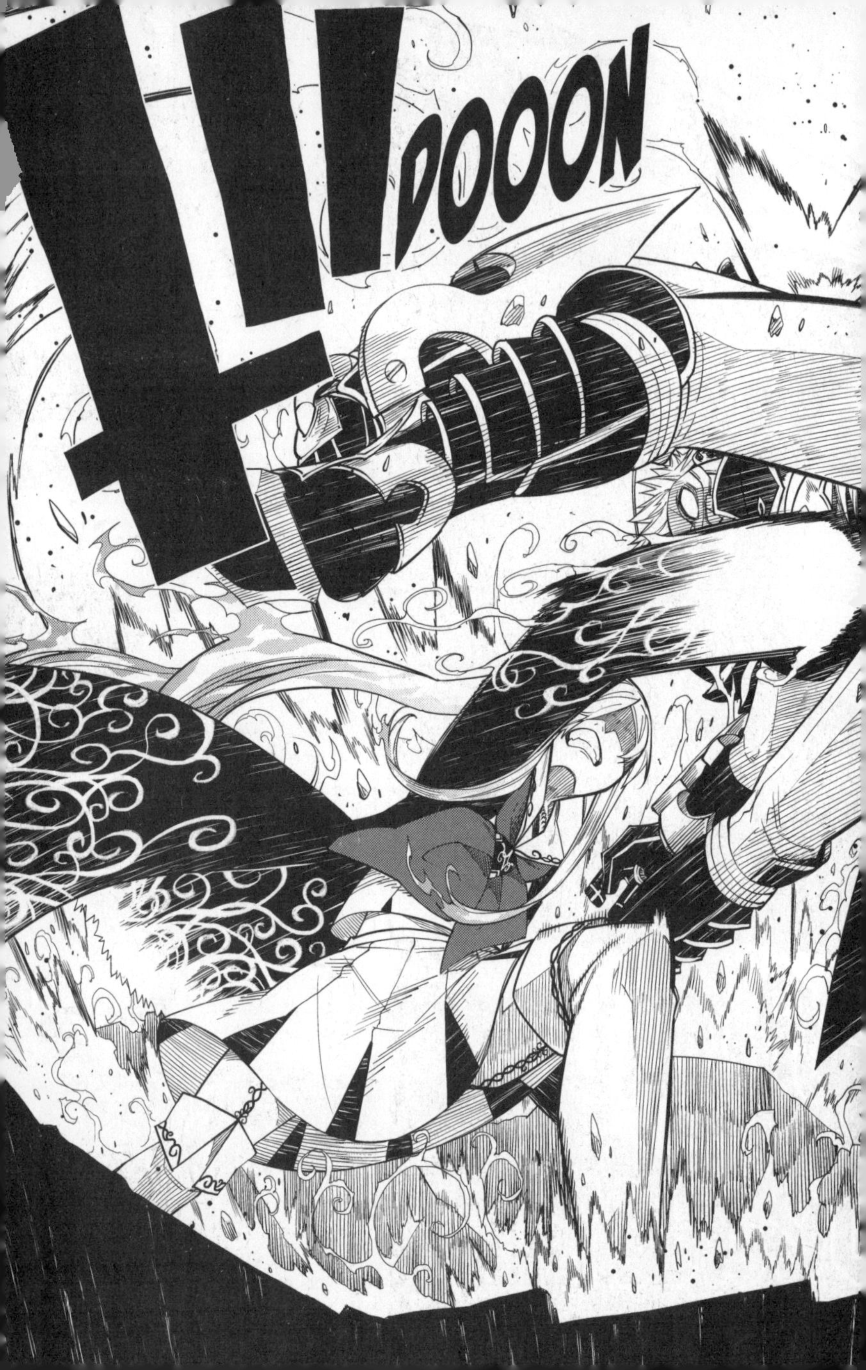
DOOON

Avatar Introduction

The Avatar of the Dawn

Vamana

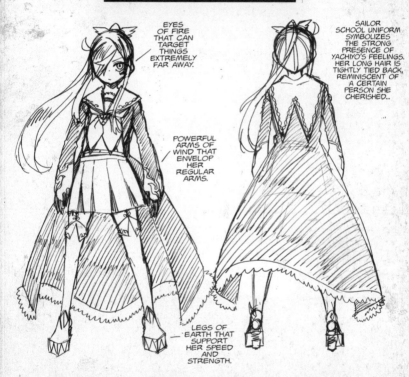

SAILOR SCHOOL UNIFORM SYMBOLIZES THE STRONG PRESENCE OF YACHIYO'S FEELINGS. HER LONG HAIR IS TIGHTLY TIED BACK, REMINISCENT OF A CERTAIN PERSON SHE CHERISHED...
EYES OF FIRE THAT CAN TARGET THINGS EXTREMELY FAR AWAY.
POWERFUL ARMS OF WIND THAT ENVELOP HER REGULAR ARMS.
LEGS OF EARTH THAT SUPPORT HER SPEED AND STRENGTH.

"From the eastern sky, the 'dawn' rose up in the three realms, and twilight fell upon the earth."

~Excerpt from *Gulgrog*, First Stanza, Chapter Fifty-Two~

◆ **Specialty:** Can combine Earth, Wind, and Fire elements

◆ **Skill:** Dealer: Imbues the body with the power of Luck

◆ **Special Skill:** Aguva Dealer

Chapter 10

That Which I Seek

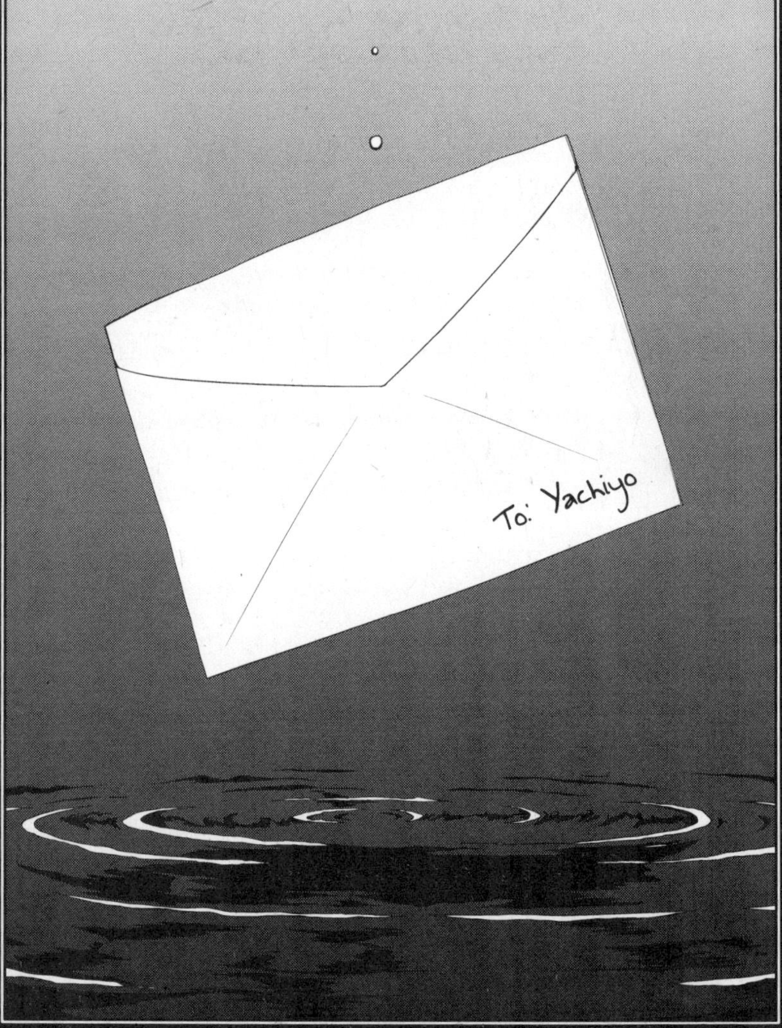
To: Yachiyo

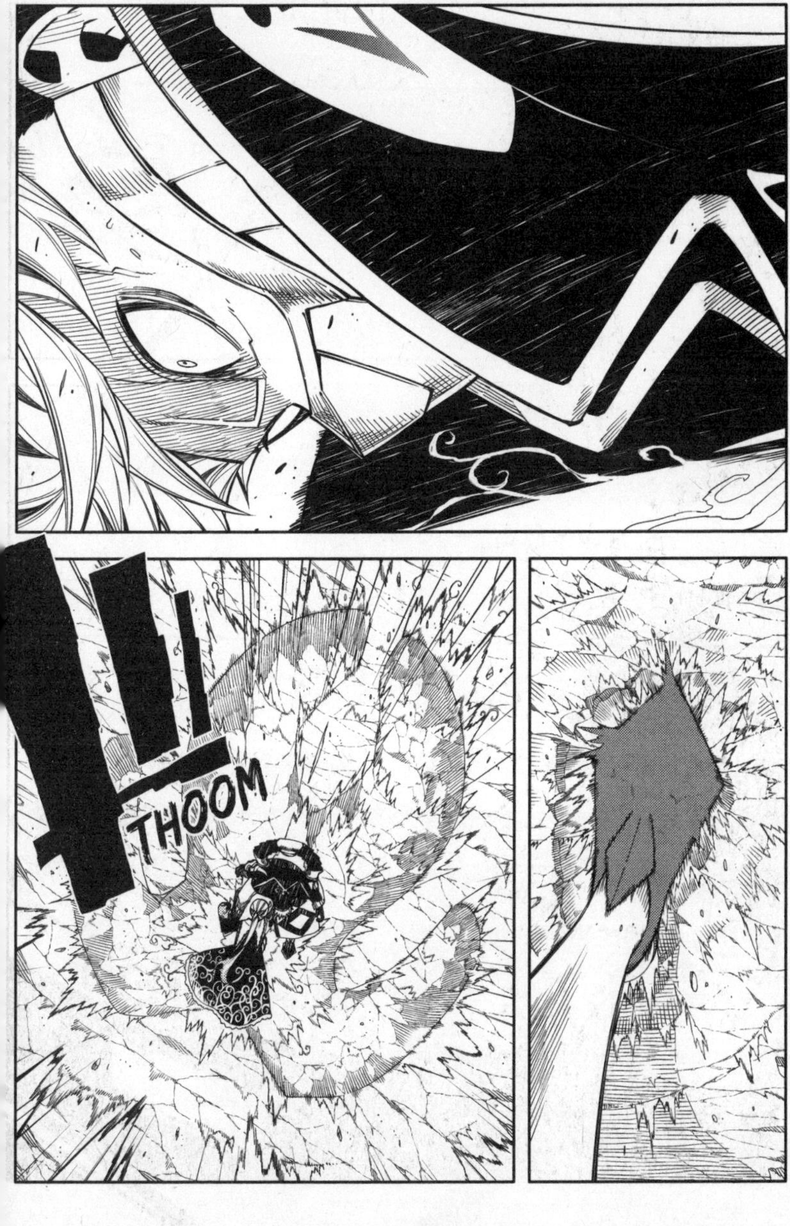
THOOM

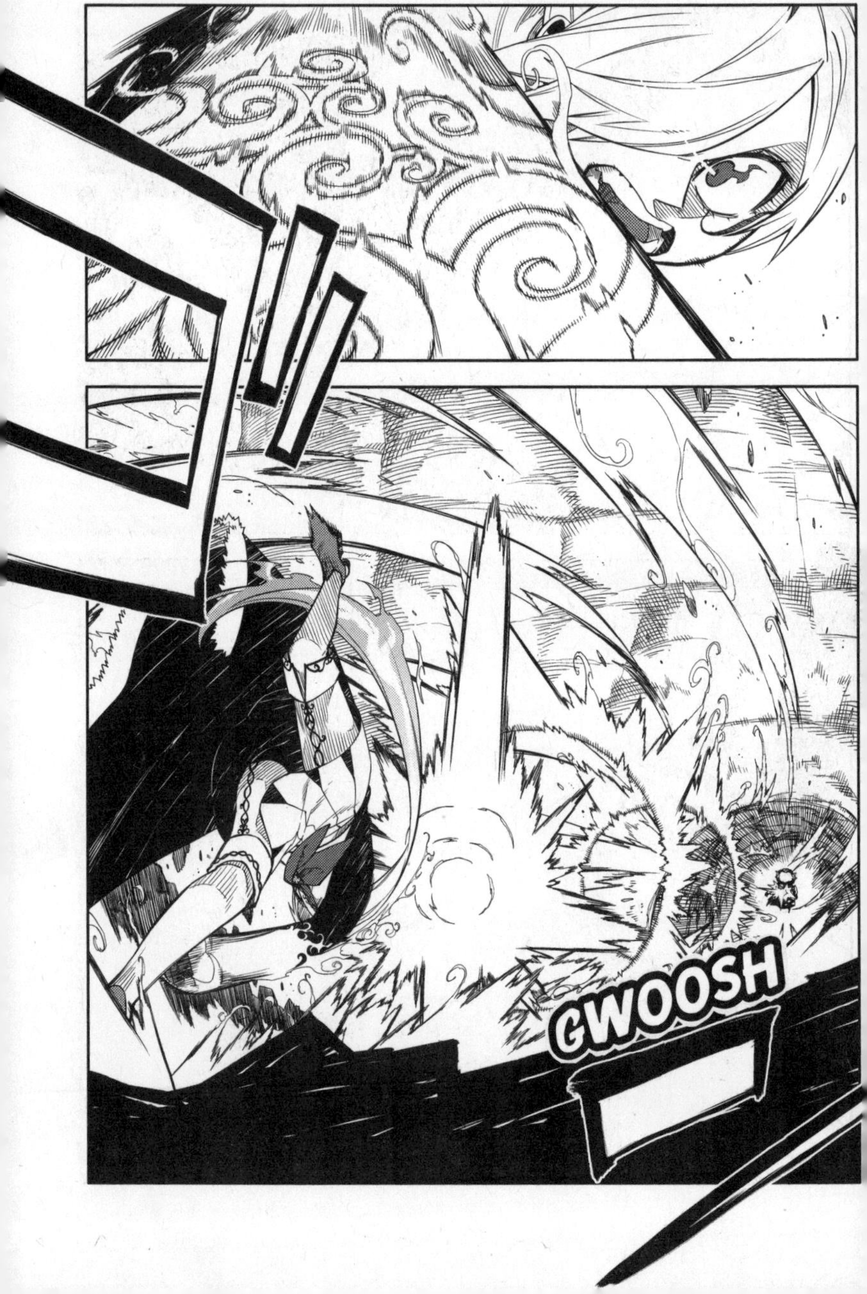
GWOOSH

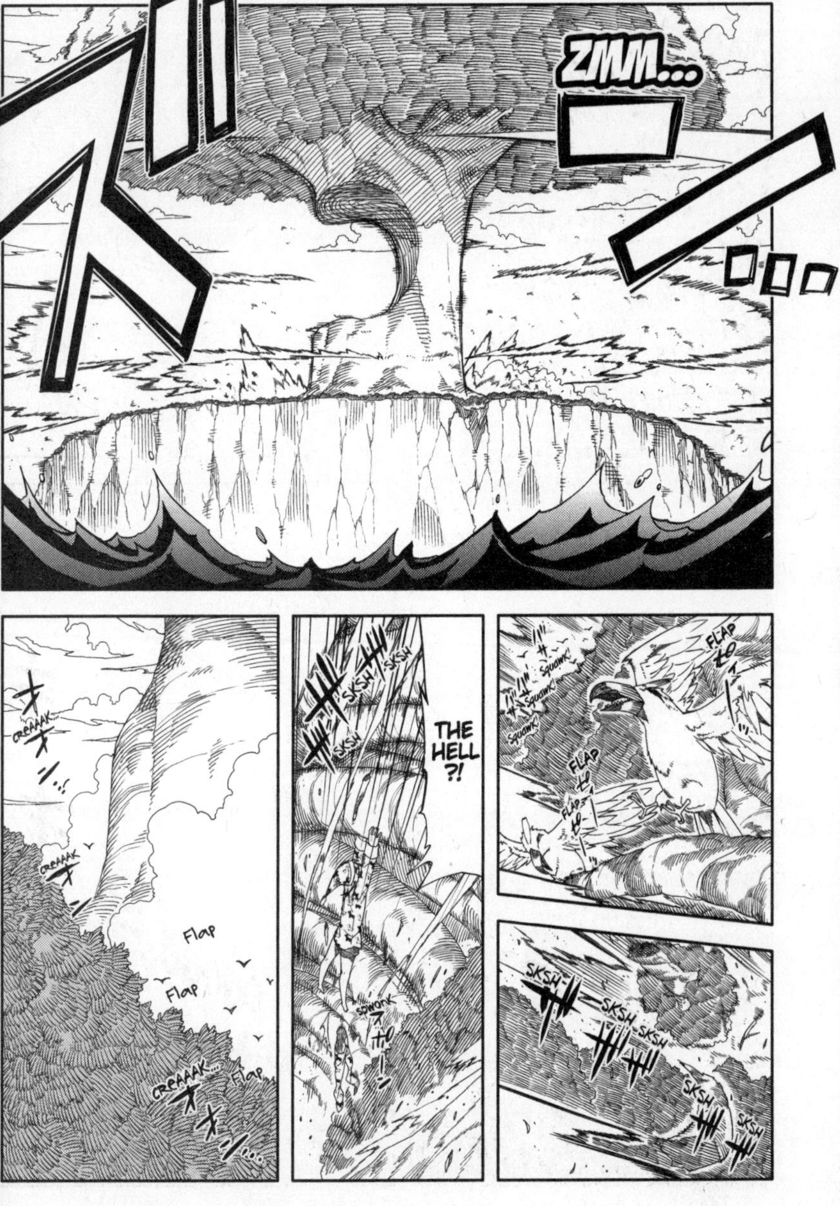
ZMM...
Squawk
Squawk
Squawk
FLAP
FLAP
FLAP
SKSH
SKSH
SKSH
SKSH
SKSH
SKSH
SKSH
SKSH
SKSH
THE HELL ?!
SQWONK
CREAAAK...
CREAAAK
Flap
Flap
CREAAAK...
Flap

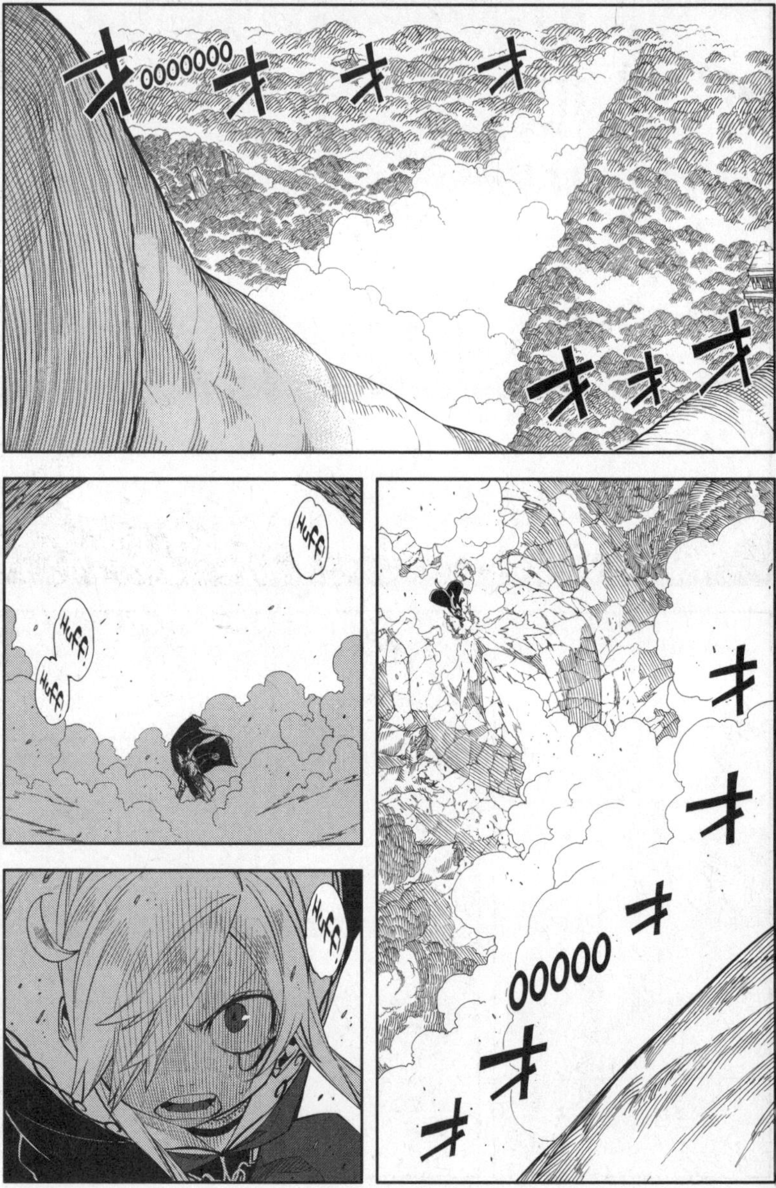

オOOOOOOOオオオ
オォオ
オオォ
OOOOO
オオォ
HUFF!
HUFF!
HUFF!
HUFF!

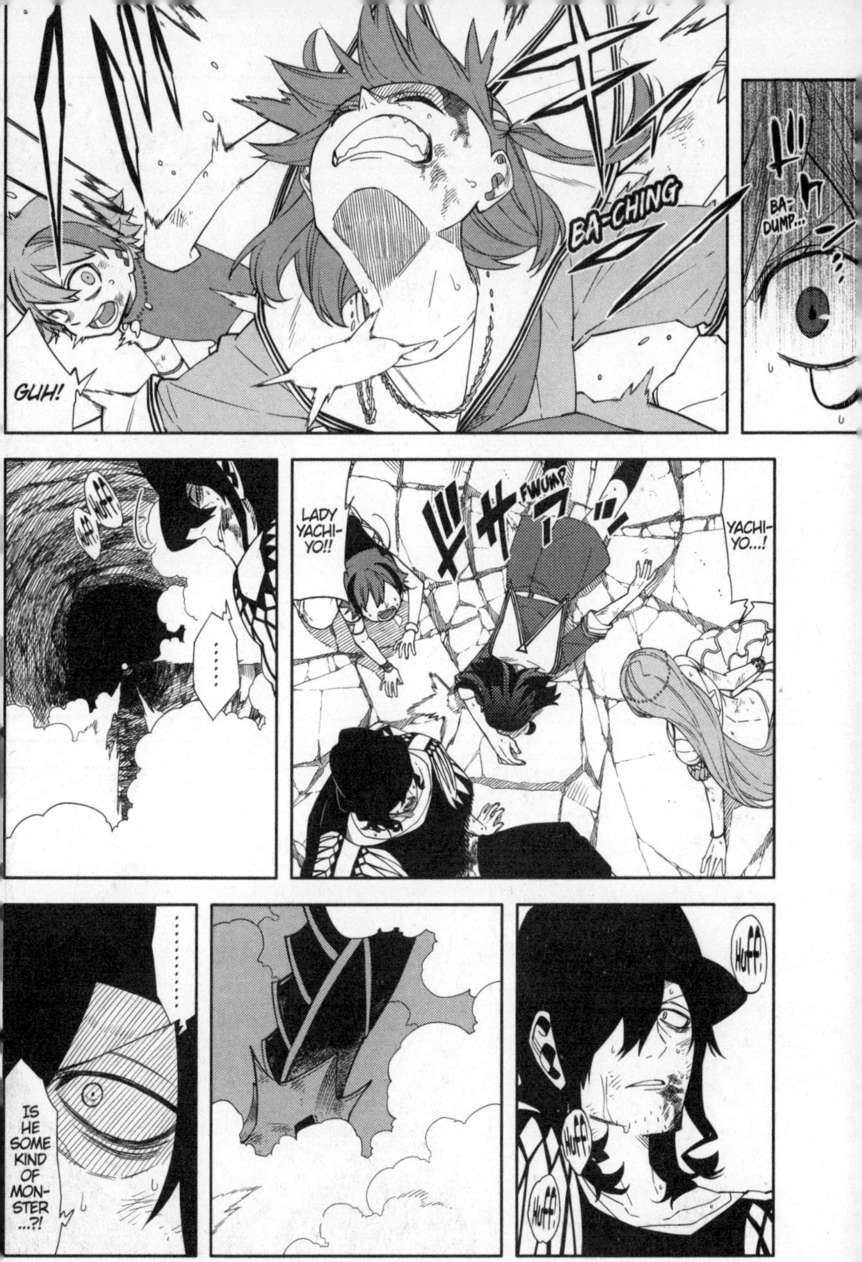
BA-DUMP...
BA-CHING
GUH!
YACHI-YO...!
FWUMP
LADY YACHI-YO!!
HUFF HUFF
......
HUFF!
HUFF!
HUFF!
......
IS HE SOME KIND OF MON-STER...?!

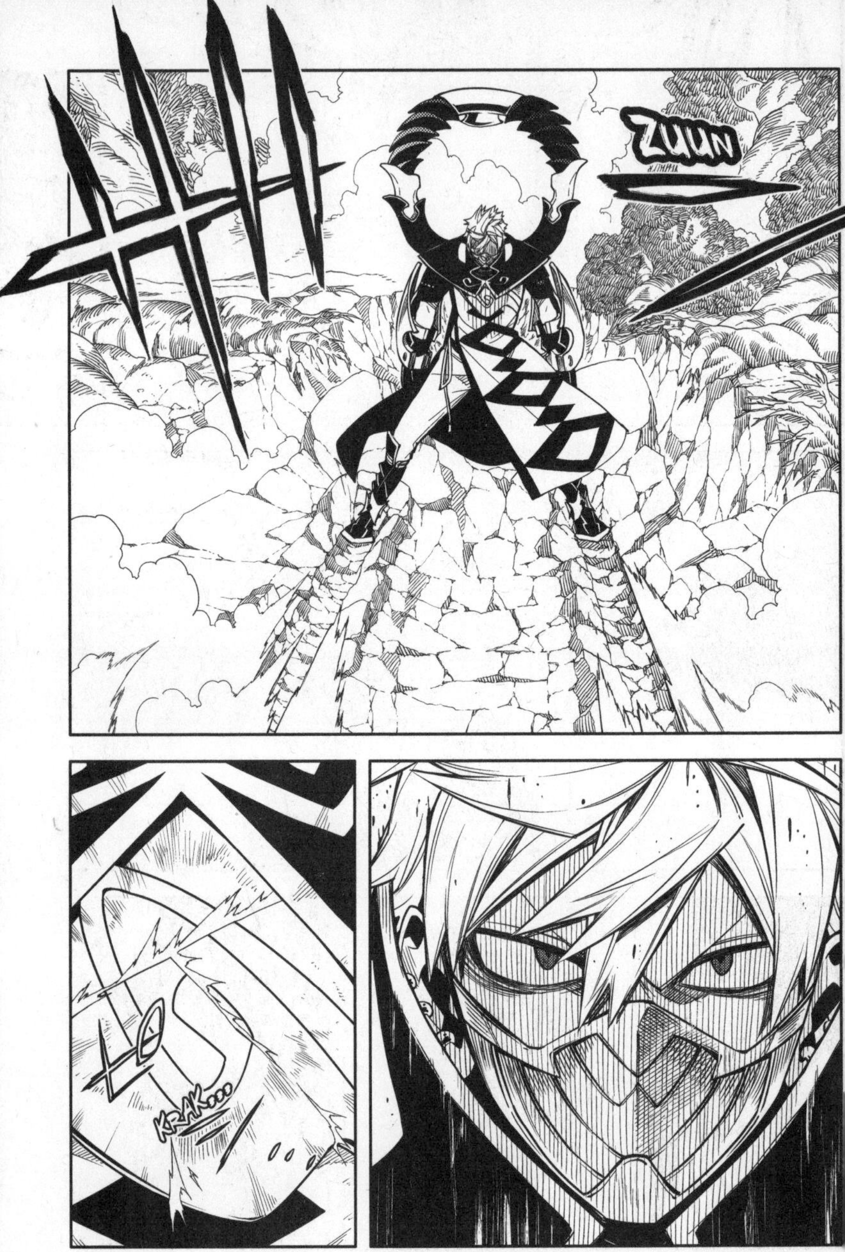
ZUUN
KRAK...

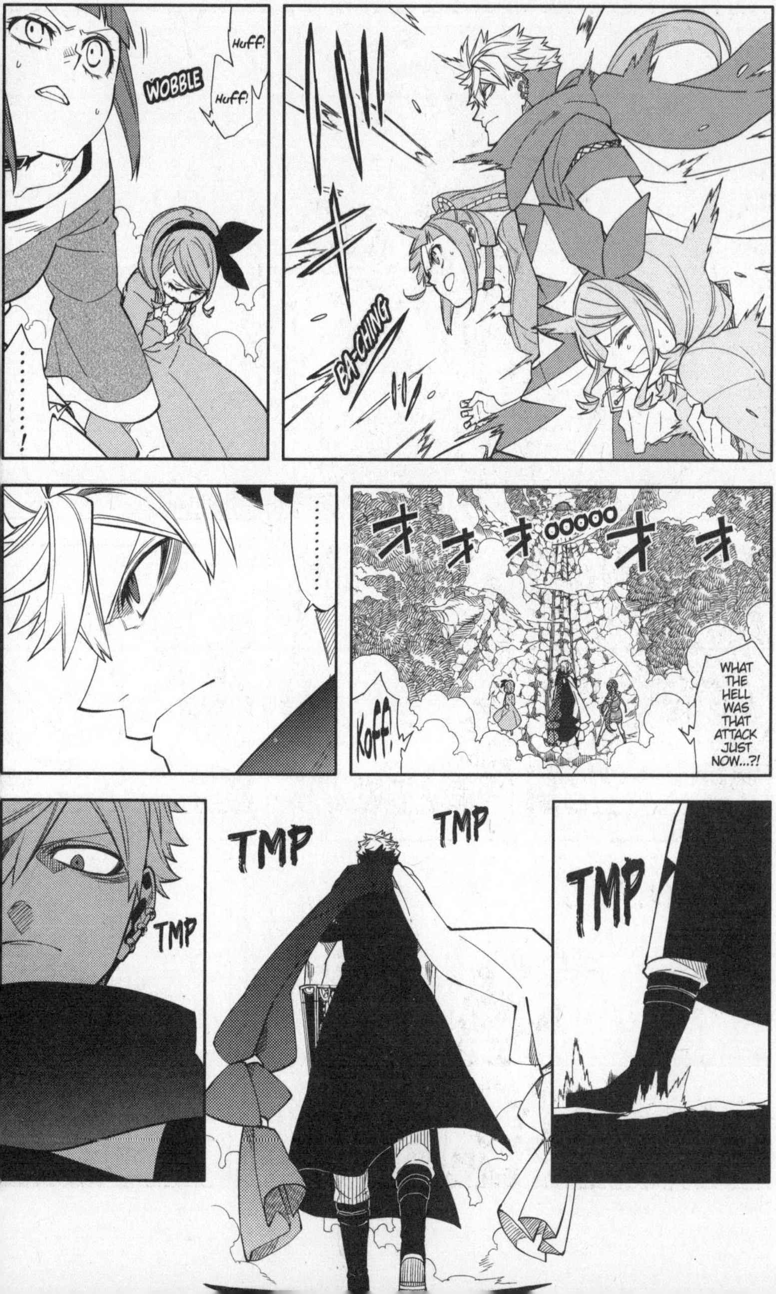
BA-CHING
Huff!
Huff!
WOBBLE
......!
オォオOOOOOオオ
WHAT THE HELL WAS THAT ATTACK JUST NOW...?!
Koff!
......
TMP
TMP
TMP
TMP

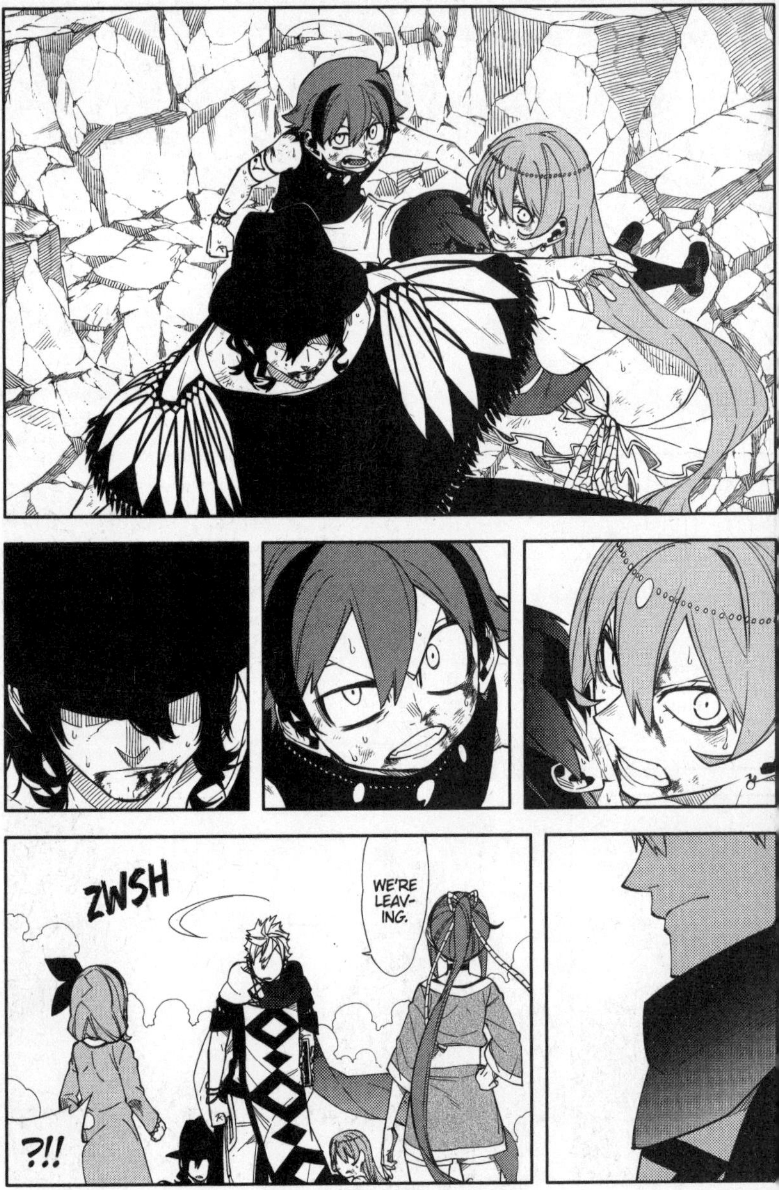
ZWSH
WE'RE LEAV-ING.
?!!

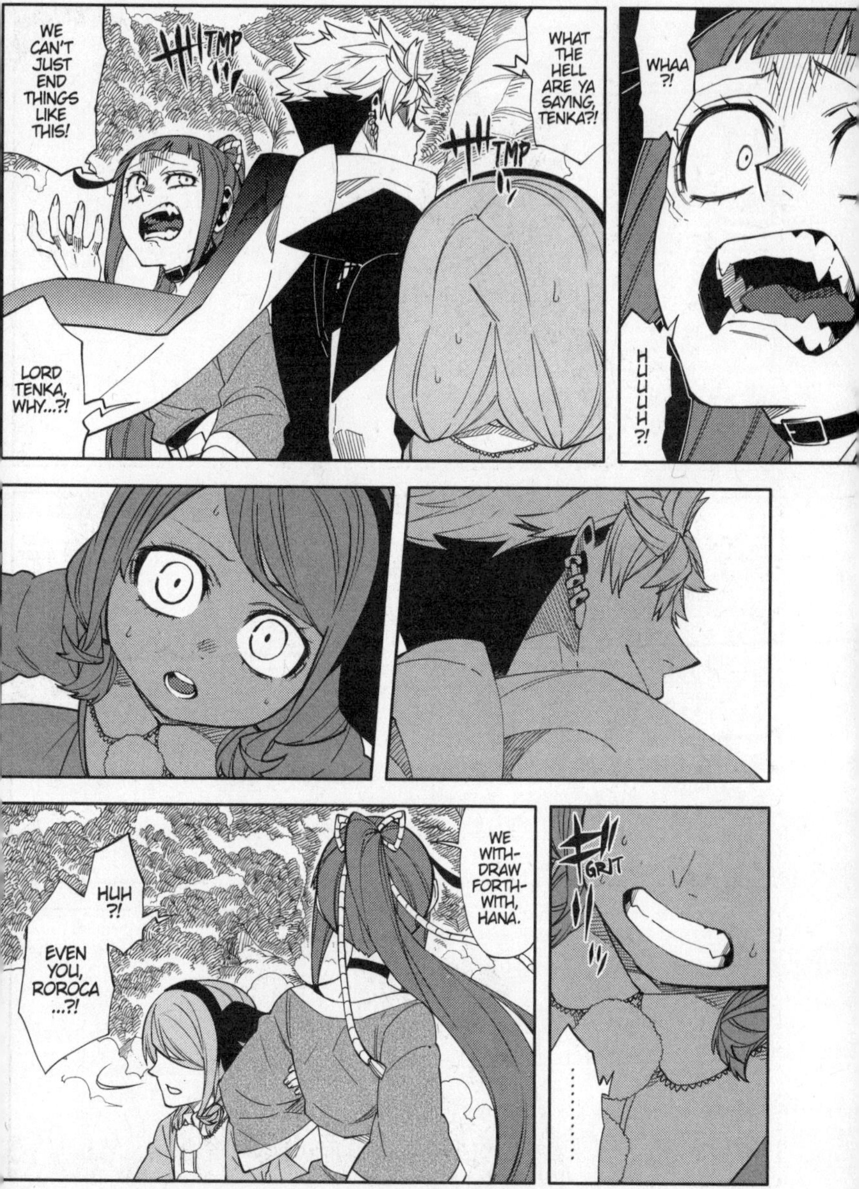
WHAA?!
HUUUH?!
WHAT THE HELL ARE YA SAYING, TENKA?!
TMP
TMP
WE CAN'T JUST END THINGS LIKE THIS!
LORD TENKA, WHY...?!
GRIT
......
WE WITH-DRAW FORTH-WITH, HANA.
HUH?!
EVEN YOU, ROROCA...?!

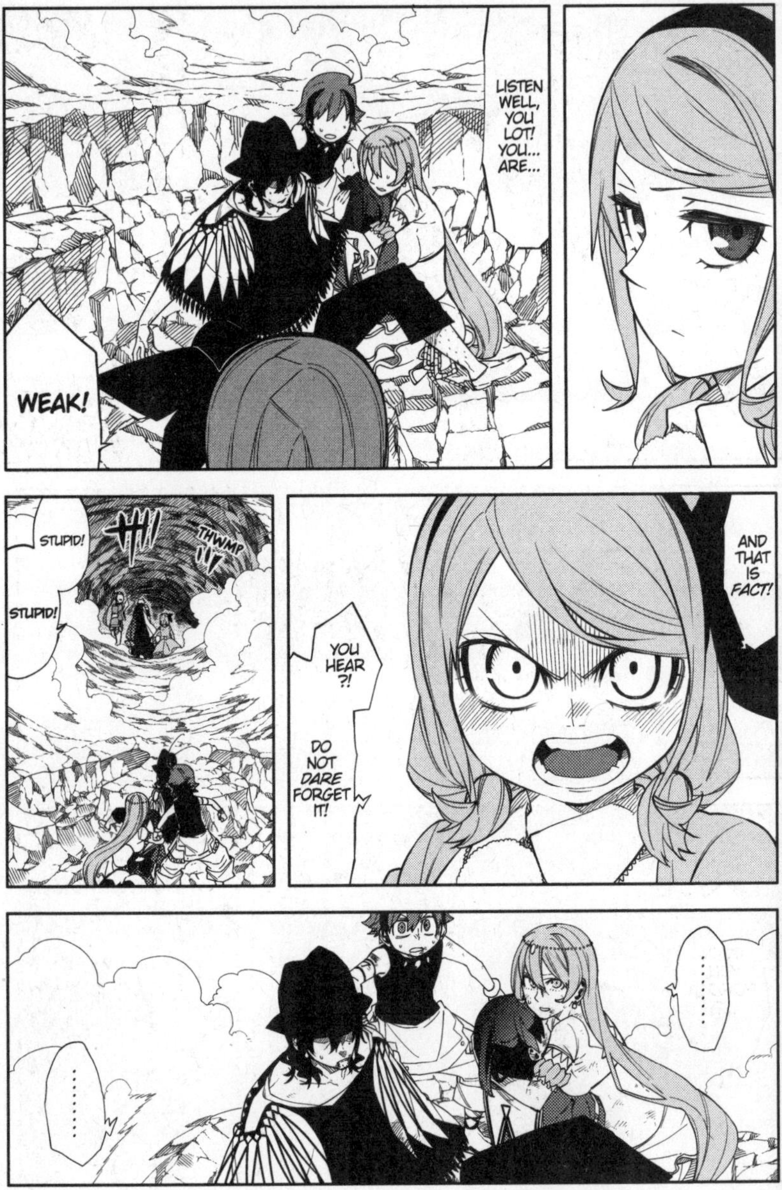
LISTEN WELL, YOU LOT! YOU... ARE...
WEAK!
AND THAT IS FACT!
YOU HEAR?!
DO NOT DARE FORGET IT!
THWMP
STUPID!
STUPID!
......
......

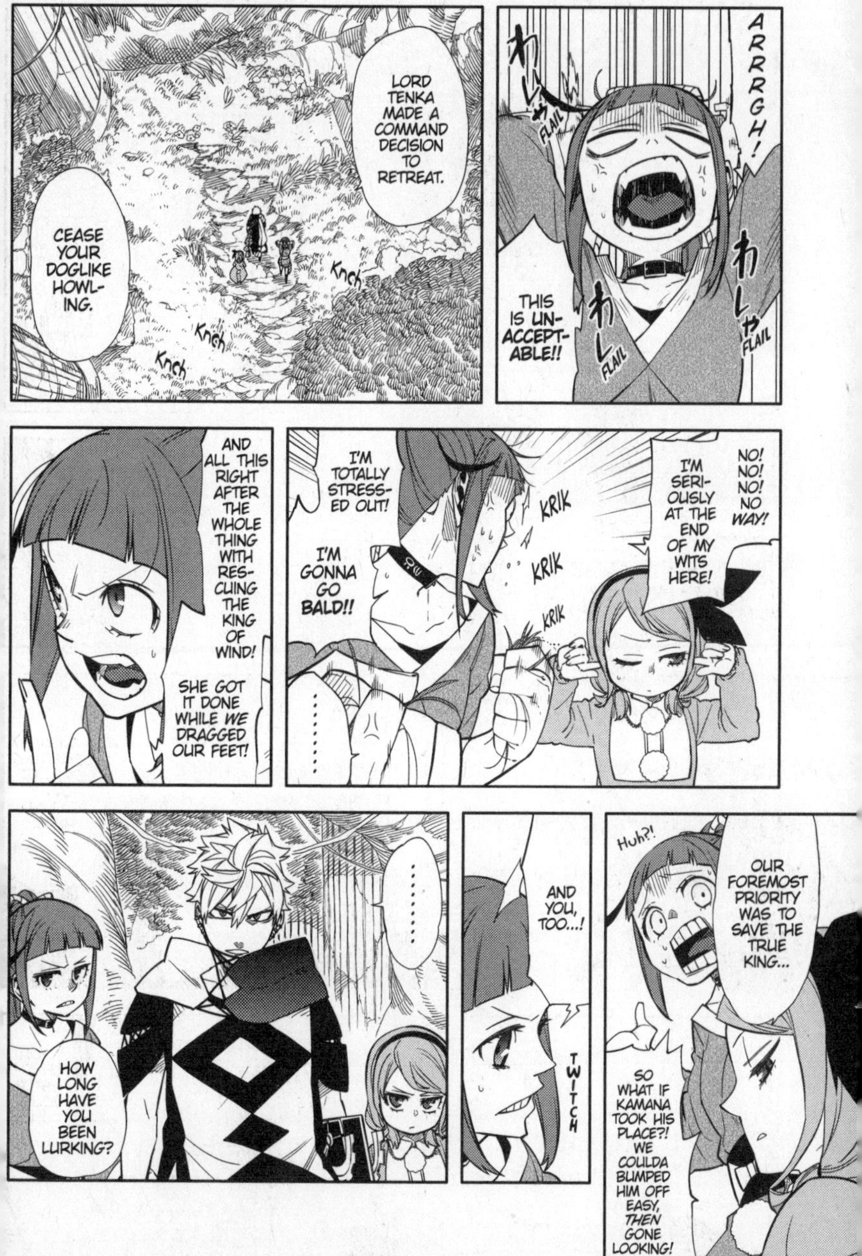
ARRRGH!
わしゃ FLAIL
わしゃ FLAIL
わしゃ FLAIL
THIS IS UN-ACCEPT-ABLE!!
LORD TENKA MADE A COMMAND DECISION TO RETREAT.
CEASE YOUR DOGLIKE HOWL-ING.
Knch
Knch
Knch
NO! NO! NO! NO WAY!
I'M SERI-OUSLY AT THE END OF MY WITS HERE!
KRIK
KRIK
KRIK
I'M TOTALLY STRESS-ED OUT!
I'M GONNA GO BALD!!
....
AND ALL THIS RIGHT AFTER THE WHOLE THING WITH RES-CUING THE KING OF WIND!
SHE GOT IT DONE WHILE WE DRAGGED OUR FEET!
Huh?!
OUR FOREMOST PRIORITY WAS TO SAVE THE TRUE KING...
SO WHAT IF KAMANA TOOK HIS PLACE?! WE COULDA BUMPED HIM OFF EASY, THEN GONE LOOKING!
AND YOU, TOO...!
TWITCH
......
HOW LONG HAVE YOU BEEN LURKING?

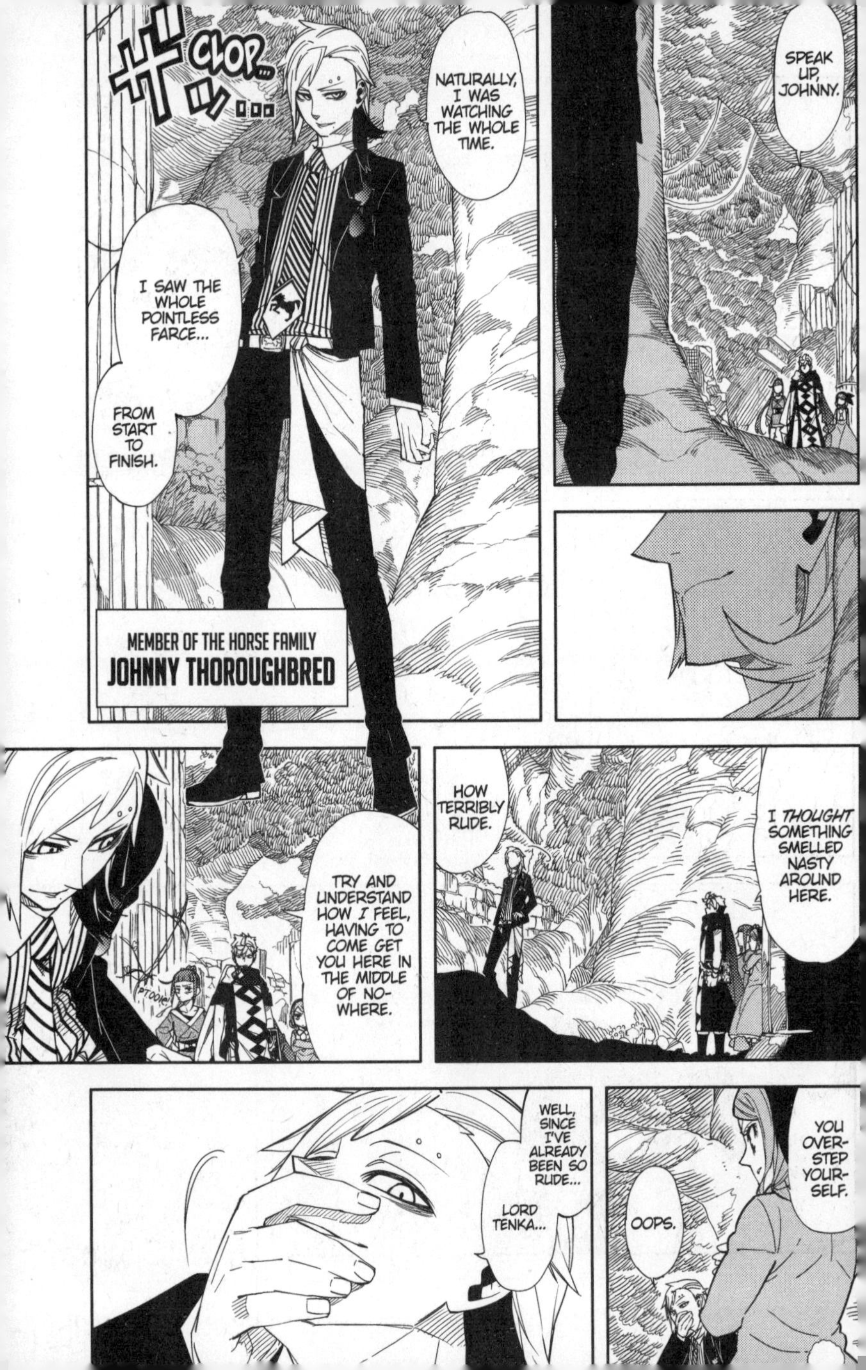
SPEAK UP, JOHNNY.
CLOP...
NATURALLY, I WAS WATCHING THE WHOLE TIME.
I SAW THE WHOLE POINTLESS FARCE...
FROM START TO FINISH.
MEMBER OF THE HORSE FAMILY
JOHNNY THOROUGHBRED
I *THOUGHT* SOMETHING SMELLED NASTY AROUND HERE.
HOW TERRIBLY RUDE.
TRY AND UNDERSTAND HOW *I* FEEL, HAVING TO COME GET YOU HERE IN THE MIDDLE OF NO-WHERE.
PTOOIE!
YOU OVER-STEP YOUR-SELF.
OOPS.
WELL, SINCE I'VE ALREADY BEEN SO RUDE...
LORD TENKA...

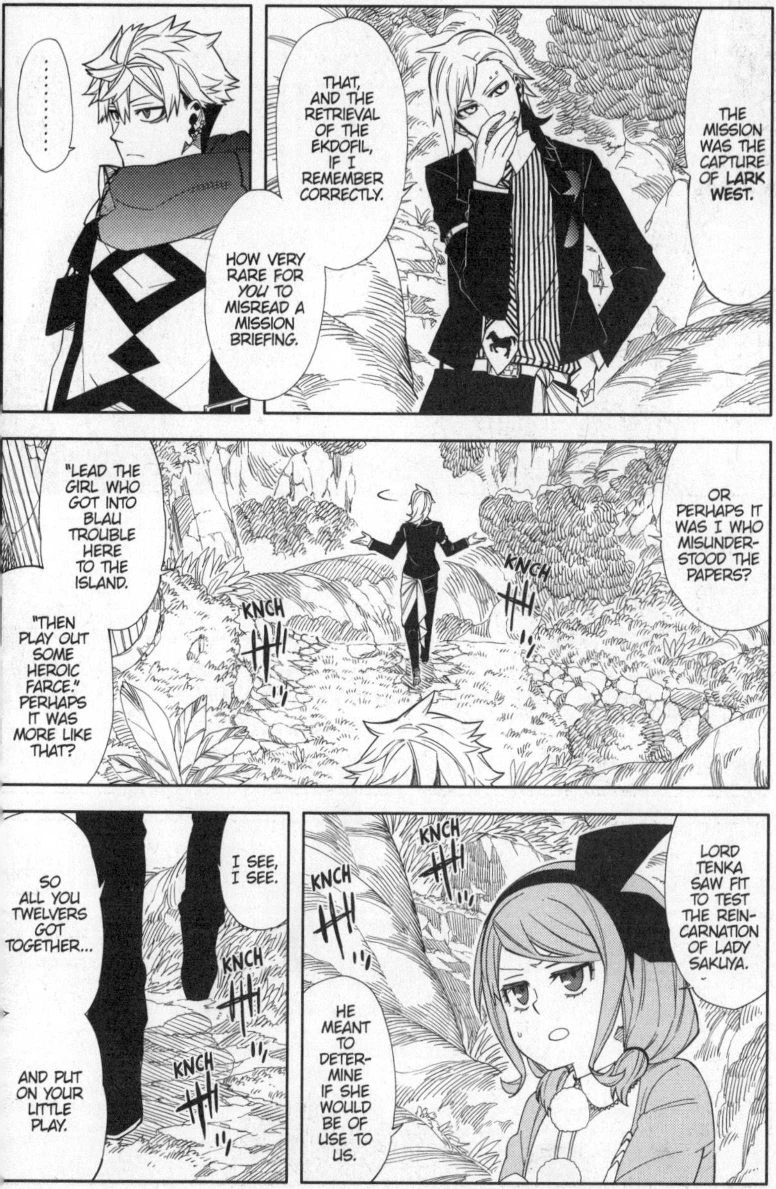
THE MISSION WAS THE CAPTURE OF LARK WEST.
THAT, AND THE RETRIEVAL OF THE EKDOFIL, IF I REMEMBER CORRECTLY.
HOW VERY RARE FOR YOU TO MISREAD A MISSION BRIEFING.
......
OR PERHAPS IT WAS I WHO MISUNDERSTOOD THE PAPERS?
KNCH
"LEAD THE GIRL WHO GOT INTO BLAU TROUBLE HERE TO THE ISLAND.
"THEN PLAY OUT SOME HEROIC FARCE." PERHAPS IT WAS MORE LIKE THAT?
KNCH
LORD TENKA SAW FIT TO TEST THE REIN-CARNATION OF LADY SAKUYA.
KNCH
KNCH
HE MEANT TO DETER-MINE IF SHE WOULD BE OF USE TO US.
I SEE, I SEE.
SO ALL YOU TWELVERS GOT TOGETHER...
KNCH
KNCH
AND PUT ON YOUR LITTLE PLAY.

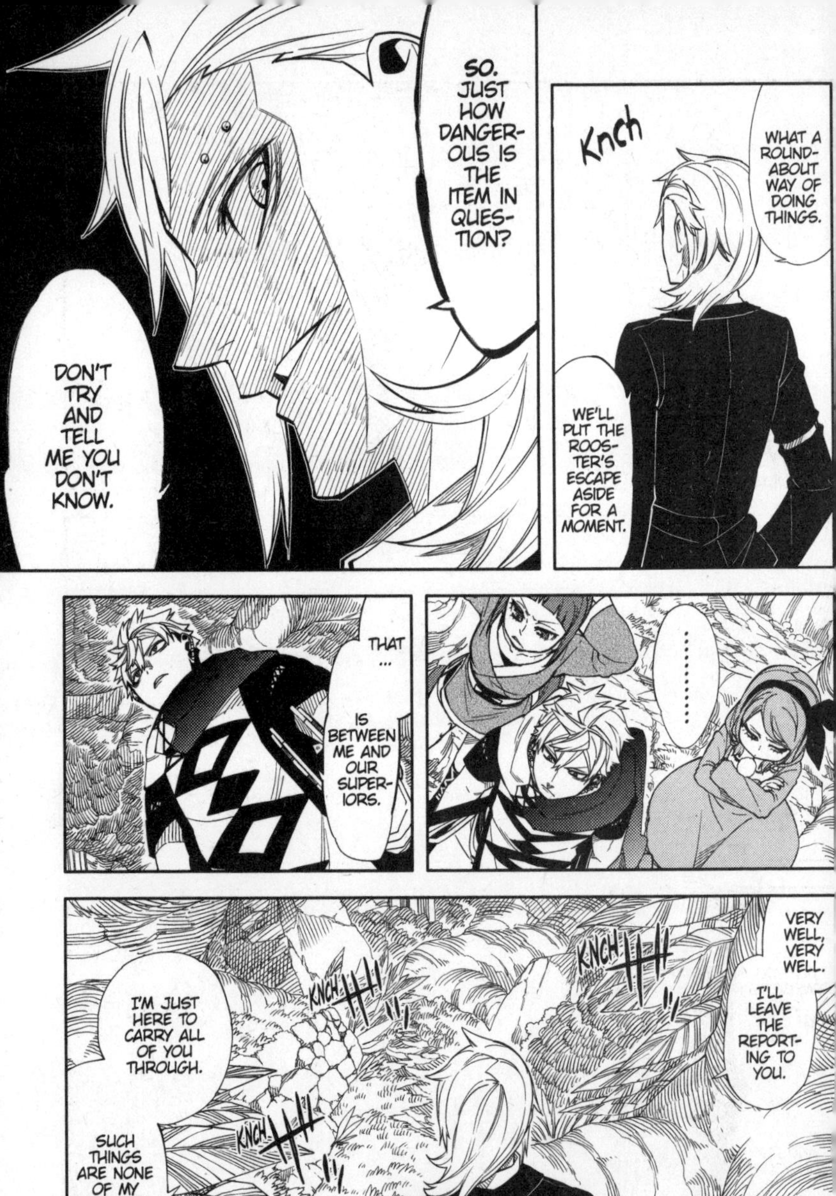
Knch
WHAT A ROUNDABOUT WAY OF DOING THINGS.
WE'LL PUT THE ROOSTER'S ESCAPE ASIDE FOR A MOMENT.
SO. JUST HOW DANGEROUS IS THE ITEM IN QUESTION?
DON'T TRY AND TELL ME YOU DON'T KNOW.
......
THAT ...
IS BETWEEN ME AND OUR SUPERIORS.
VERY WELL, VERY WELL.
I'LL LEAVE THE REPORTING TO YOU.
KNCH
KNCH
I'M JUST HERE TO CARRY ALL OF YOU THROUGH.
KNCH
SUCH THINGS ARE NONE OF MY CONCERN.

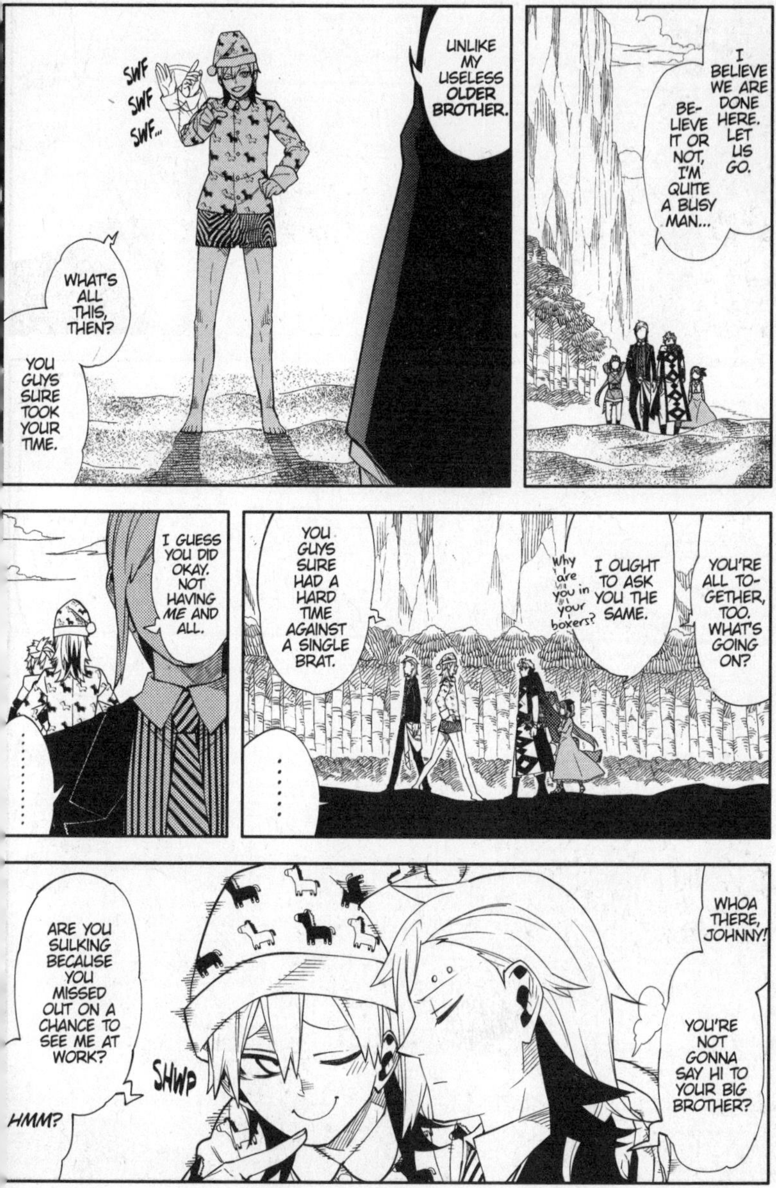
I BELIEVE WE ARE DONE HERE. LET US GO.
BELIEVE IT OR NOT, I'M QUITE A BUSY MAN...
UNLIKE MY USELESS OLDER BROTHER.
SWF SWF SWF...
WHAT'S ALL THIS, THEN?
YOU GUYS SURE TOOK YOUR TIME.
YOU'RE ALL TOGETHER, TOO. WHAT'S GOING ON?
I OUGHT TO ASK YOU THE SAME.
Why are you in your boxers?
YOU GUYS SURE HAD A HARD TIME AGAINST A SINGLE BRAT.
......
I GUESS YOU DID OKAY. NOT HAVING *ME* AND ALL.
......
WHOA THERE, JOHNNY!
YOU'RE NOT GONNA SAY HI TO YOUR BIG BROTHER?
SHWP
ARE YOU SULKING BECAUSE YOU MISSED OUT ON A CHANCE TO SEE ME AT WORK?
HMM?

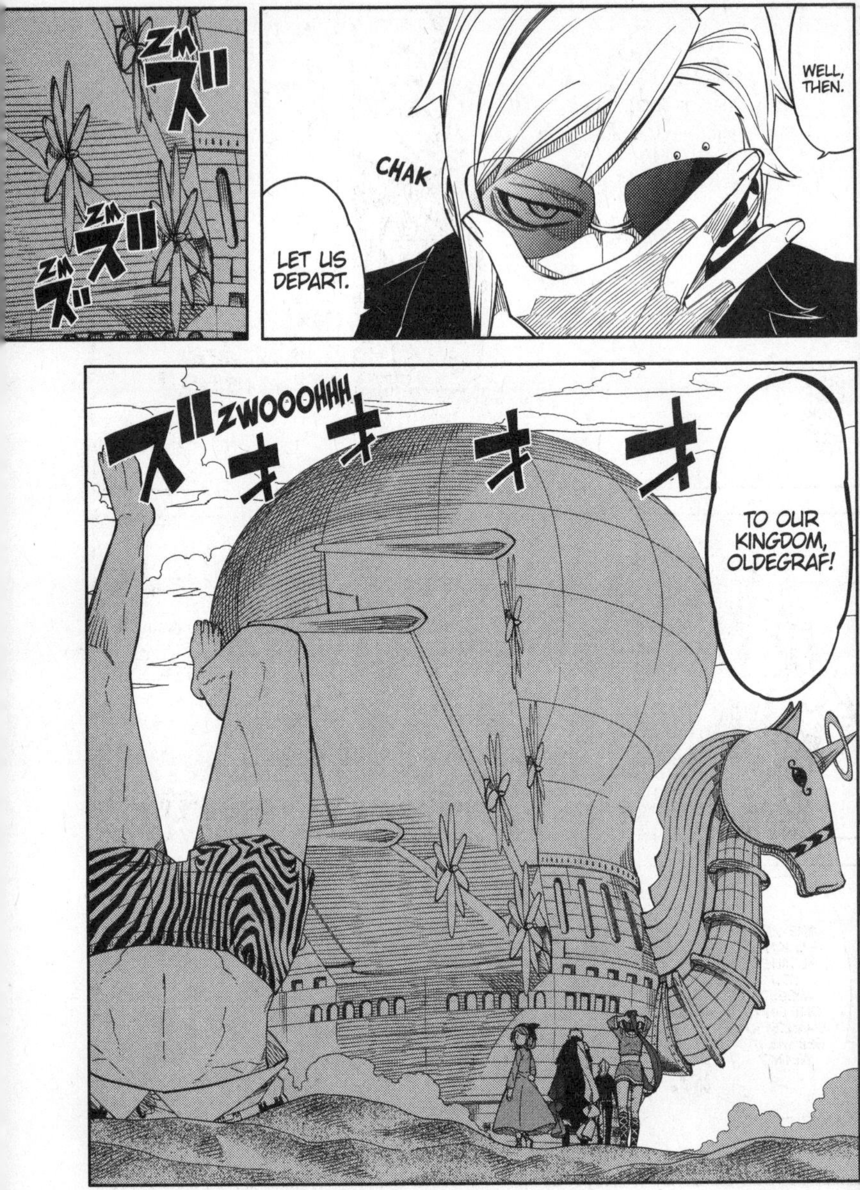
WELL, THEN.
CHAK
LET US DEPART.
ZM
ZM
ZM
ZWOOOHHH
TO OUR KINGDOM, OLDEGRAF!

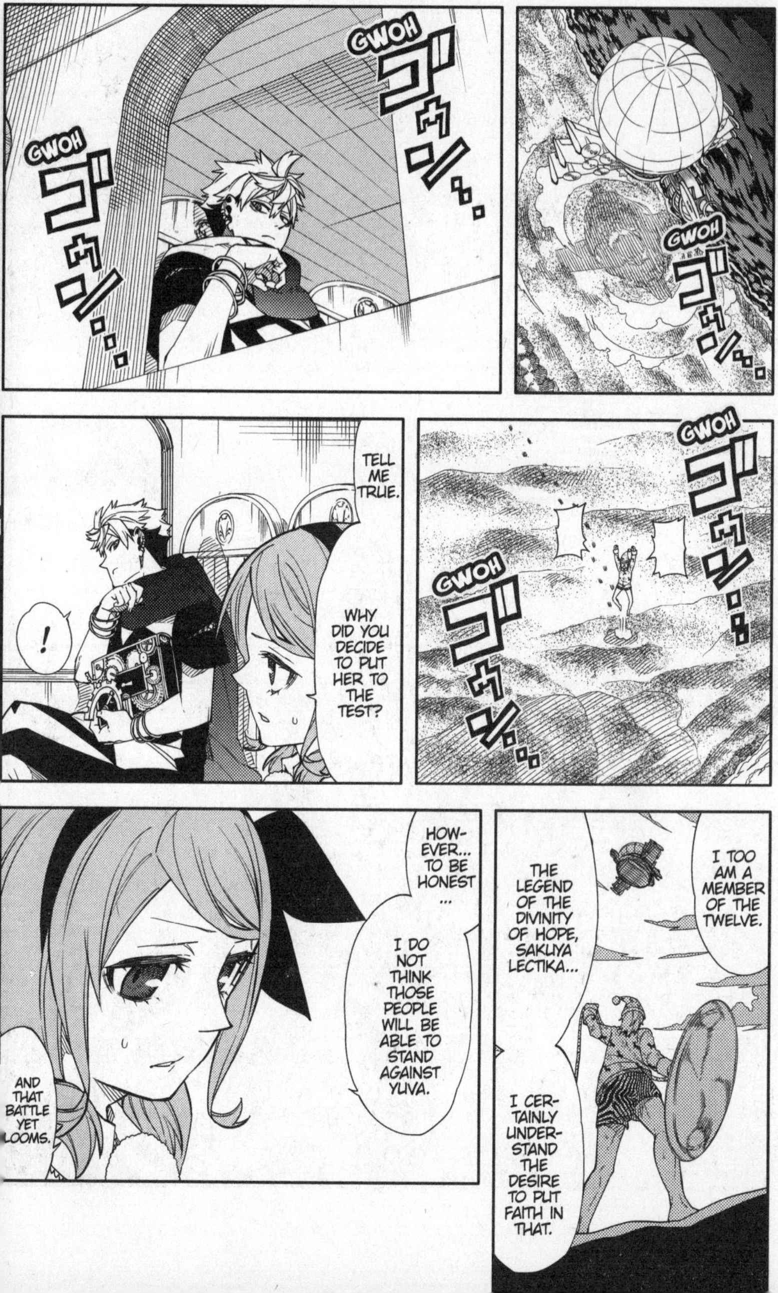
GWOH
ゴウン。。
GWOH
ゴウン。。
GWOH
ゴウン。。
GWOH
ゴウン。。
GWOH
ゴウン。。
TELL ME TRUE.
WHY DID YOU DECIDE TO PUT HER TO THE TEST?
!
I TOO AM A MEMBER OF THE TWELVE.
THE LEGEND OF THE DIVINITY OF HOPE, SAKUYA LECTIKA...
I CERTAINLY UNDERSTAND THE DESIRE TO PUT FAITH IN THAT.
HOW-EVER... TO BE HONEST ...
I DO NOT THINK THOSE PEOPLE WILL BE ABLE TO STAND AGAINST YUVA.
AND THAT BATTLE YET LOOMS.

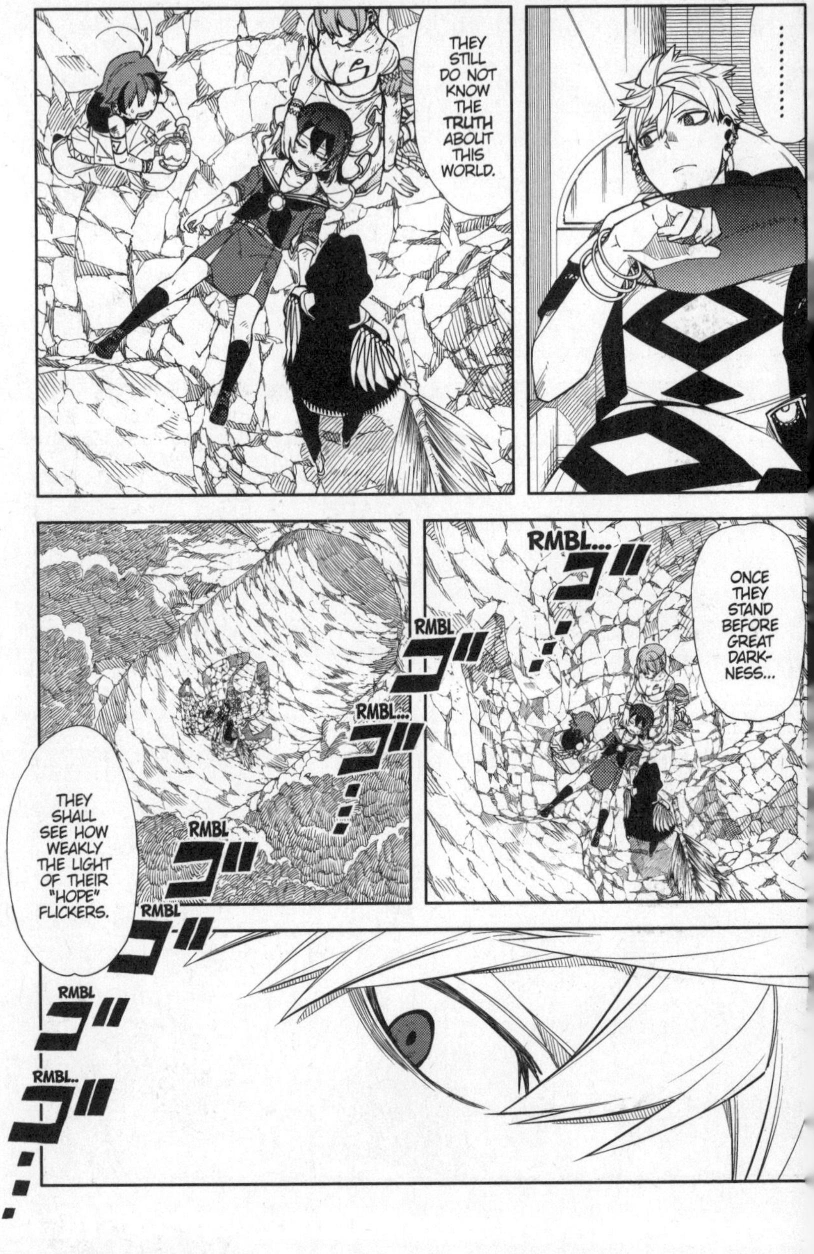
......
THEY STILL DO NOT KNOW THE TRUTH ABOUT THIS WORLD.
RMBL... ゴ
ONCE THEY STAND BEFORE GREAT DARK-NESS...
RMBL ゴ
RMBL... ゴ
RMBL ゴ
THEY SHALL SEE HOW WEAKLY THE LIGHT OF THEIR "HOPE" FLICKERS.
RMBL ゴー
RMBL ゴ
RMBL... ゴ

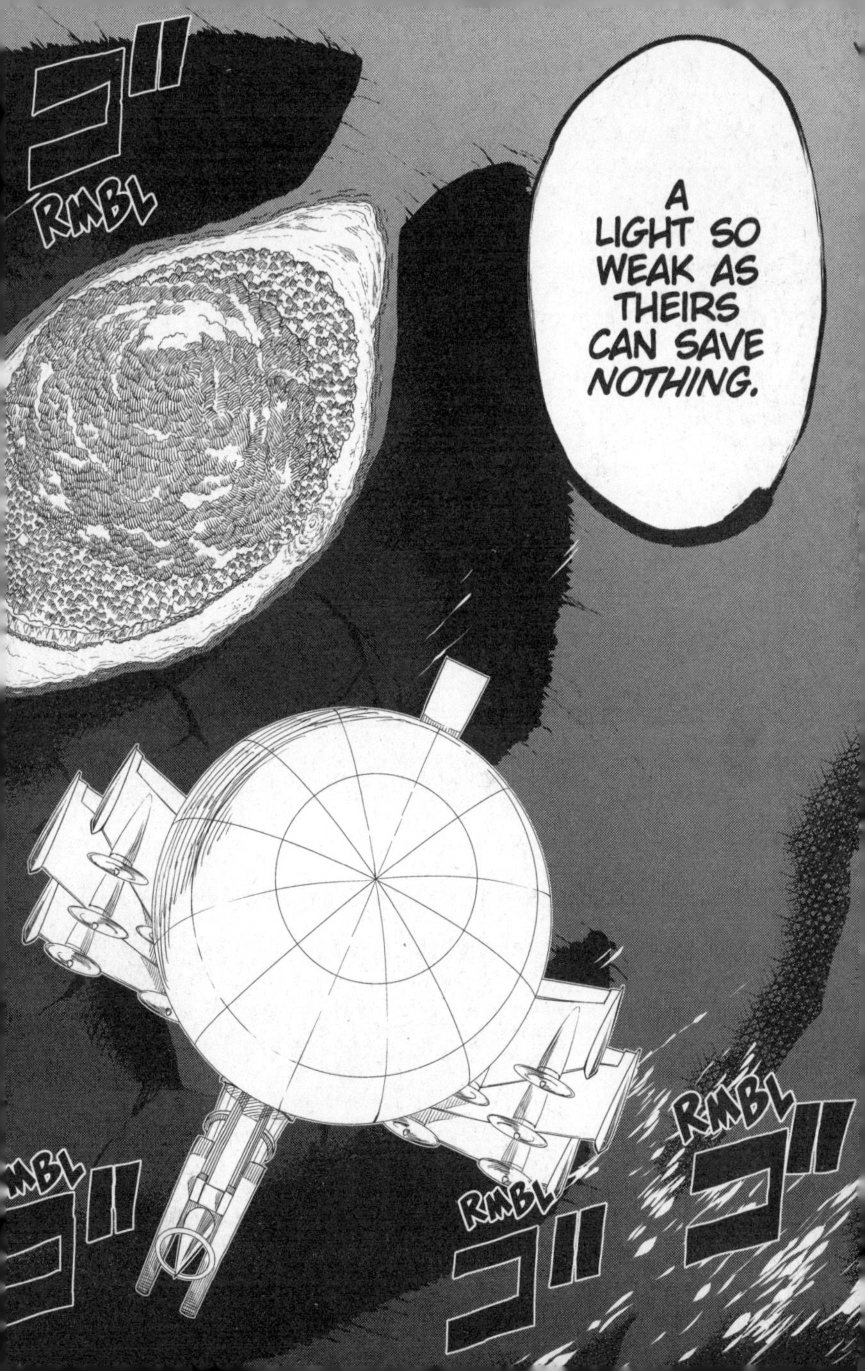
A LIGHT SO WEAK AS THEIRS CAN SAVE NOTHING.
ゴ
RMBL
ゴ
RMBL
ゴ
RMBL
ゴ
MBL

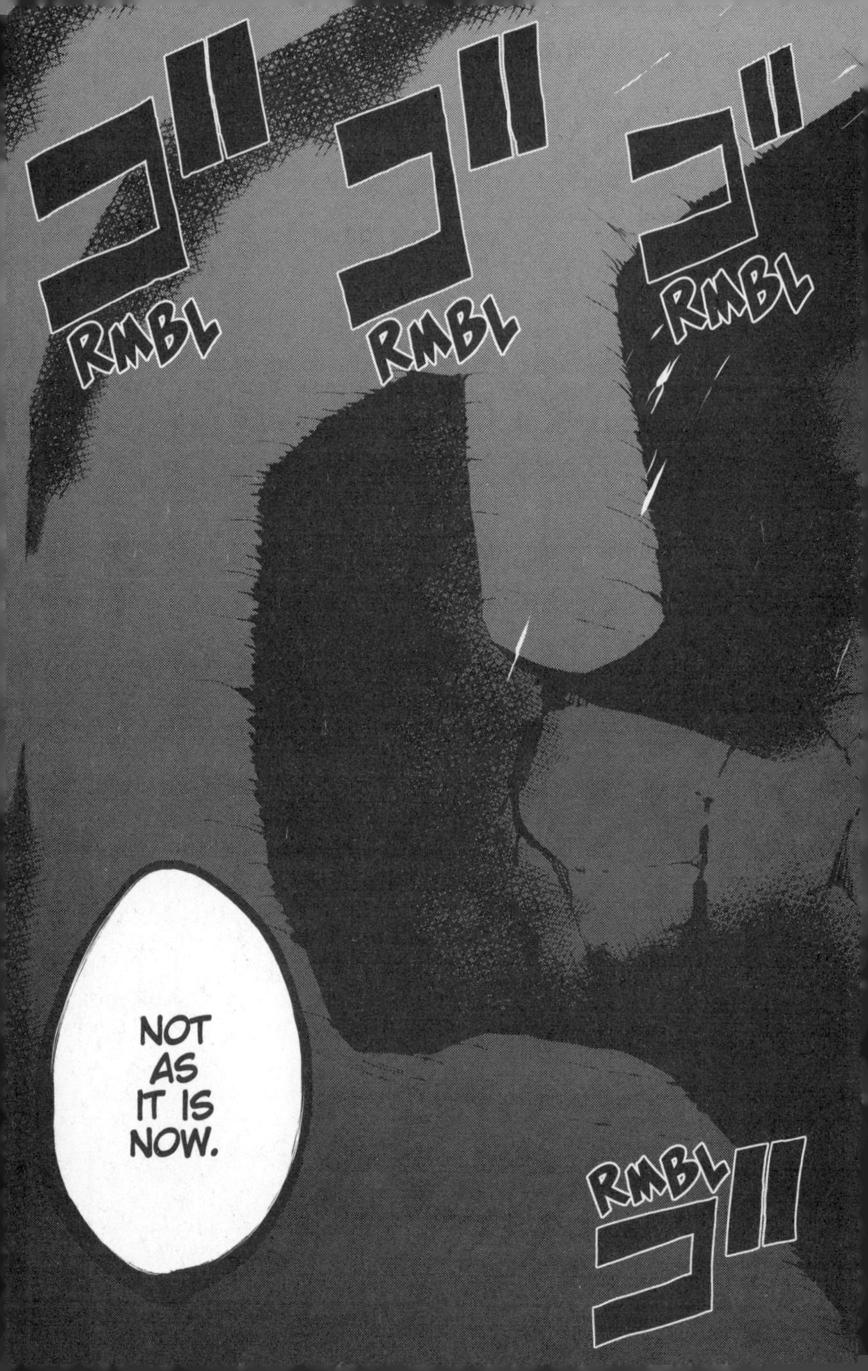
ゴ RMBL
ゴ RMBL
ゴ RMBL
RMBL ゴ
NOT AS IT IS NOW.

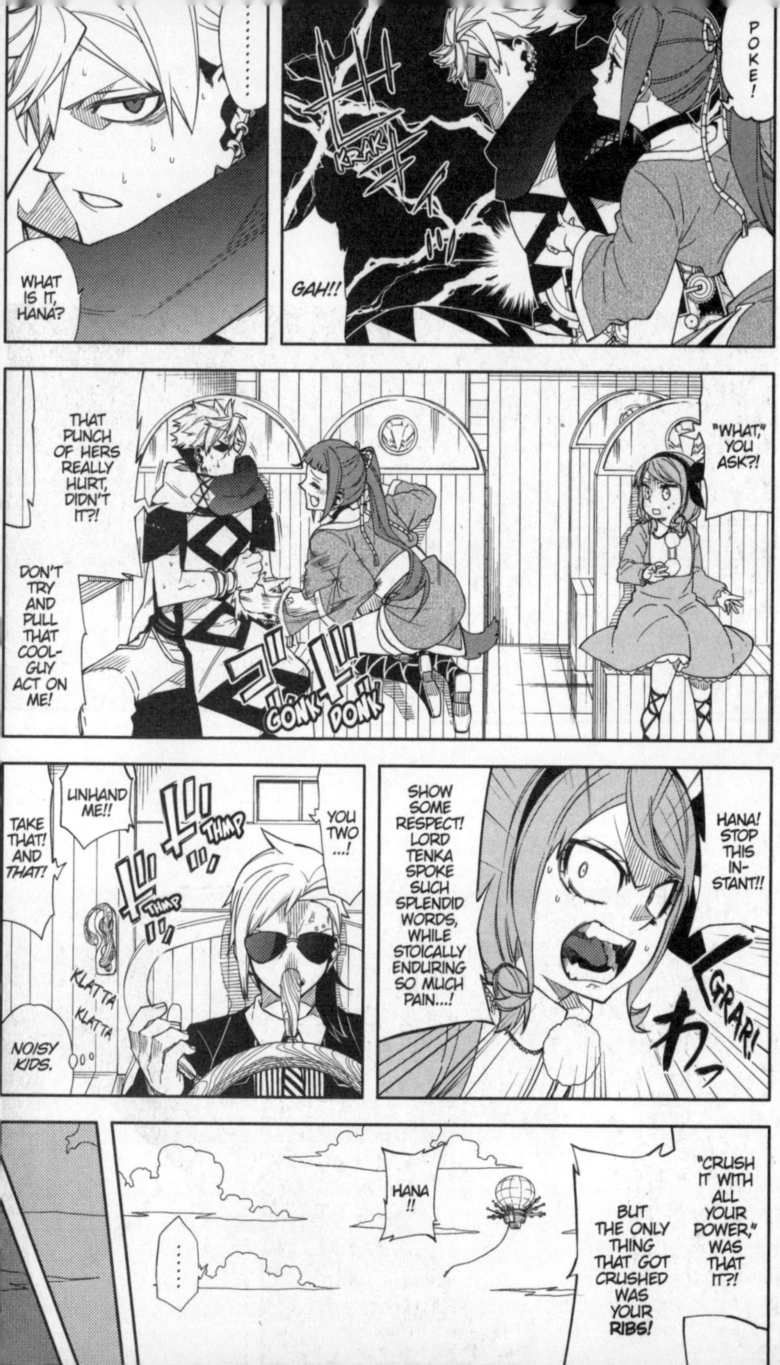
POKE!
KRAK
GAH!!
......
WHAT IS IT, HANA?
"WHAT," YOU ASK?!
THAT PUNCH OF HERS REALLY HURT, DIDN'T IT?!
DON'T TRY AND PULL THAT COOL-GUY ACT ON ME!
GONK
DONK
HANA! STOP THIS IN-STANT!!
GRAR!
SHOW SOME RESPECT! LORD TENKA SPOKE SUCH SPLENDID WORDS, WHILE STOICALLY ENDURING SO MUCH PAIN...!
YOU TWO ...!
UNHAND ME!!
THMP
TAKE THAT! AND THAT!
THMP
KLATTA KLATTA
NOISY KIDS.
"CRUSH IT WITH ALL YOUR POWER," WAS THAT IT?!
BUT THE ONLY THING THAT GOT CRUSHED WAS YOUR RIBS!
HANA !!
......

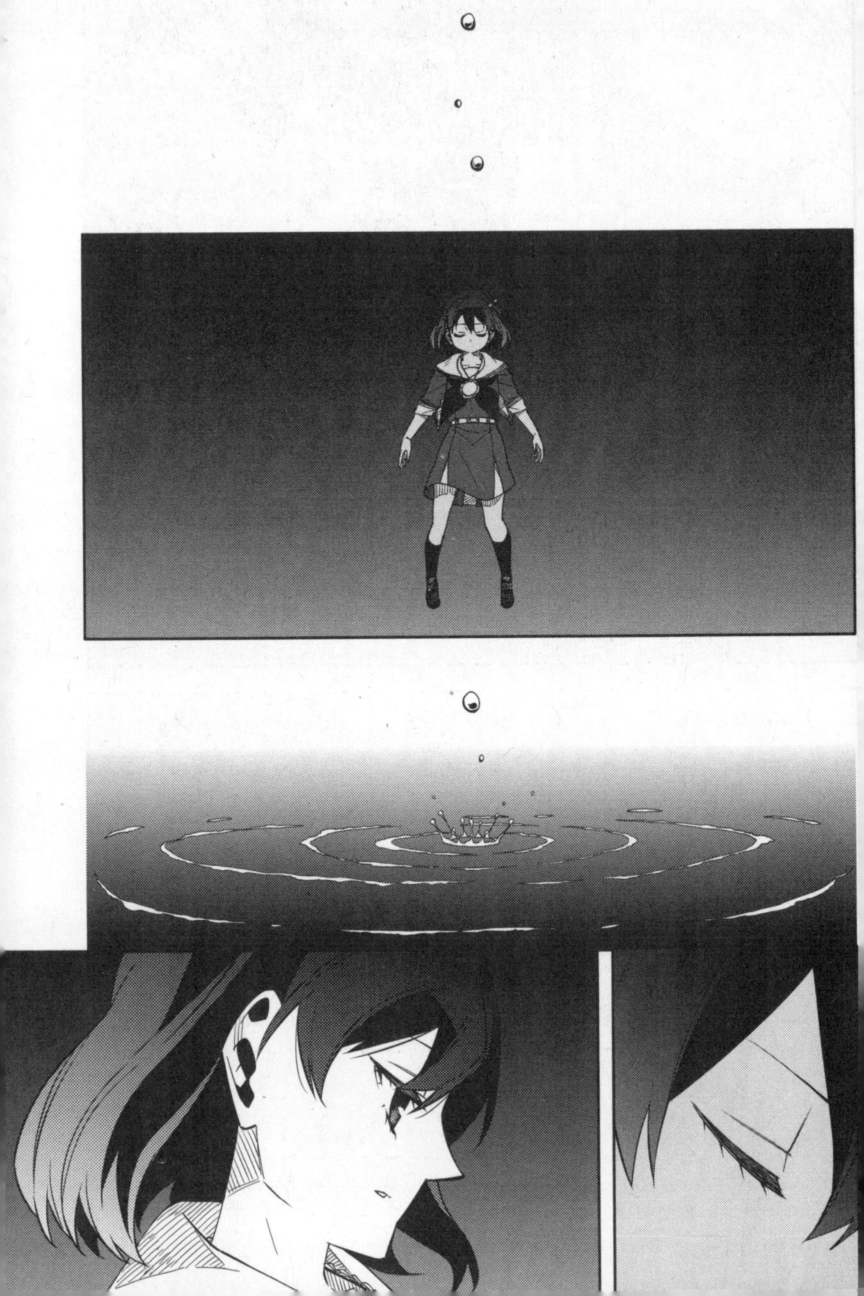

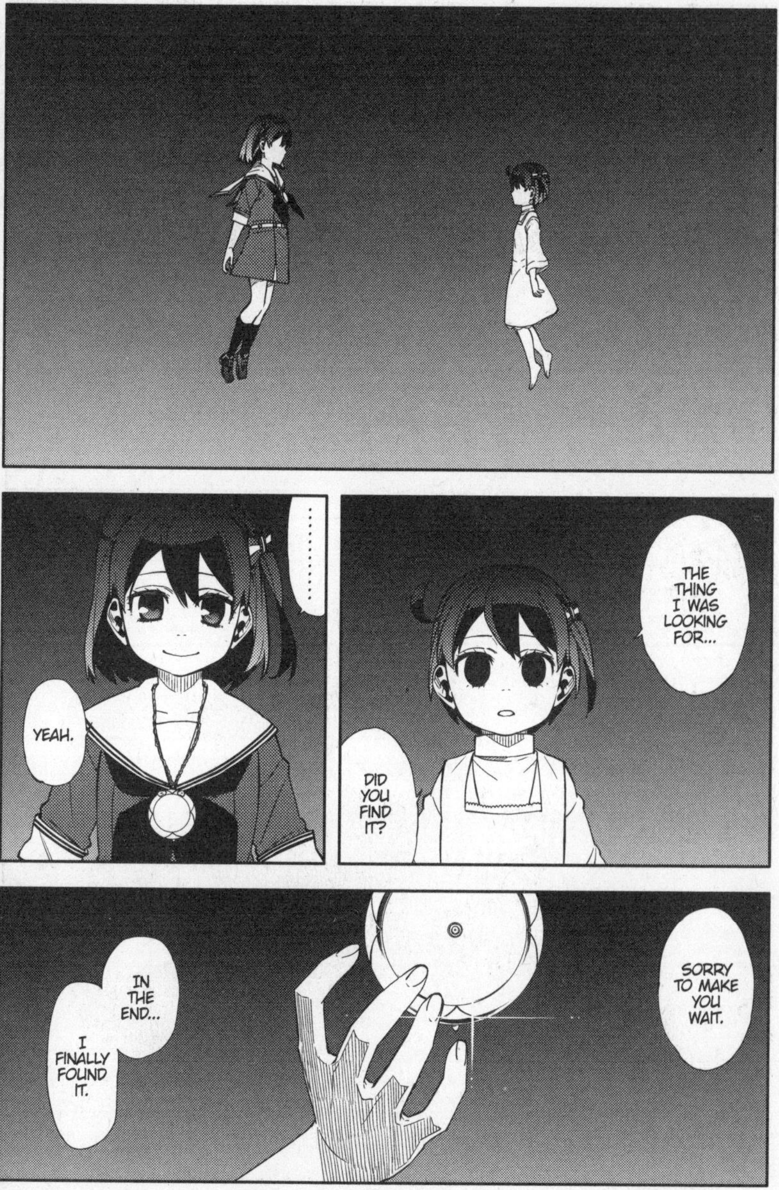
THE THING I WAS LOOKING FOR...
DID YOU FIND IT?
......
YEAH.
SORRY TO MAKE YOU WAIT.
IN THE END...
I FINALLY FOUND IT.

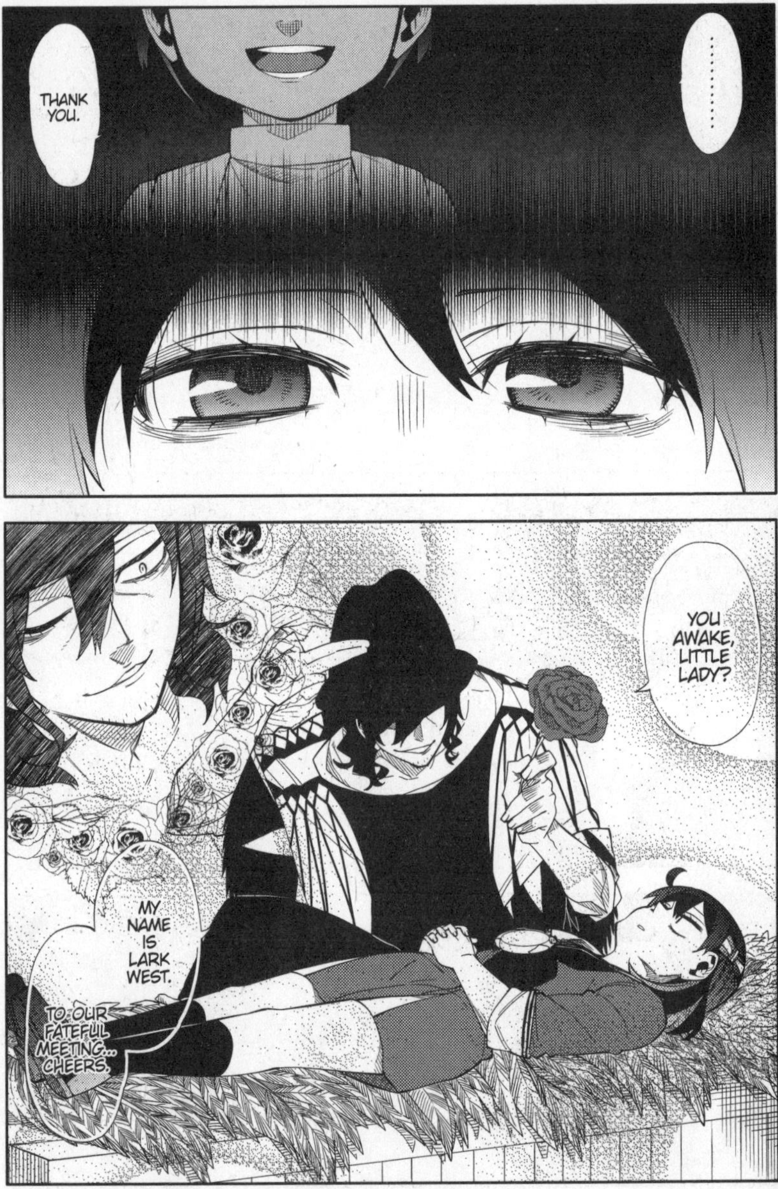
……
THANK YOU.
YOU AWAKE, LITTLE LADY?
MY NAME IS LARK WEST.
TO OUR FATEFUL MEETING... CHEERS.

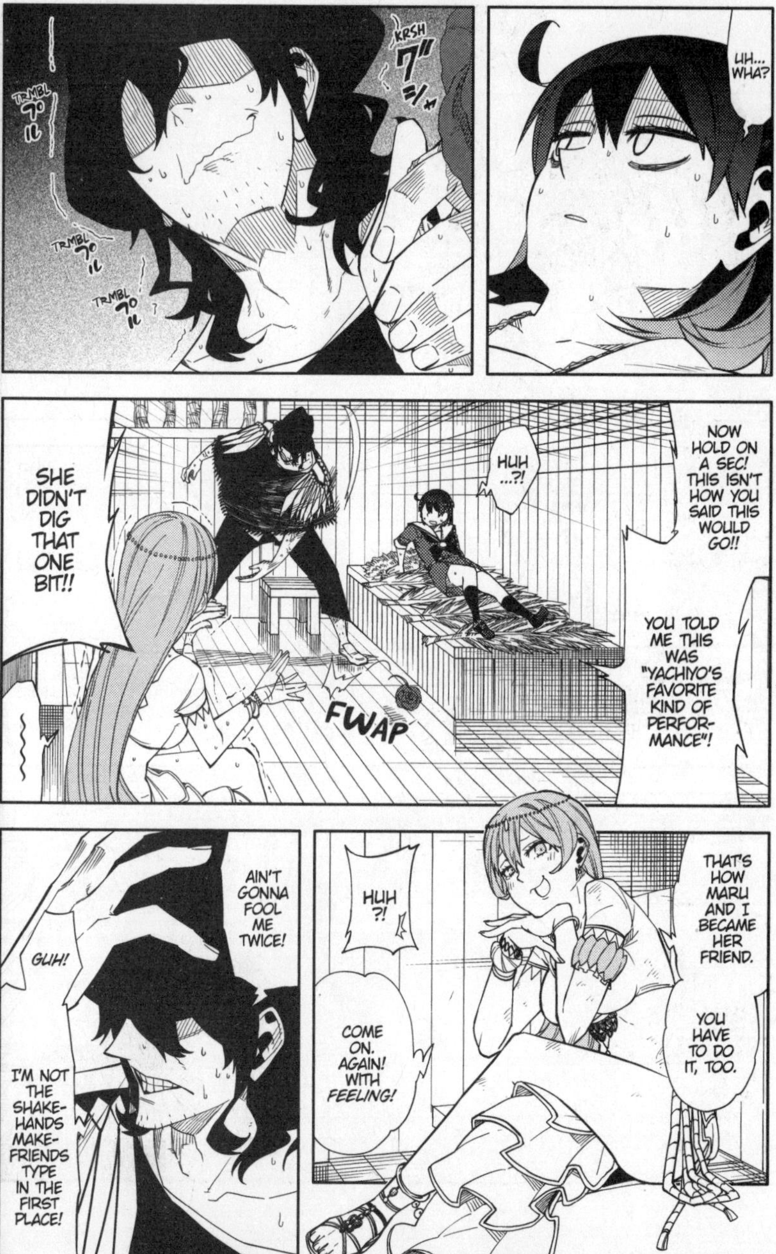
UH... WHA?
KRSH
TRMBL
TRMBL
TRMBL
NOW HOLD ON A SEC! THIS ISN'T HOW YOU SAID THIS WOULD GO!!
HUH ...?!
YOU TOLD ME THIS WAS "YACHIYO'S FAVORITE KIND OF PERFOR-MANCE"!
SHE DIDN'T DIG THAT ONE BIT!!
FWAP
THAT'S HOW MARU AND I BECAME HER FRIEND.
HUH ?!
YOU HAVE TO DO IT, TOO.
COME ON. AGAIN! WITH FEELING!
AIN'T GONNA FOOL ME TWICE!
GUH!
I'M NOT THE SHAKE-HANDS MAKE-FRIENDS TYPE IN THE FIRST PLACE!

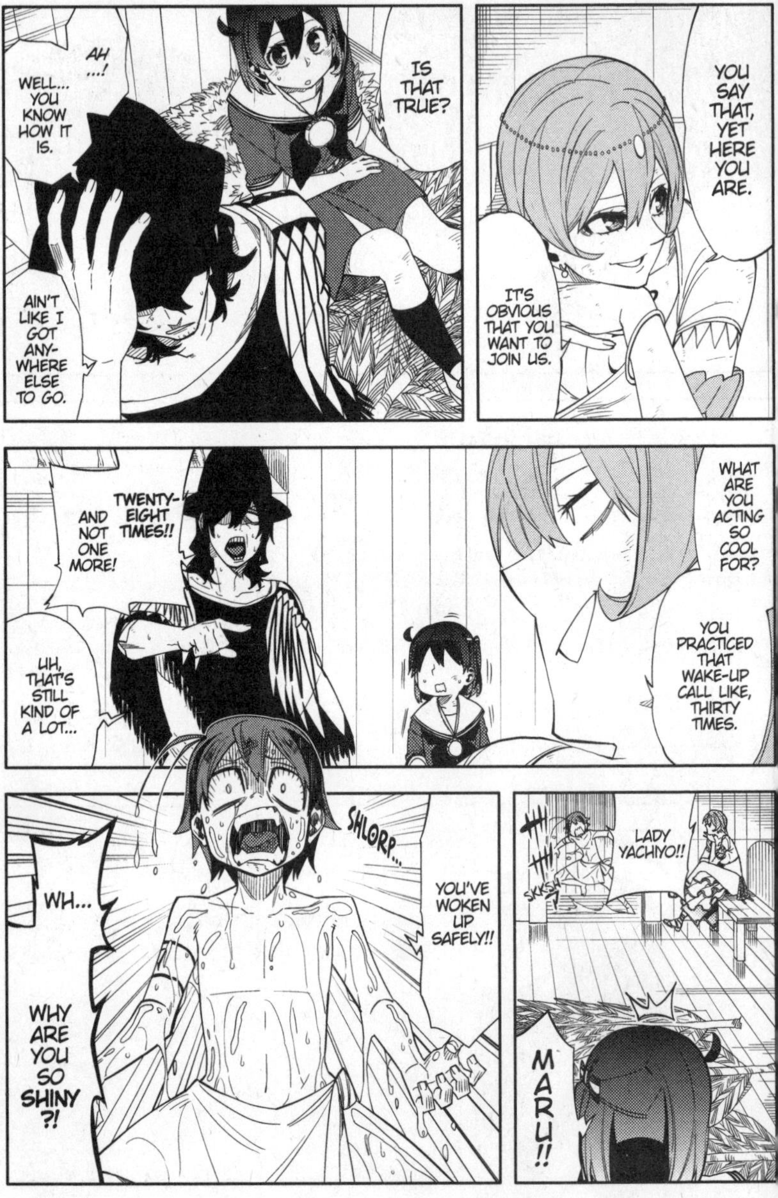
YOU SAY THAT, YET HERE YOU ARE.
IT'S OBVIOUS THAT YOU WANT TO JOIN US.
IS THAT TRUE?
AH ...!
WELL... YOU KNOW HOW IT IS.
AIN'T LIKE I GOT ANYWHERE ELSE TO GO.
WHAT ARE YOU ACTING SO COOL FOR?
YOU PRACTICED THAT WAKE-UP CALL LIKE, THIRTY TIMES.
TWENTY-EIGHT TIMES!!
AND NOT ONE MORE!
UH, THAT'S STILL KIND OF A LOT...
LADY YACHIYO!!
SKKSH
MARU!!
SHLORP...
YOU'VE WOKEN UP SAFELY!!
WH...
WHY ARE YOU SO SHINY?!

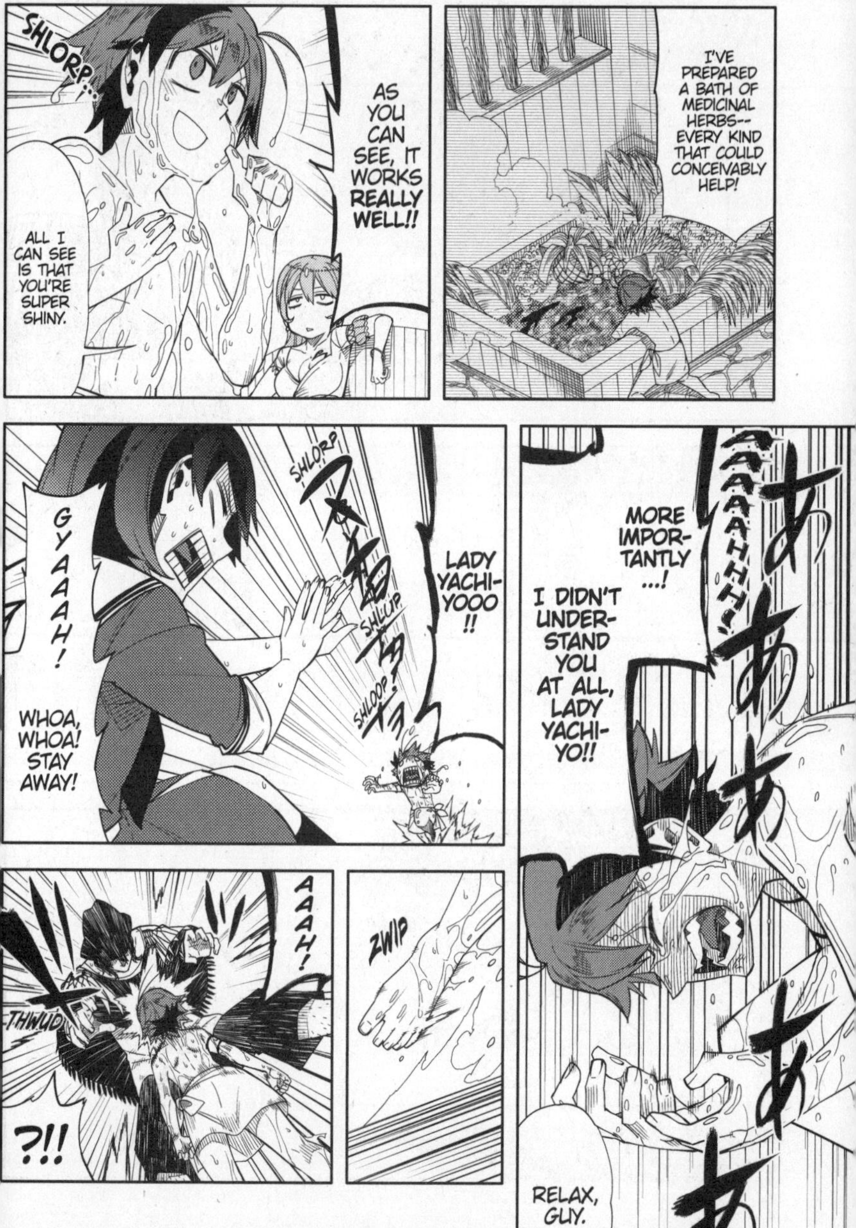
I'VE PREPARED A BATH OF MEDICINAL HERBS-- EVERY KIND THAT COULD CONCEIVABLY HELP!
SHLORP...
AS YOU CAN SEE, IT WORKS REALLY WELL!!
ALL I CAN SEE IS THAT YOU'RE SUPER SHINY.
AAAAAAAHHHH!
ああああああ
MORE IMPORTANTLY...!
I DIDN'T UNDERSTAND YOU AT ALL, LADY YACHIYO!!
RELAX, GUY.
LADY YACHIYOOO!!
SHLORP
SHLUP
SHLOOP
GYAAAAH!
WHOA, WHOA! STAY AWAY!
ZWIP
AAAAH!
THWUD
?!!

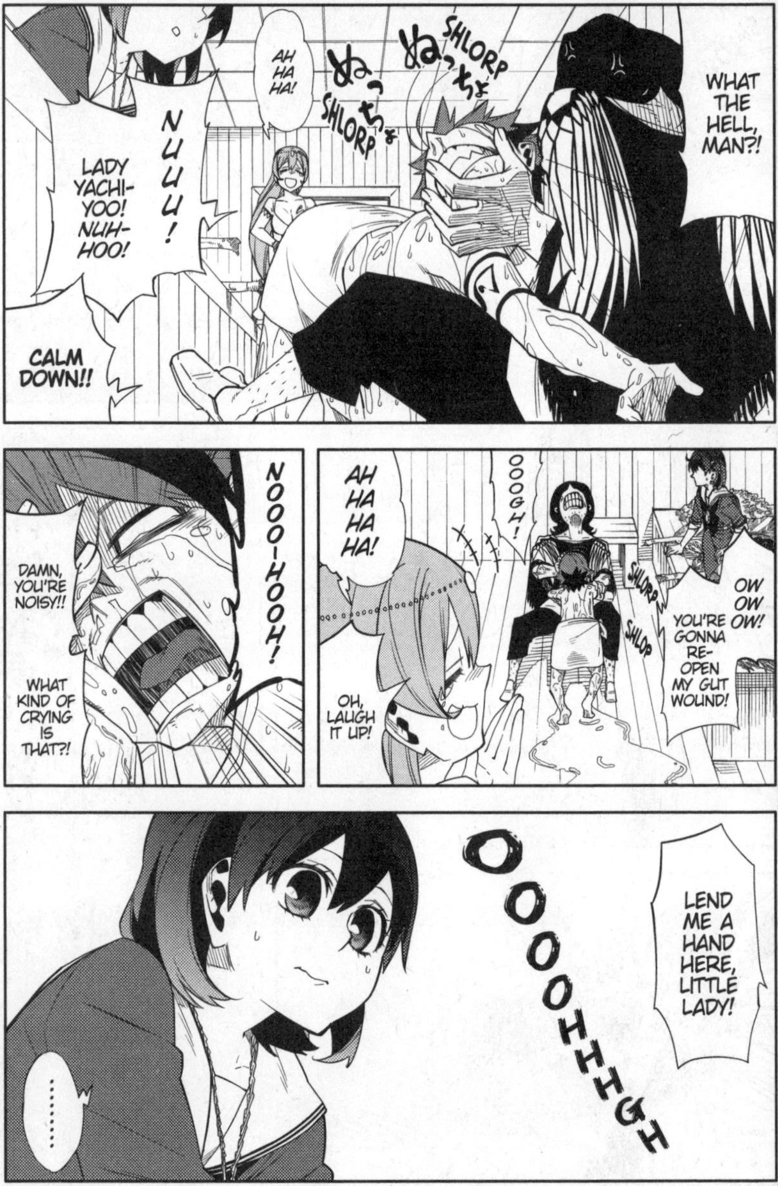
WHAT THE HELL, MAN?!
ぬっちょ
SHLORP
ぬっちょ
SHLORP
AH HA HA!
NUUUU!
LADY YACHI-YOO! NUH-HOO!
CALM DOWN!!
OW OW OW! YOU'RE GONNA RE-OPEN MY GUT WOUND!
SHLORP
SHLOP
OOOGH!
AH HA HA HA HA!
OH, LAUGH IT UP!
NOOOO-HOOOH!
DAMN, YOU'RE NOISY!!
WHAT KIND OF CRYING IS THAT?!
LEND ME A HAND HERE, LITTLE LADY!
OOOOOHHHGH
......

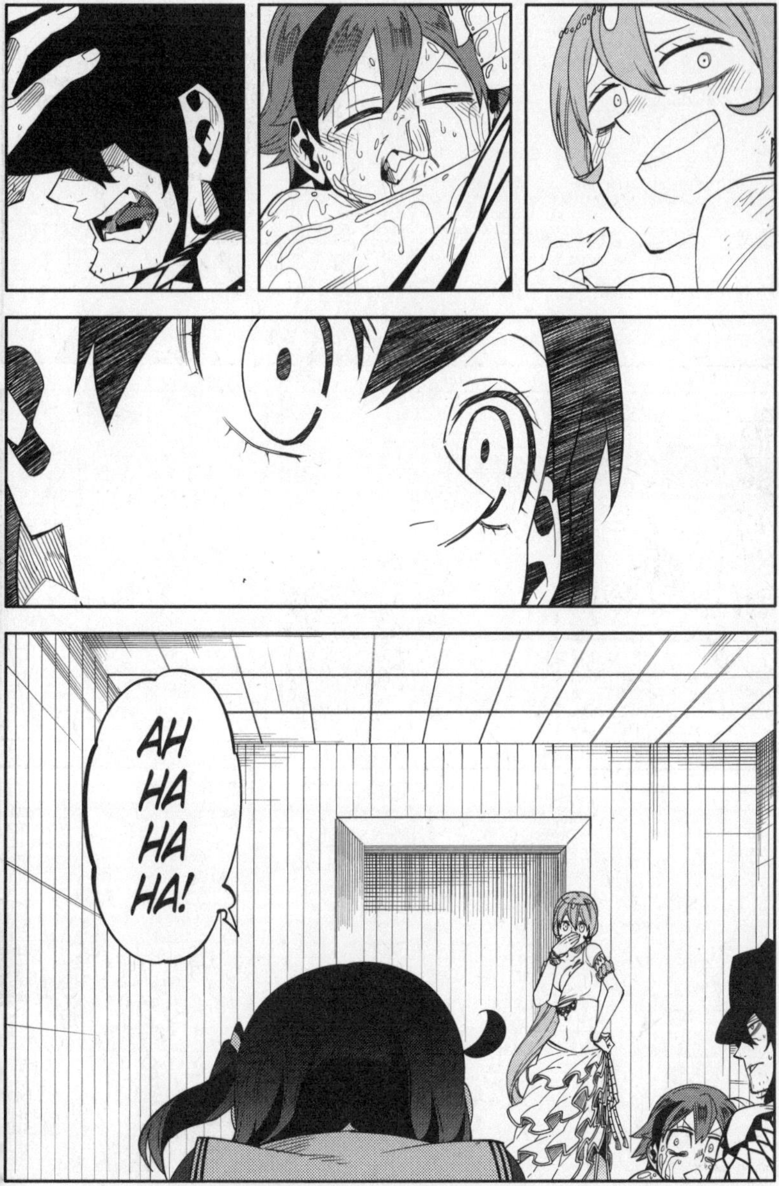
AH HA HA HA!

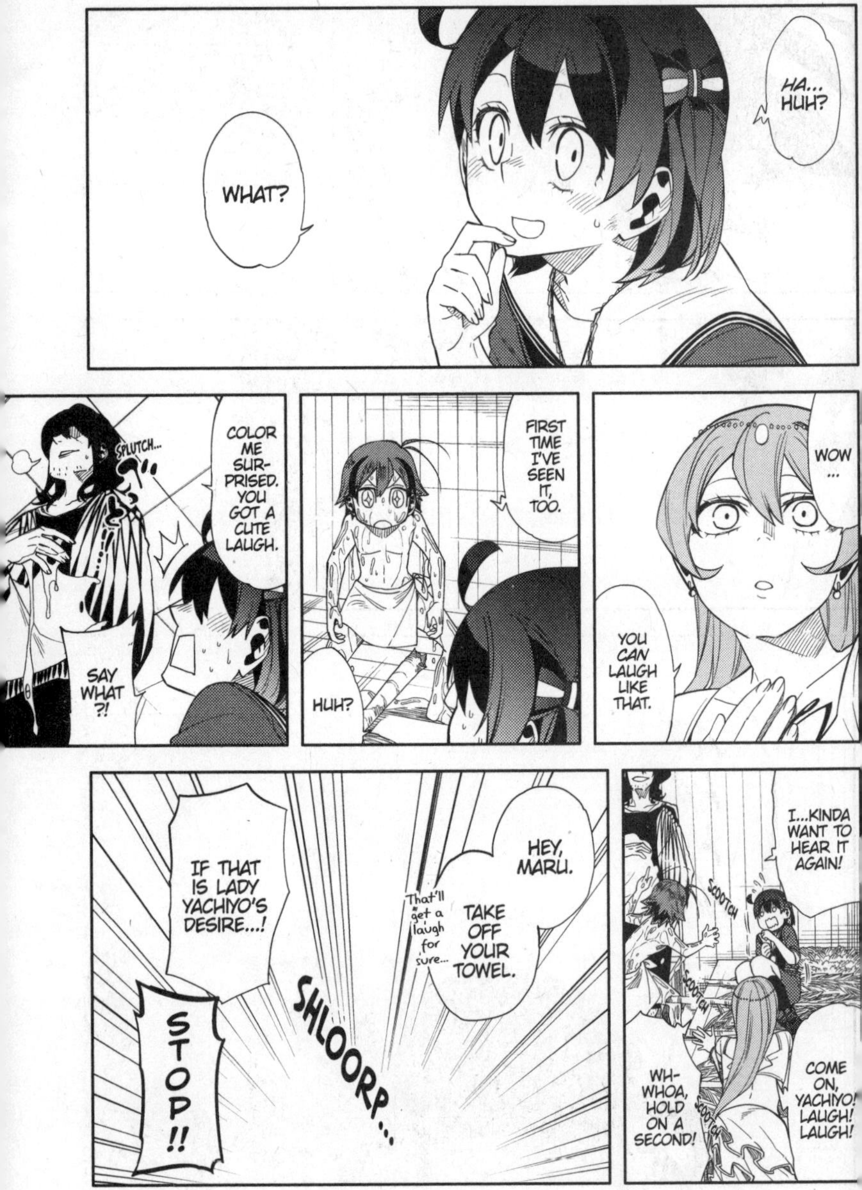
HA... HUH?
WHAT?
WOW ...
YOU CAN LAUGH LIKE THAT.
FIRST TIME I'VE SEEN IT, TOO.
HUH?
COLOR ME SUR-PRISED. YOU GOT A CUTE LAUGH.
SPLUTCH...
SAY WHAT?!
I...KINDA WANT TO HEAR IT AGAIN!
SCOOTCH
SCOOTCH
COME ON, YACHIYO! LAUGH! LAUGH!
SCOOTCH
WH-WHOA, HOLD ON A SECOND!
HEY, MARU.
TAKE OFF YOUR TOWEL.
That'll get a laugh for sure...
SHLOORP...
IF THAT IS LADY YACHIYO'S DESIRE...!
STOP!!

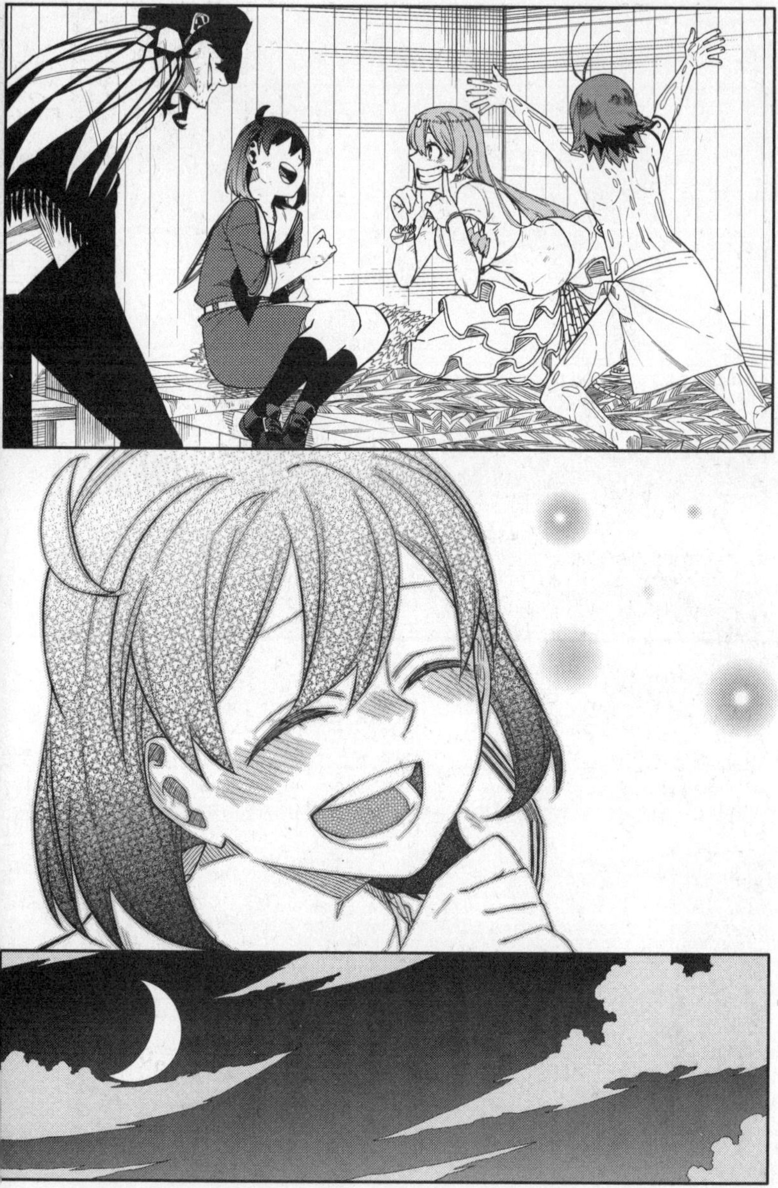

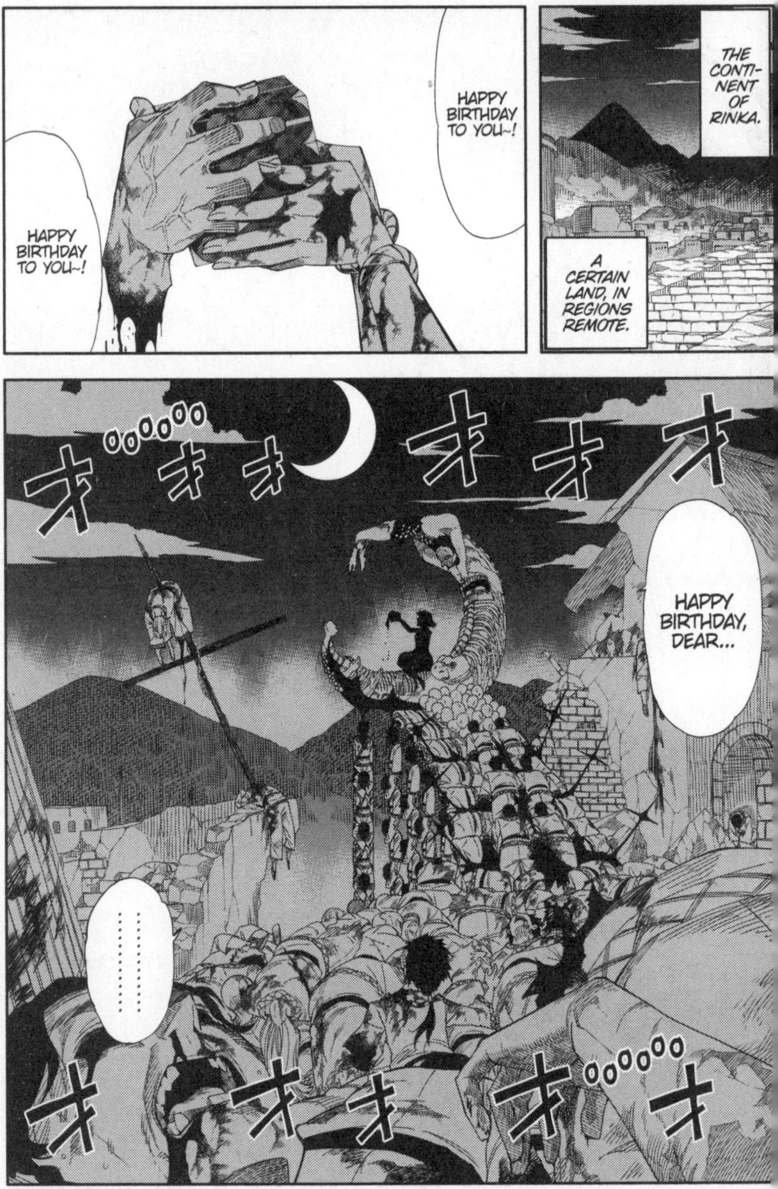
THE CONTINENT OF RINKA.
A CERTAIN LAND, IN REGIONS REMOTE.
HAPPY BIRTHDAY TO YOU~!
HAPPY BIRTHDAY TO YOU~!
オォォォオオオ
OOOOOO
HAPPY BIRTHDAY, DEAR...
....
オォォオオ
OOOOOO

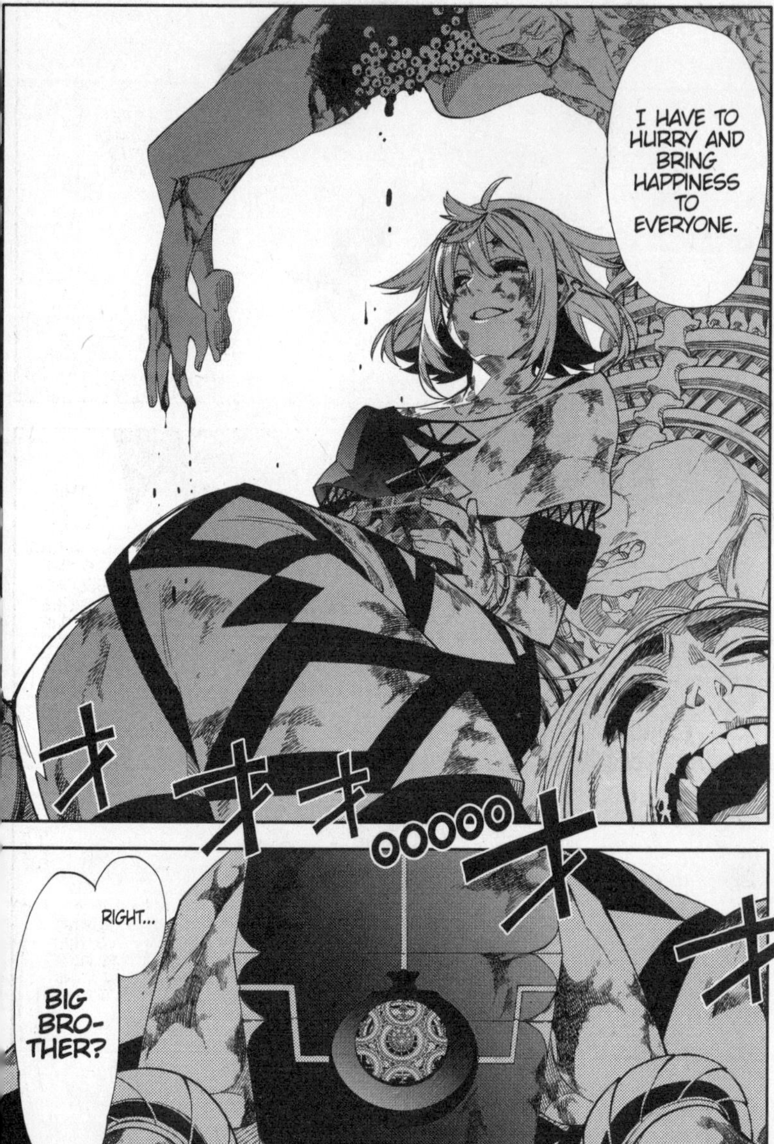
I HAVE TO HURRY AND BRING HAPPINESS TO EVERYONE.
OOOOO
RIGHT...
BIG BRO-THER?

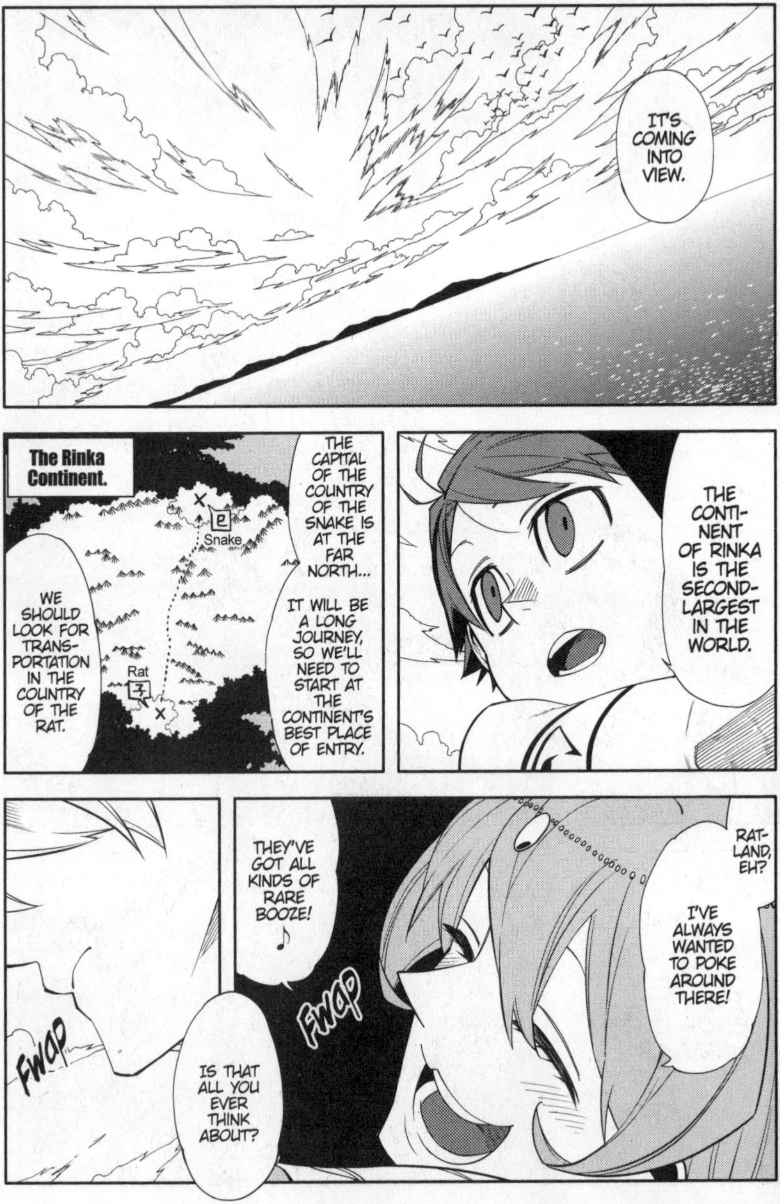
IT'S COMING INTO VIEW.
THE CONTINENT OF RINKA IS THE SECOND-LARGEST IN THE WORLD.
The Rinka Continent.
THE CAPITAL OF THE COUNTRY OF THE SNAKE IS AT THE FAR NORTH...
IT WILL BE A LONG JOURNEY, SO WE'LL NEED TO START AT THE CONTINENT'S BEST PLACE OF ENTRY.
Snake
Rat
WE SHOULD LOOK FOR TRANSPORTATION IN THE COUNTRY OF THE RAT.
RAT-LAND, EH?
I'VE ALWAYS WANTED TO POKE AROUND THERE!
THEY'VE GOT ALL KINDS OF RARE BOOZE! ♪
FWAP
IS THAT ALL YOU EVER THINK ABOUT?
FWAP

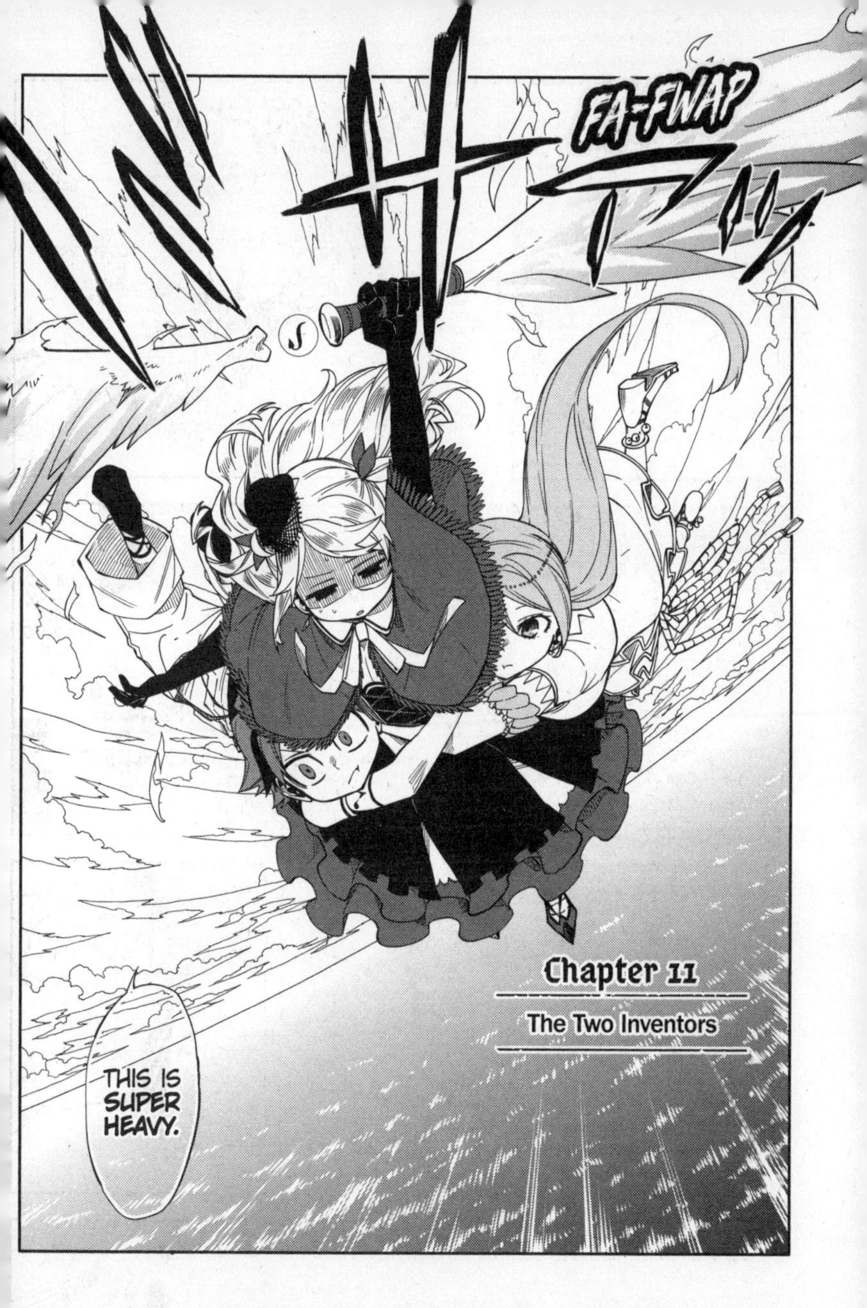
FA-FWAP
Chapter 11
The Two Inventors
THIS IS SUPER HEAVY.

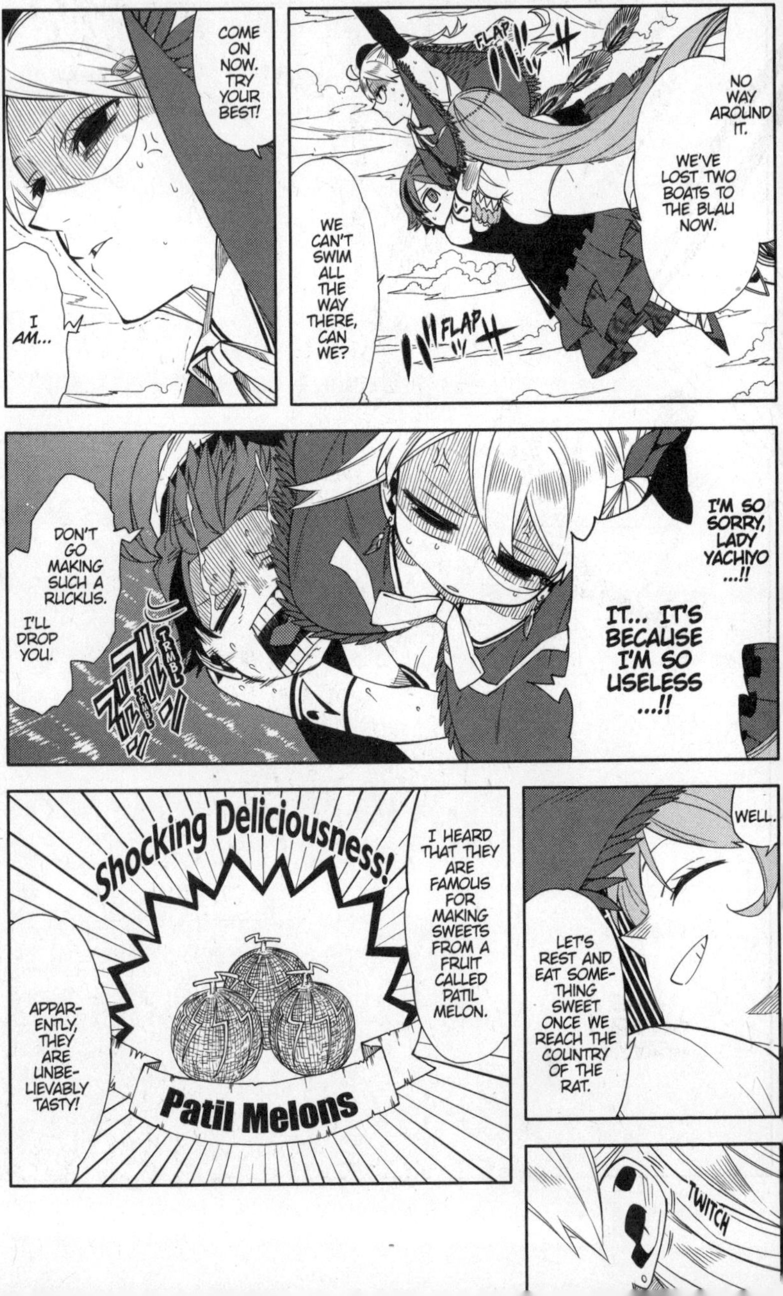
FLAP!!
NO WAY AROUND IT.
WE'VE LOST TWO BOATS TO THE BLAU NOW.
WE CAN'T SWIM ALL THE WAY THERE, CAN WE?
FLAP!!
COME ON NOW. TRY YOUR BEST!
I AM...
I'M SO SORRY, LADY YACHIYO...!!
IT... IT'S BECAUSE I'M SO USELESS...!!
DON'T GO MAKING SUCH A RUCKUS.
I'LL DROP YOU.
TRMBL
TRMBL
WELL.
LET'S REST AND EAT SOME-THING SWEET ONCE WE REACH THE COUNTRY OF THE RAT.
TWITCH
I HEARD THAT THEY ARE FAMOUS FOR MAKING SWEETS FROM A FRUIT CALLED PATIL MELON.
Shocking Deliciousness!
Patil Melons
APPAR-ENTLY, THEY ARE UNBE-LIEVABLY TASTY!

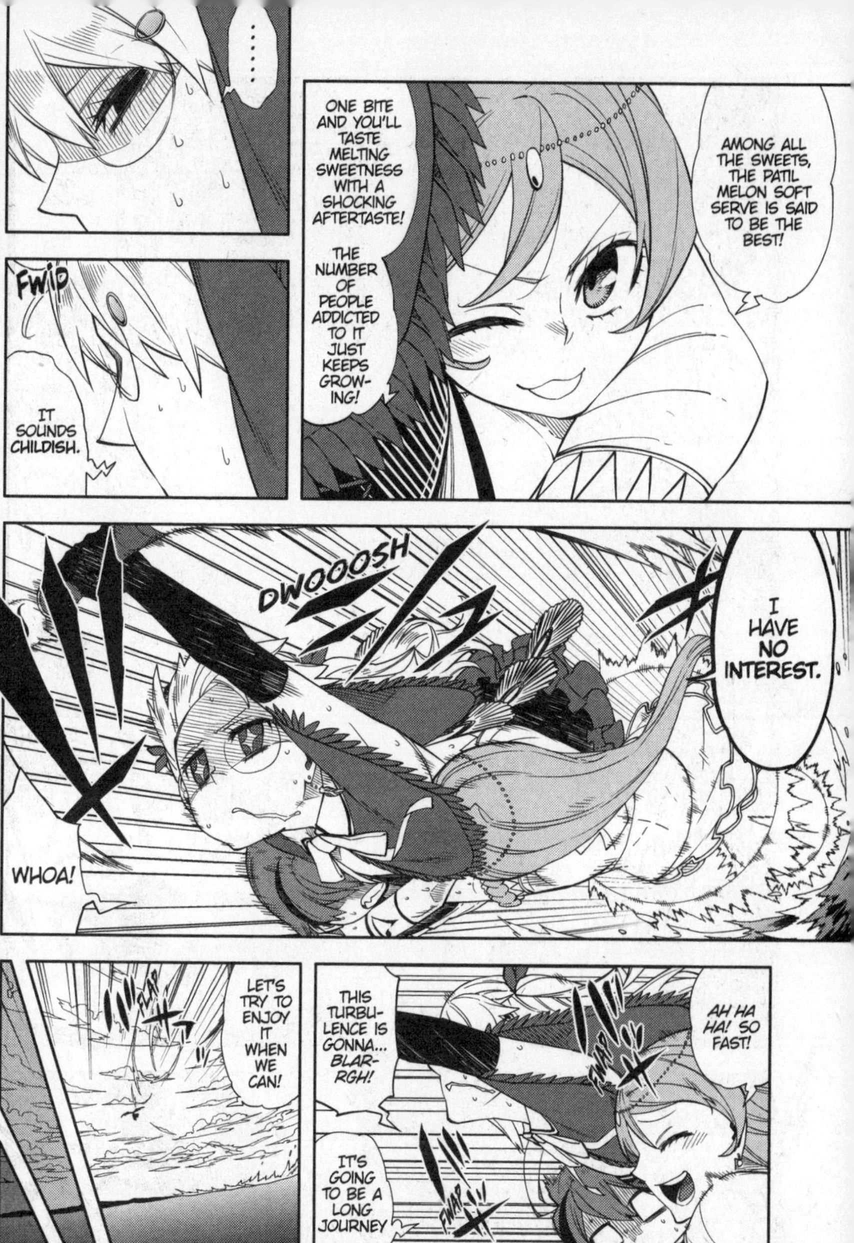
AMONG ALL THE SWEETS, THE PATIL MELON SOFT SERVE IS SAID TO BE THE BEST!
ONE BITE AND YOU'LL TASTE MELTING SWEETNESS WITH A SHOCKING AFTERTASTE!
THE NUMBER OF PEOPLE ADDICTED TO IT JUST KEEPS GROWING!
......
FWIP
IT SOUNDS CHILDISH.
I HAVE NO INTEREST.
DWOOOSH
WHOA!
AH HA HA! SO FAST!
FWAP
THIS TURBULENCE IS GONNA... BLARGH!
IT'S GOING TO BE A LONG JOURNEY...
FWAP
FLAP
LET'S TRY TO ENJOY IT WHEN WE CAN!

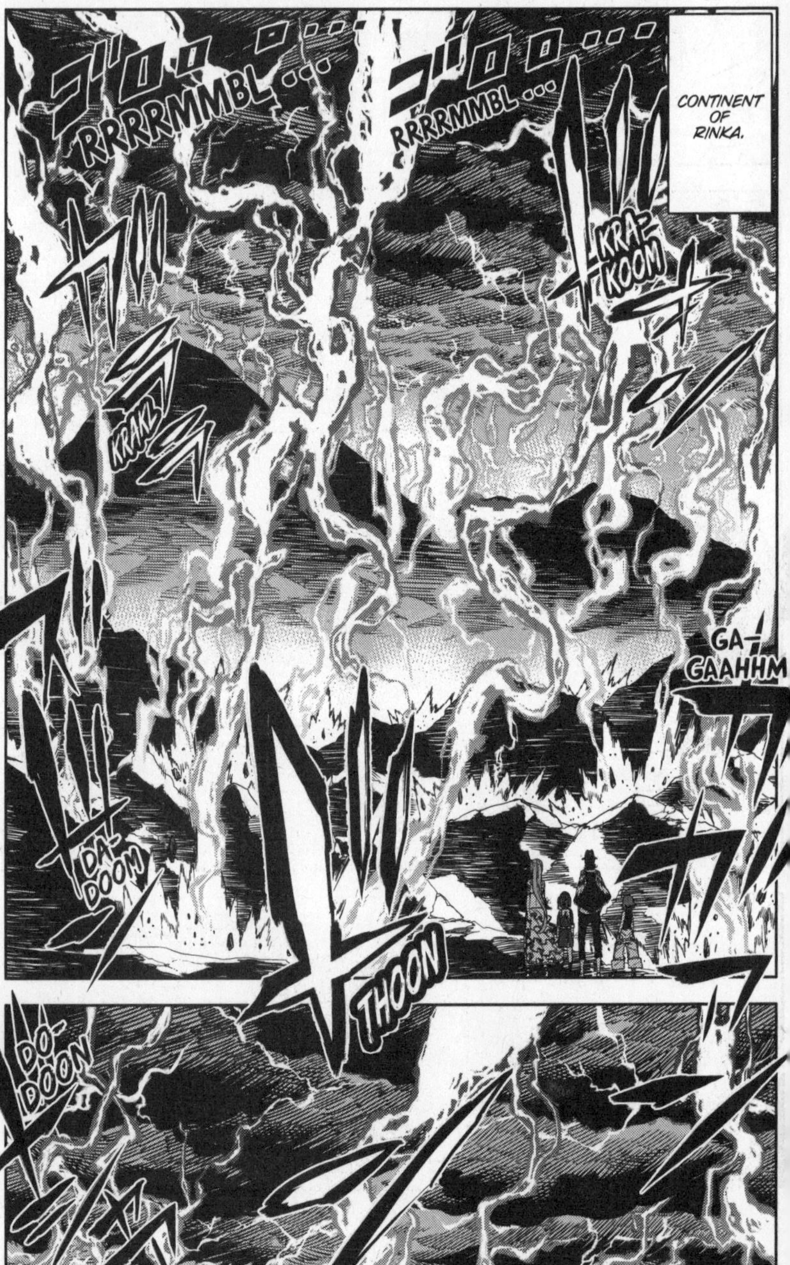
CONTINENT OF RINKA.
ゴロロ...
RRRRMMBL...
ゴロロ...
RRRRMMBL...
KRA-KOOM
KRAKL
GA-GAAHHM
THOON
DA-DOOM
DO-DOON

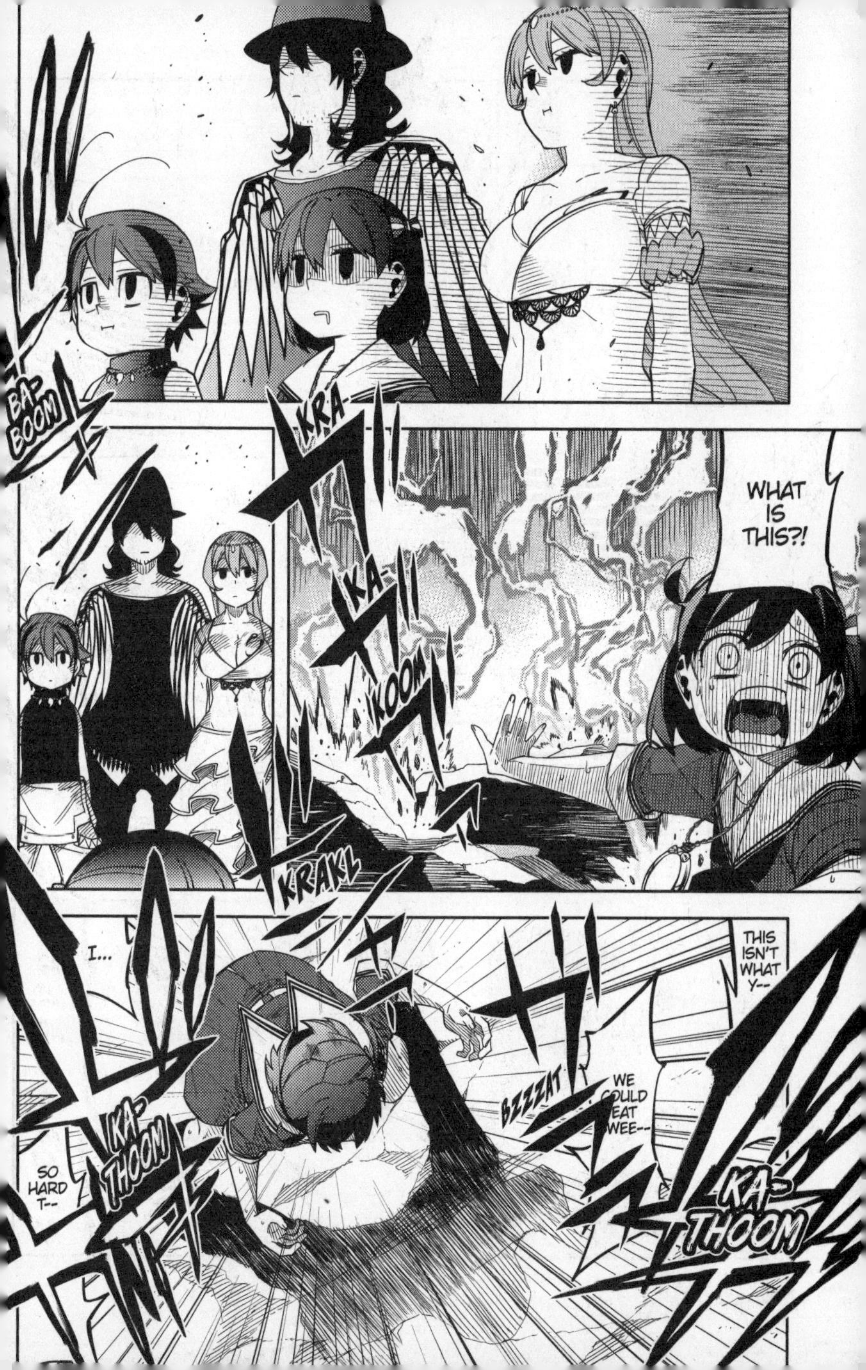
BA-BOOM
WHAT IS THIS?!
KRA KA KOOM
KRAKL
THIS ISN'T WHAT Y--
KA-THOOM
WE COULD EAT WEE--
BZZZAT
I...
KA-THOOM
SO HARD T--

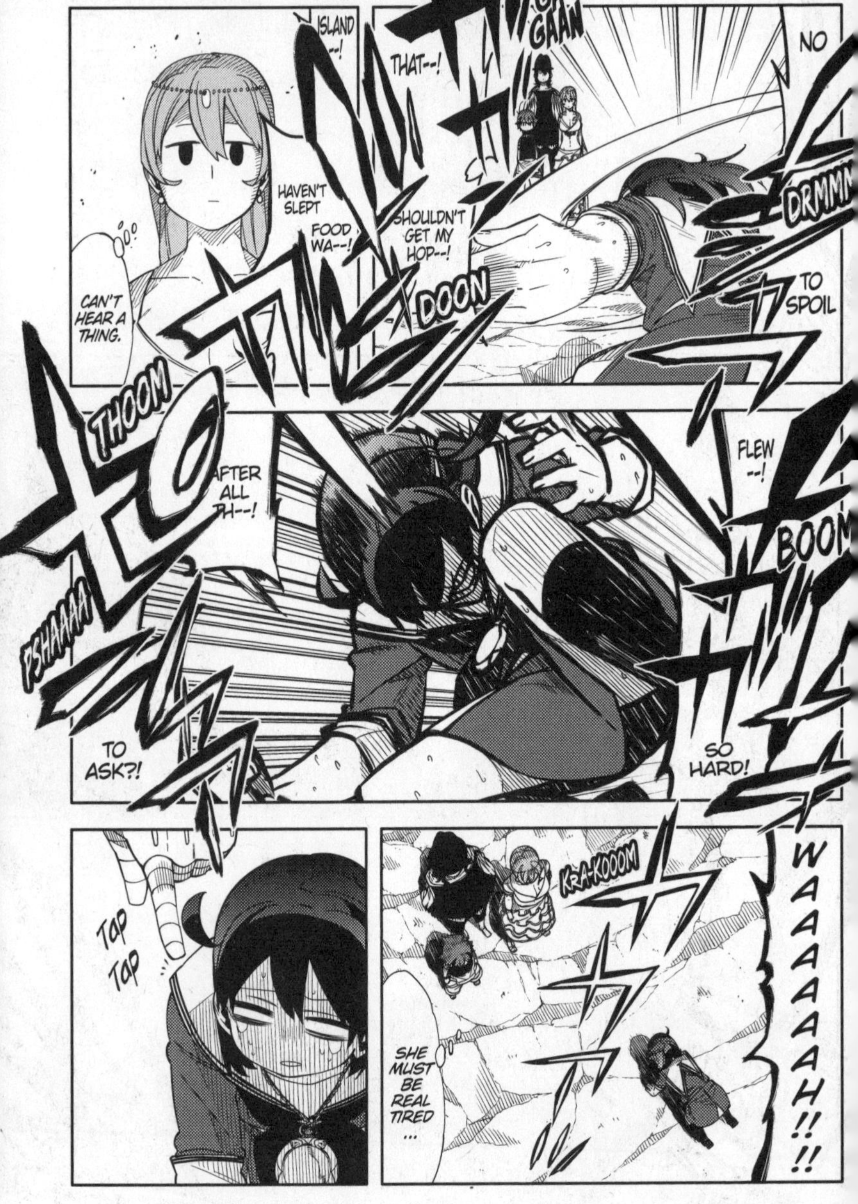
GA-GAAN
NO
TO SPOIL
THAT--!
SHOULDN'T GET MY HOP--!
DRMMM
DOON
ISLAND--!
HAVEN'T SLEPT
FOOD WA--!
CAN'T HEAR A THING.
THOOM
FLEW--!
BOOM
SO HARD!
AFTER ALL TH--!
TO ASK?!
PSHAAAA
WAAAAAAAH!!!!
KRA-KOOOM
SHE MUST BE REAL TIRED...
Tap Tap

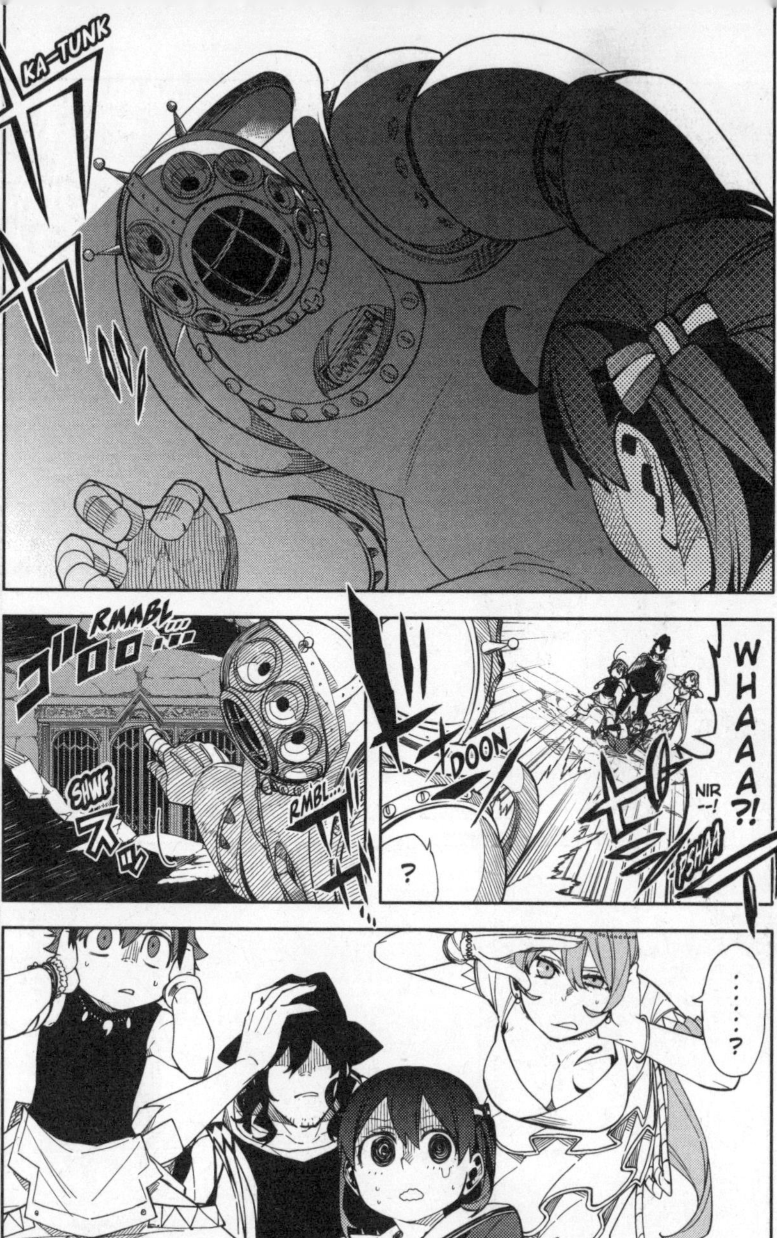
KA-TUNK
WHAAAA?!
NIR--!
FSHAA
DOON
?
RMMBL...
RMBL...
SHWF
......?

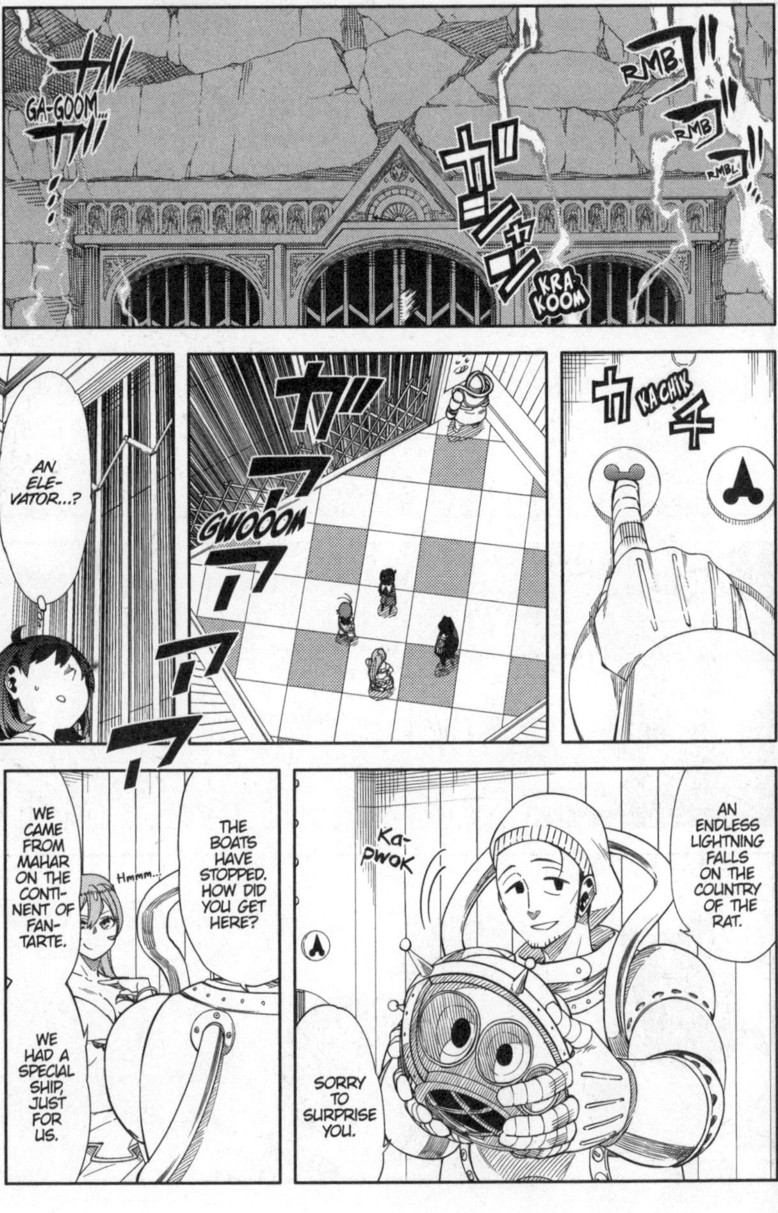
RMB
RMB
RMBL
KRA KOOM
GA-GOOM...
KACHIK
GWOOOM
AN ELEVATOR...?
AN ENDLESS LIGHTNING FALLS ON THE COUNTRY OF THE RAT.
Ka-pwok
SORRY TO SURPRISE YOU.
THE BOATS HAVE STOPPED. HOW DID YOU GET HERE?
WE CAME FROM MAHAR ON THE CONTINENT OF FANTARTE.
Hmmm...
WE HAD A SPECIAL SHIP, JUST FOR US.

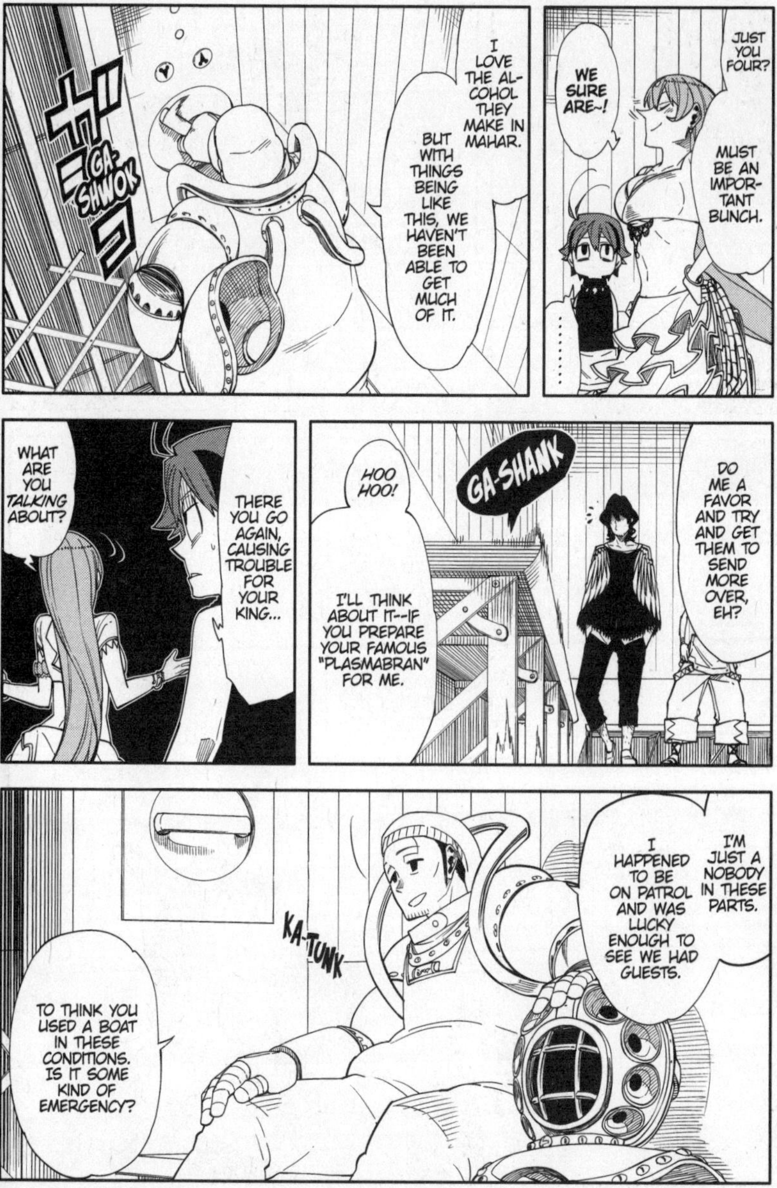
JUST YOU FOUR?
MUST BE AN IMPORTANT BUNCH.
WE SURE ARE~!
...
I LOVE THE ALCOHOL THEY MAKE IN MAHAR.
BUT WITH THINGS BEING LIKE THIS, WE HAVEN'T BEEN ABLE TO GET MUCH OF IT.
GA-SHWOK
DO ME A FAVOR AND TRY AND GET THEM TO SEND MORE OVER, EH?
GA-SHANK
HOO HOO!
I'LL THINK ABOUT IT--IF YOU PREPARE YOUR FAMOUS "PLASMABRAN" FOR ME.
THERE YOU GO AGAIN, CAUSING TROUBLE FOR YOUR KING...
WHAT ARE YOU *TALKING* ABOUT?
I'M JUST A NOBODY IN THESE PARTS.
I HAPPENED TO BE ON PATROL AND WAS LUCKY ENOUGH TO SEE WE HAD GUESTS.
KA-TUNK
TO THINK YOU USED A BOAT IN THESE CONDITIONS. IS IT SOME KIND OF EMERGENCY?

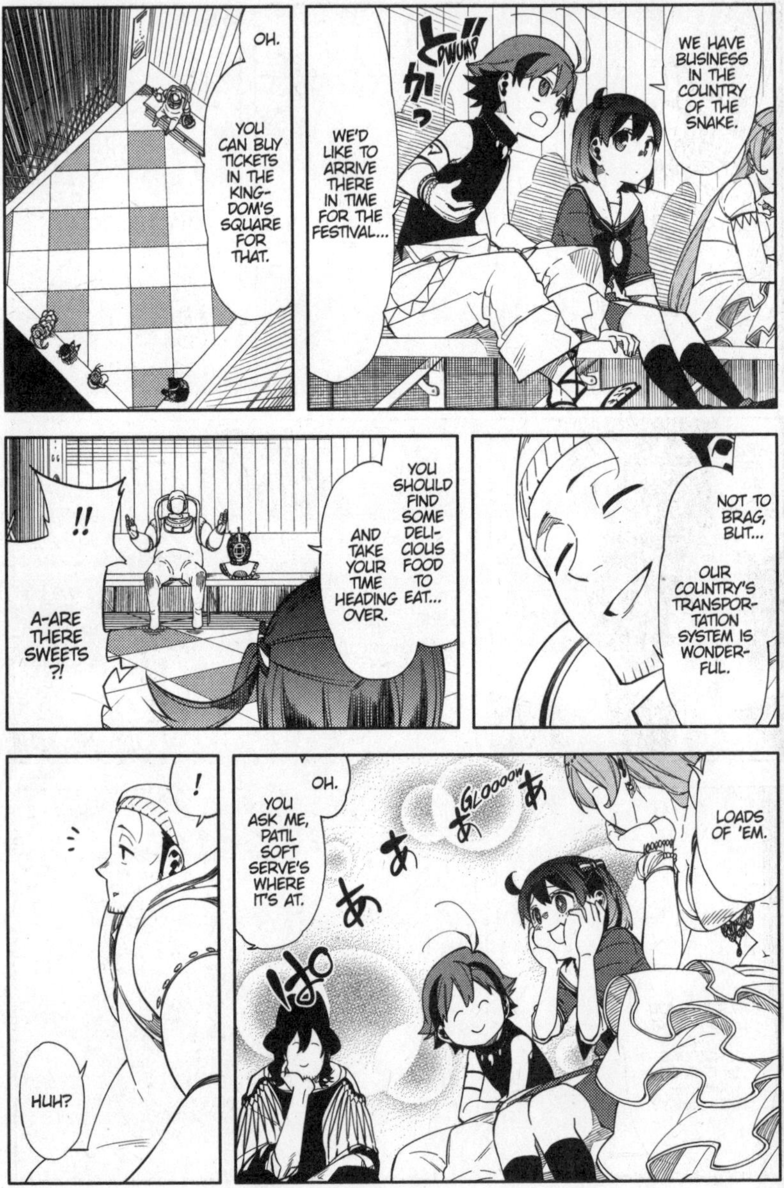
WE HAVE BUSINESS IN THE COUNTRY OF THE SNAKE.
DWUMP
WE'D LIKE TO ARRIVE THERE IN TIME FOR THE FESTIVAL...
OH.
YOU CAN BUY TICKETS IN THE KINGDOM'S SQUARE FOR THAT.
NOT TO BRAG, BUT...
OUR COUNTRY'S TRANSPORTATION SYSTEM IS WONDERFUL.
YOU SHOULD FIND SOME DELICIOUS FOOD TO EAT...
AND TAKE YOUR TIME HEADING OVER.
!!
A-ARE THERE SWEETS?!
LOADS OF 'EM.
GLOOOOW
OH.
YOU ASK ME, PATIL SOFT SERVE'S WHERE IT'S AT.
!
HUH?

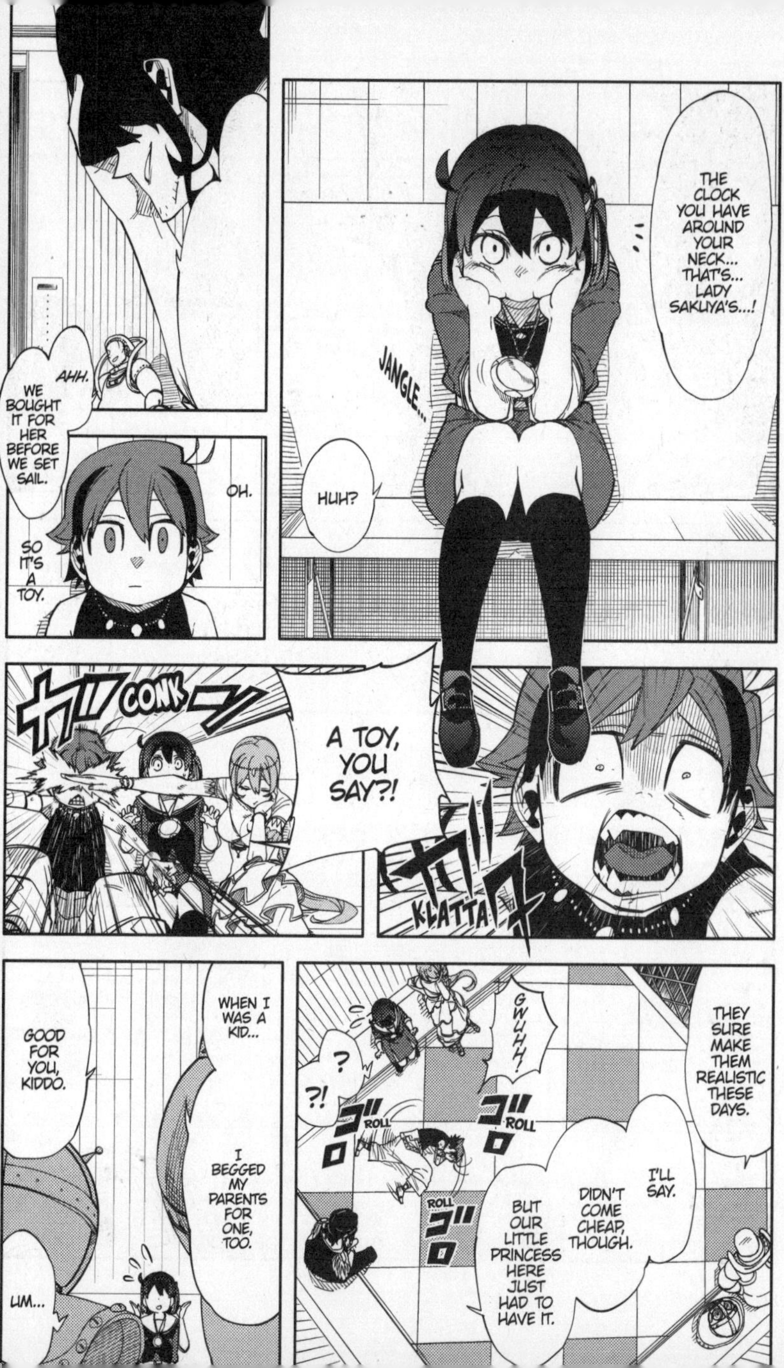

THE CLOCK YOU HAVE AROUND YOUR NECK... THAT'S... LADY SAKUYA'S...!
JANGLE...
HUH?
AHH. WE BOUGHT IT FOR HER BEFORE WE SET SAIL.
OH.
SO IT'S A TOY.
A TOY, YOU SAY?!
KLATTA
CONK
THEY SURE MAKE THEM REALISTIC THESE DAYS.
GWUHH!
?
?!
ROLL
ROLL
ROLL
I'LL SAY.
DIDN'T COME CHEAP, THOUGH.
BUT OUR LITTLE PRINCESS HERE JUST HAD TO HAVE IT.
WHEN I WAS A KID...
I BEGGED MY PARENTS FOR ONE, TOO.
GOOD FOR YOU, KIDDO.
UM...

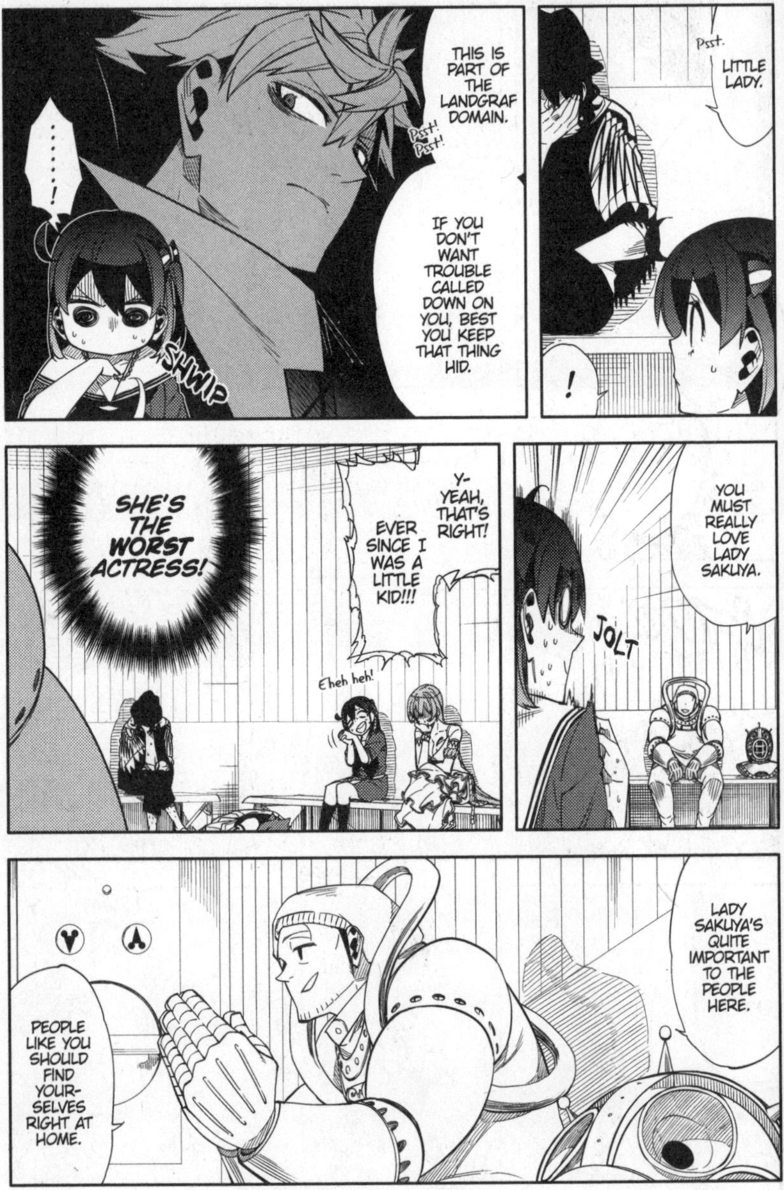
Psst.
LITTLE LADY.
!
THIS IS PART OF THE LANDGRAF DOMAIN.
Psst! Psst!
IF YOU DON'T WANT TROUBLE CALLED DOWN ON YOU, BEST YOU KEEP THAT THING HID.
......!
SHWIP
YOU MUST REALLY LOVE LADY SAKUYA.
JOLT
Y-YEAH, THAT'S RIGHT!
EVER SINCE I WAS A LITTLE KID!!!
Eheh heh!
SHE'S THE WORST ACTRESS!
LADY SAKUYA'S QUITE IMPORTANT TO THE PEOPLE HERE.
PEOPLE LIKE YOU SHOULD FIND YOUR-SELVES RIGHT AT HOME.

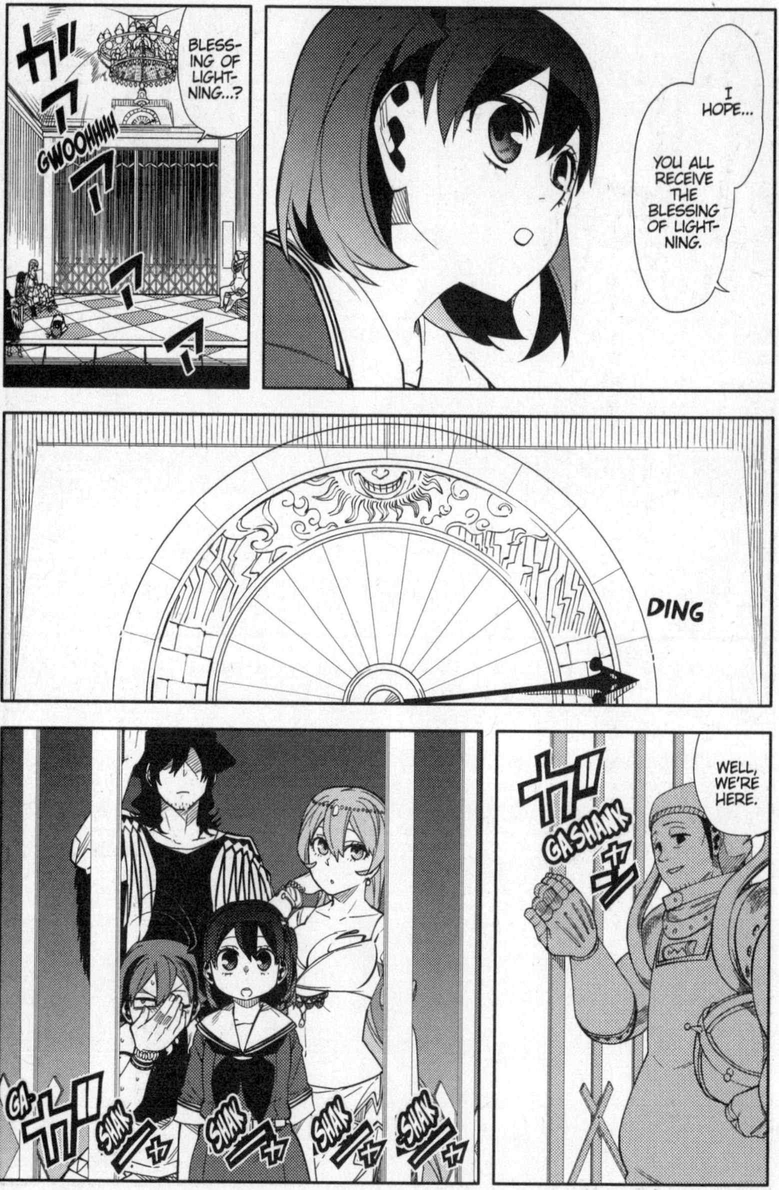
I HOPE...
YOU ALL RECEIVE THE BLESSING OF LIGHT-NING.
GWOOHHHH
BLESS-ING OF LIGHT-NING...?
DING
GASHANK
WELL, WE'RE HERE.
GA-
SHAK
SHAK
SHAK
SHAK

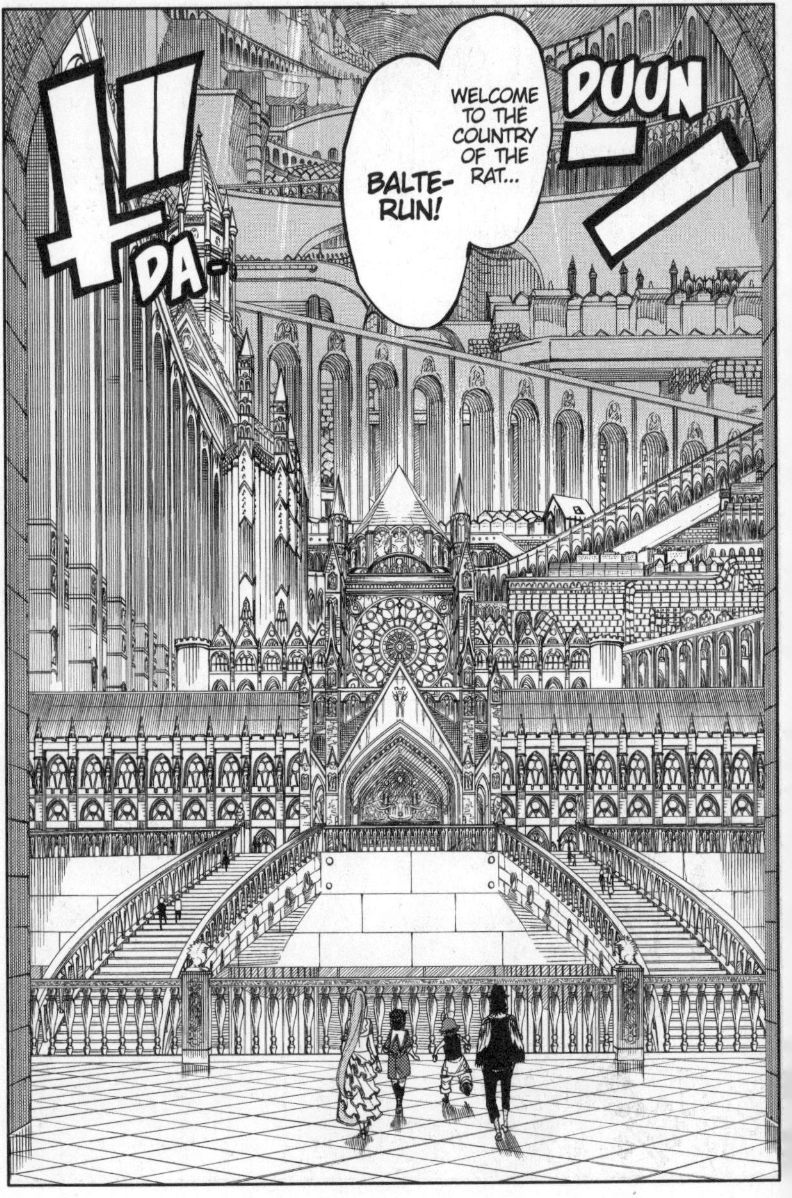
WELCOME TO THE COUNTRY OF THE RAT... BALTE-RUN!
DA-
DUUN

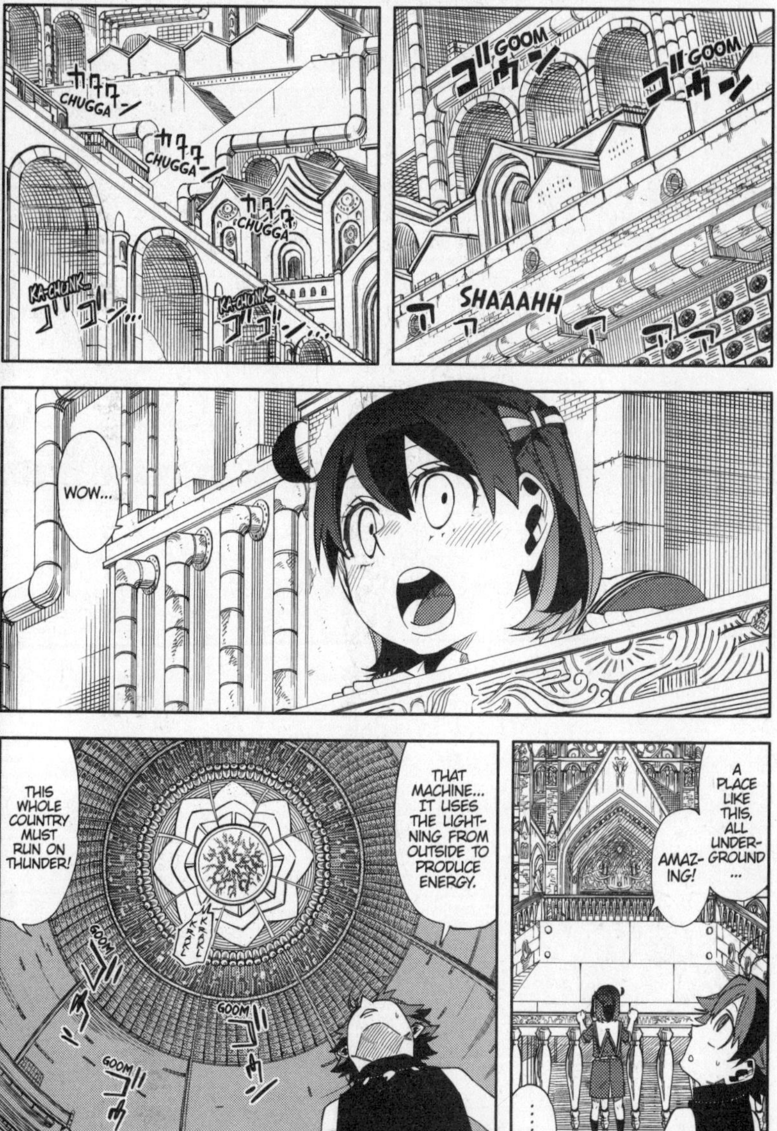
GOOM
GOOM
SHAAAHH
CHUGGA
CHUGGA
CHUGGA
KA-CHUNK...
KA-CHUNK...
WOW...
A PLACE LIKE THIS, ALL UNDERGROUND...
AMAZING!
......
THAT MACHINE... IT USES THE LIGHTNING FROM OUTSIDE TO PRODUCE ENERGY.
THIS WHOLE COUNTRY MUST RUN ON THUNDER!
KRAKL KRAKL
GOOM
GOOM
GOOM

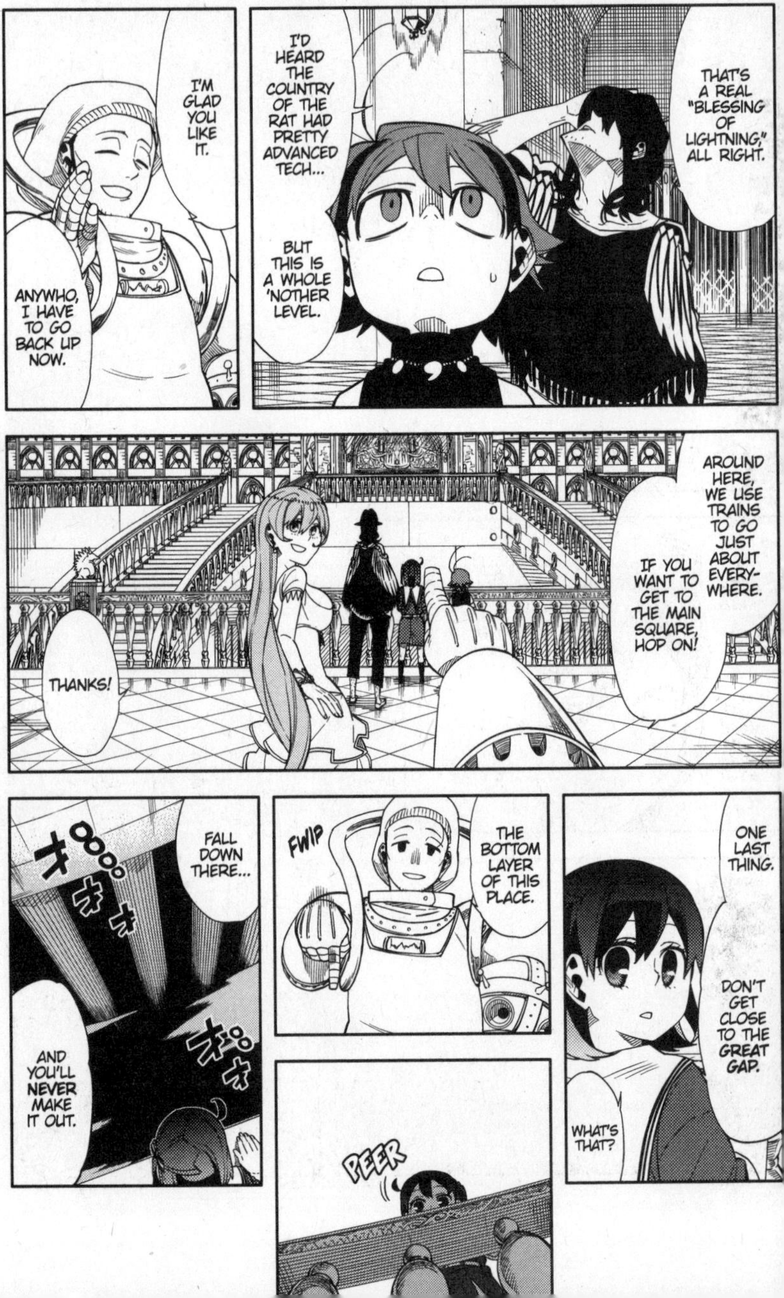
THAT'S A REAL "BLESSING OF LIGHTNING," ALL RIGHT.
I'D HEARD THE COUNTRY OF THE RAT HAD PRETTY ADVANCED TECH...
BUT THIS IS A WHOLE 'NOTHER LEVEL.
I'M GLAD YOU LIKE IT.
ANYWHO, I HAVE TO GO BACK UP NOW.
AROUND HERE, WE USE TRAINS TO GO JUST ABOUT EVERYWHERE.
IF YOU WANT TO GET TO THE MAIN SQUARE, HOP ON!
THANKS!
ONE LAST THING.
DON'T GET CLOSE TO THE GREAT GAP.
WHAT'S THAT?
FWIP
THE BOTTOM LAYER OF THIS PLACE.
PEER
FALL DOWN THERE...
OOOO
AND YOU'LL NEVER MAKE IT OUT.

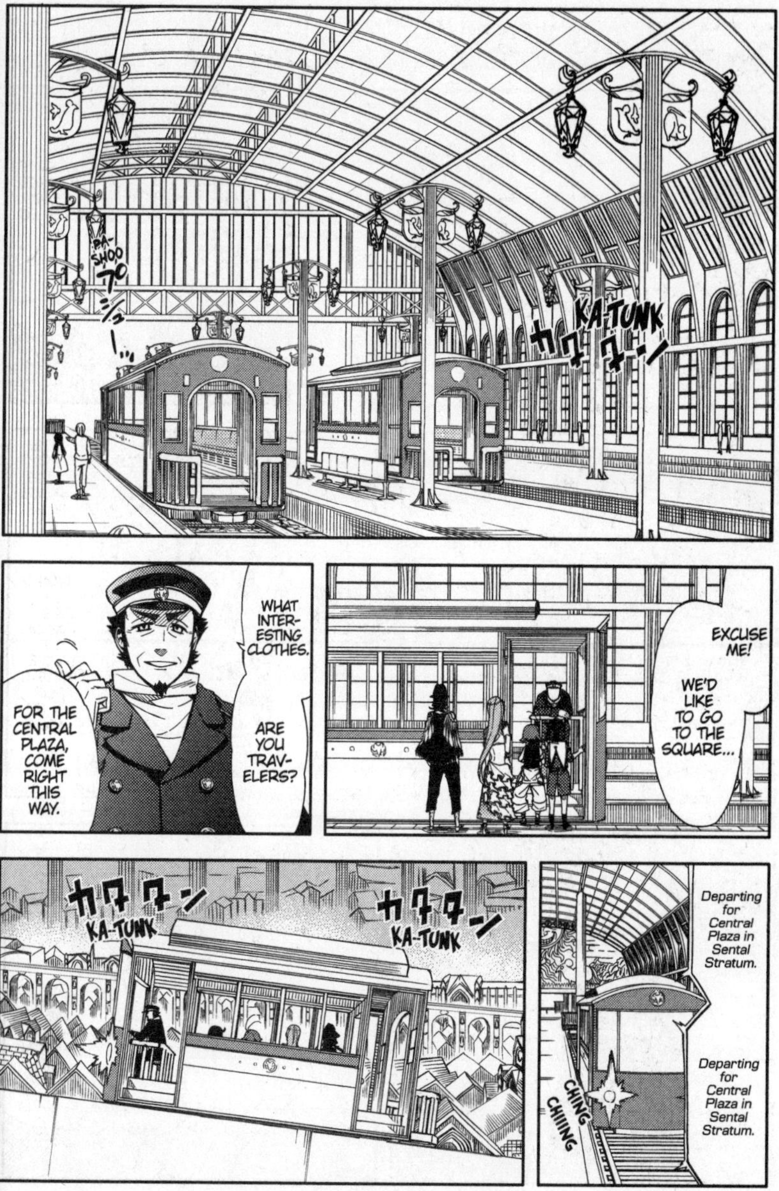
KA-TUNK
PA-SHOO
EXCUSE ME!
WE'D LIKE TO GO TO THE SQUARE...
WHAT INTERESTING CLOTHES.
ARE YOU TRAVELERS?
FOR THE CENTRAL PLAZA, COME RIGHT THIS WAY.
Departing for Central Plaza in Sental Stratum.
Departing for Central Plaza in Sental Stratum.
CHING CHING
KA-TUNK
KA-TUNK

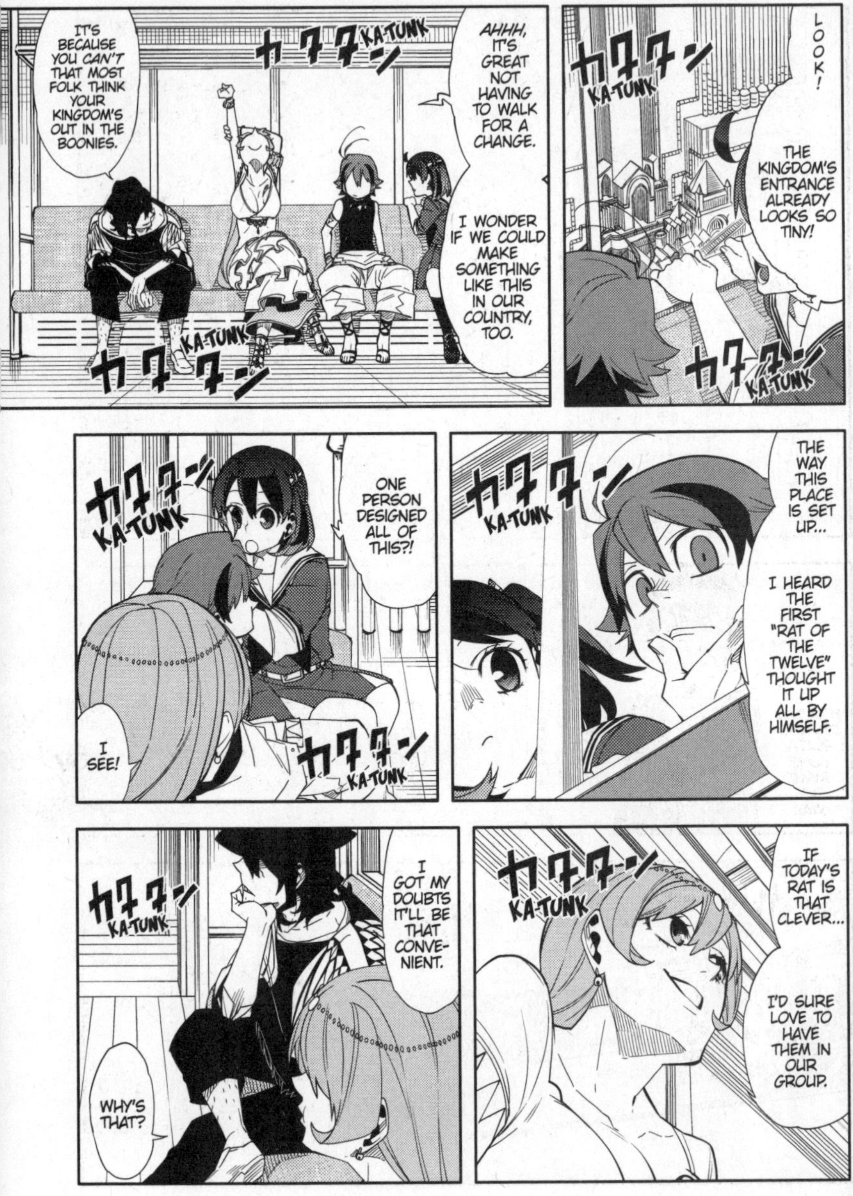

LOOK!
THE KINGDOM'S ENTRANCE ALREADY LOOKS SO TINY!
KA-TUNK
KA-TUNK
AHHH, IT'S GREAT NOT HAVING TO WALK FOR A CHANGE.
I WONDER IF WE COULD MAKE SOMETHING LIKE THIS IN OUR COUNTRY, TOO.
KA-TUNK
IT'S BECAUSE YOU CAN'T THAT MOST FOLK THINK YOUR KINGDOM'S OUT IN THE BOONIES.
KA-TUNK
THE WAY THIS PLACE IS SET UP...
I HEARD THE FIRST "RAT OF THE TWELVE" THOUGHT IT UP ALL BY HIMSELF.
KA-TUNK
ONE PERSON DESIGNED ALL OF THIS?!
KA-TUNK
I SEE!
KA-TUNK
IF TODAY'S RAT IS THAT CLEVER...
I'D SURE LOVE TO HAVE THEM IN OUR GROUP.
KA-TUNK
I GOT MY DOUBTS IT'LL BE THAT CONVE-NIENT.
KA-TUNK
WHY'S THAT?

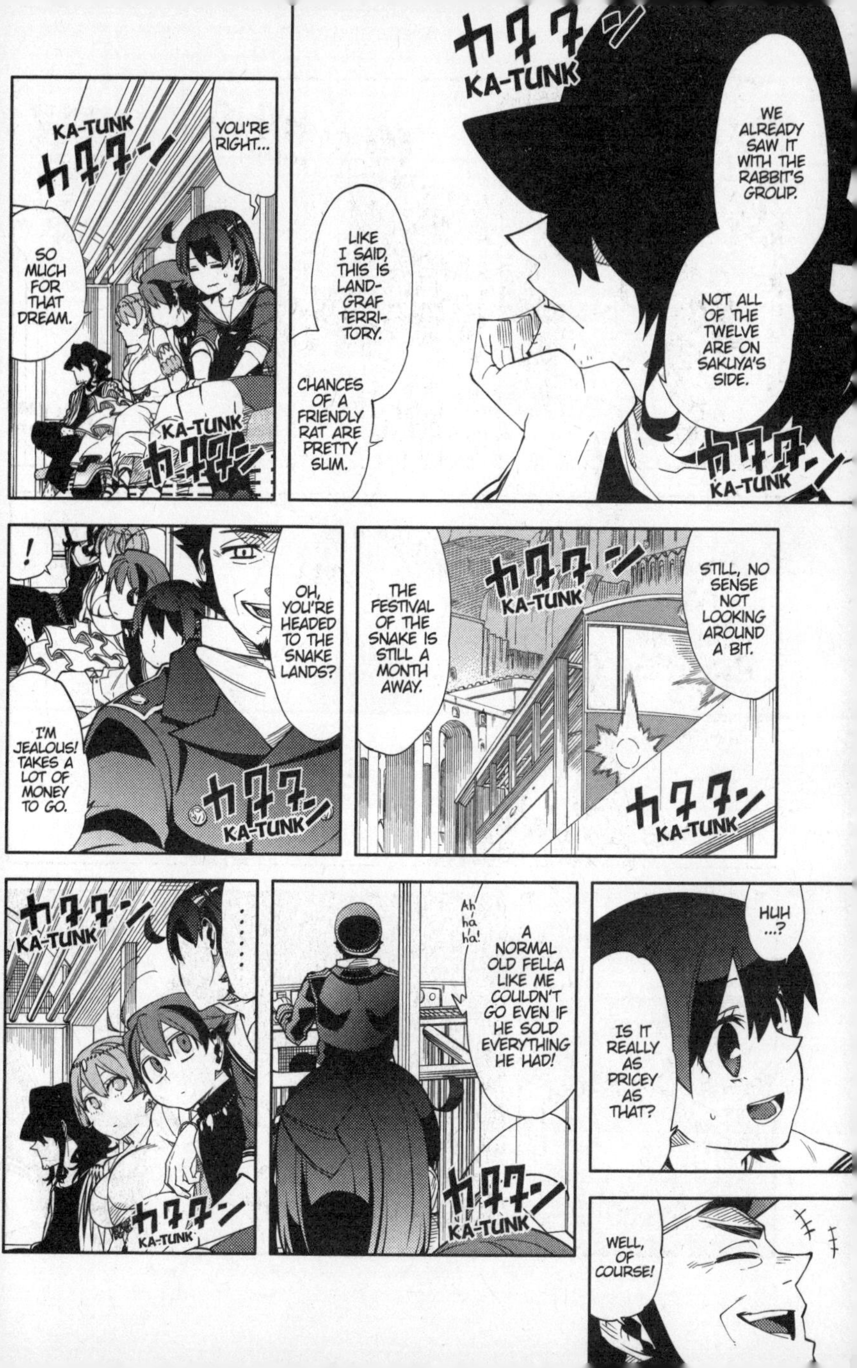
カタタン
KA-TUNK
WE ALREADY SAW IT WITH THE RABBIT'S GROUP.
NOT ALL OF THE TWELVE ARE ON SAKUYA'S SIDE.
LIKE I SAID, THIS IS LANDGRAF TERRITORY.
CHANCES OF A FRIENDLY RAT ARE PRETTY SLIM.
カタタン
KA-TUNK
YOU'RE RIGHT...
KA-TUNK
カタタン
SO MUCH FOR THAT DREAM.
KA-TUNK
カタタン
STILL, NO SENSE NOT LOOKING AROUND A BIT.
カタタン
KA-TUNK
THE FESTIVAL OF THE SNAKE IS STILL A MONTH AWAY.
カタタン
KA-TUNK
OH, YOU'RE HEADED TO THE SNAKE LANDS?
!
I'M JEALOUS! TAKES A LOT OF MONEY TO GO.
カタタン
KA-TUNK
HUH ...?
IS IT REALLY AS PRICEY AS THAT?
WELL, OF COURSE!
Ah ha ha!
A NORMAL OLD FELLA LIKE ME COULDN'T GO EVEN IF HE SOLD EVERYTHING HE HAD!
カタタン
KA-TUNK
......
カタタン
KA-TUNK
カタタン
KA-TUNK

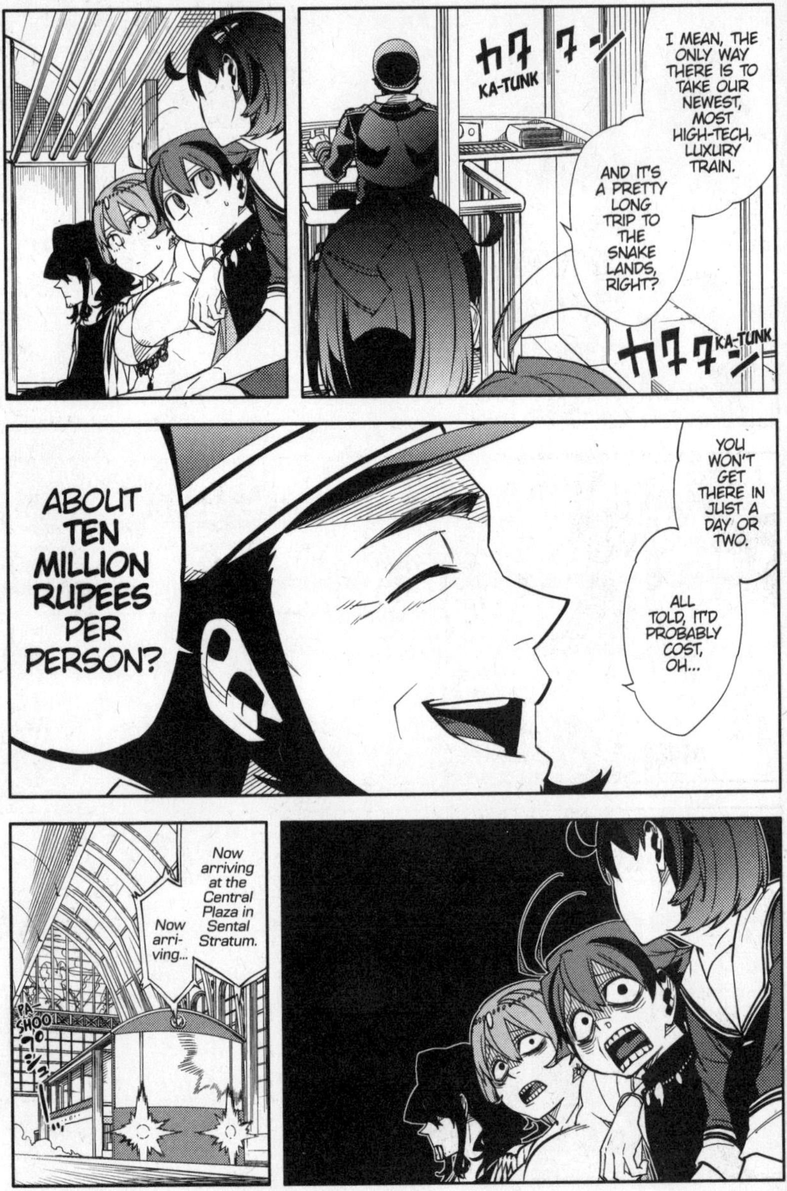
I MEAN, THE ONLY WAY THERE IS TO TAKE OUR NEWEST, MOST HIGH-TECH, LUXURY TRAIN.
KA-TUNK
AND IT'S A PRETTY LONG TRIP TO THE SNAKE LANDS, RIGHT?
KA-TUNK
YOU WON'T GET THERE IN JUST A DAY OR TWO.
ALL TOLD, IT'D PROBABLY COST, OH...
ABOUT TEN MILLION RUPEES PER PERSON?
Now arriving at the Central Plaza in Sental Stratum.
Now arri- ving...
PA SHOO

BY THE WAY...

HOW MUCH MONEY HAVE WE GOT RIGHT NOW, ALL TOGETHER?

CHATTER ワイ

CHATTER ワイ

HUSTLE ガヤ

BUSTLE ガヤ

RUMMAGE

RUMMAGE

RUMMAGE

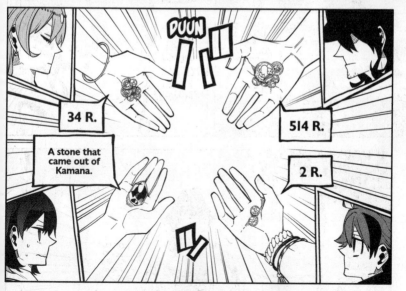

DUUN

34 R.

514 R.

A stone that came out of Kamana.

2 R.

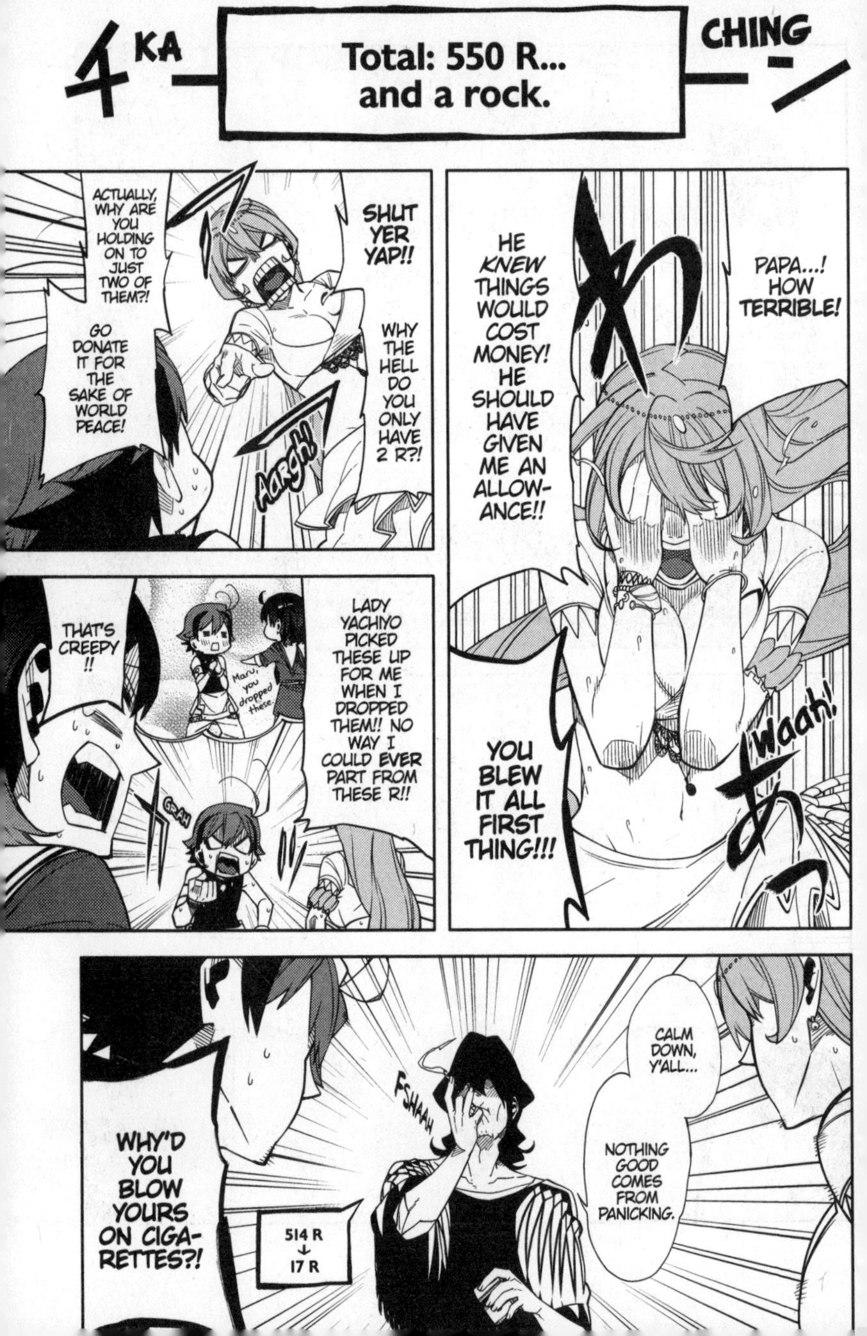
KA
Total: 550 R... and a rock.
CHING
PAPA...! HOW TERRIBLE!
HE KNEW THINGS WOULD COST MONEY! HE SHOULD HAVE GIVEN ME AN ALLOWANCE!!
YOU BLEW IT ALL FIRST THING!!!
Waah!
SHUT YER YAP!!
ACTUALLY, WHY ARE YOU HOLDING ON TO JUST TWO OF THEM?!
WHY THE HELL DO YOU ONLY HAVE 2 R?!
GO DONATE IT FOR THE SAKE OF WORLD PEACE!
Aargh!
LADY YACHIYO PICKED THESE UP FOR ME WHEN I DROPPED THEM!! NO WAY I COULD EVER PART FROM THESE R!!
Maru, you dropped these.
THAT'S CREEPY!!
GRAH
CALM DOWN, Y'ALL...
NOTHING GOOD COMES FROM PANICKING.
FSHAAH
WHY'D YOU BLOW YOURS ON CIGARETTES?!
514 R → 17 R

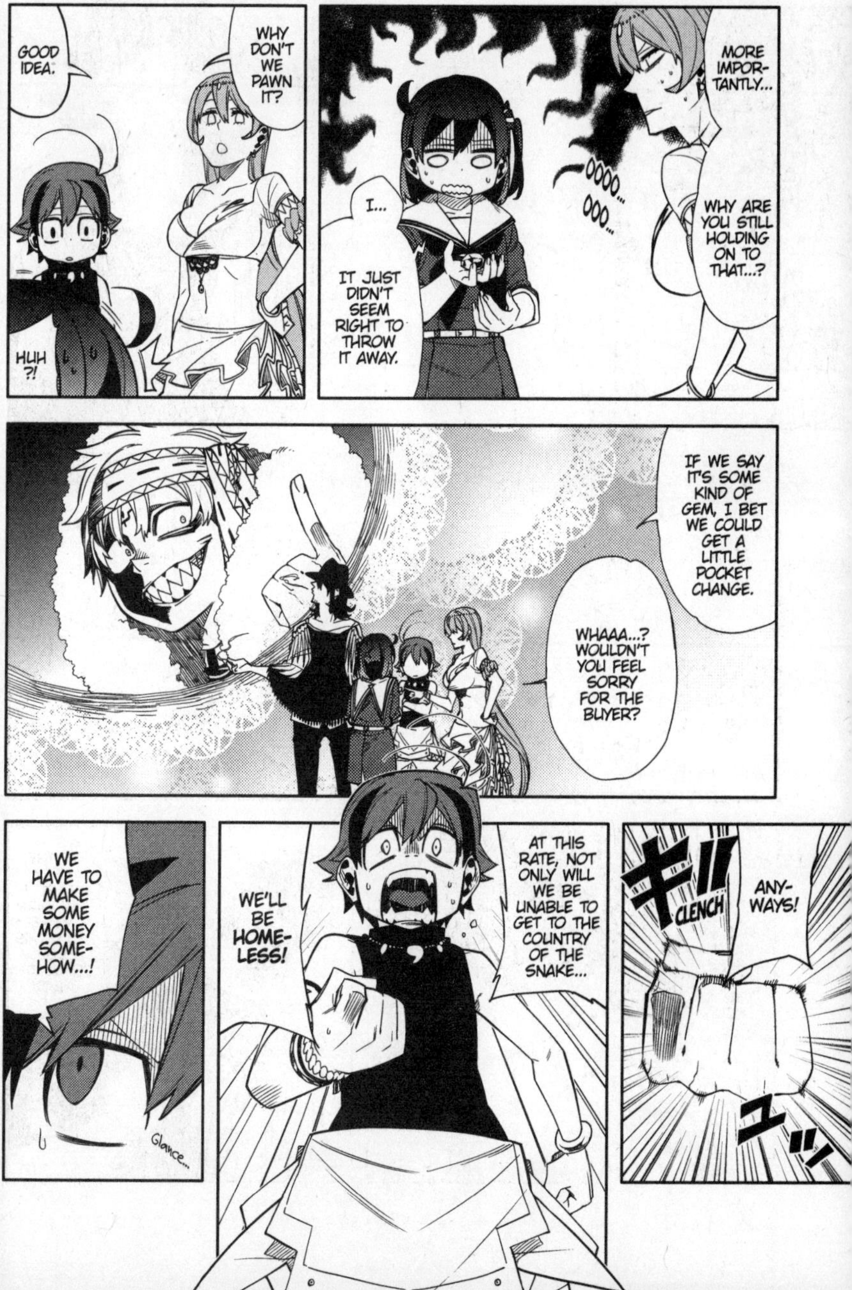

MORE IMPORTANTLY...
OOOO... OOO...
WHY ARE YOU STILL HOLDING ON TO THAT...?
I...
IT JUST DIDN'T SEEM RIGHT TO THROW IT AWAY.
WHY DON'T WE PAWN IT?
GOOD IDEA.
HUH?!
IF WE SAY IT'S SOME KIND OF GEM, I BET WE COULD GET A LITTLE POCKET CHANGE.
WHAAA...? WOULDN'T YOU FEEL SORRY FOR THE BUYER?
CLENCH
ANY-WAYS!
AT THIS RATE, NOT ONLY WILL WE BE UNABLE TO GET TO THE COUNTRY OF THE SNAKE...
WE'LL BE HOME-LESS!
WE HAVE TO MAKE SOME MONEY SOME-HOW...!
Glance...

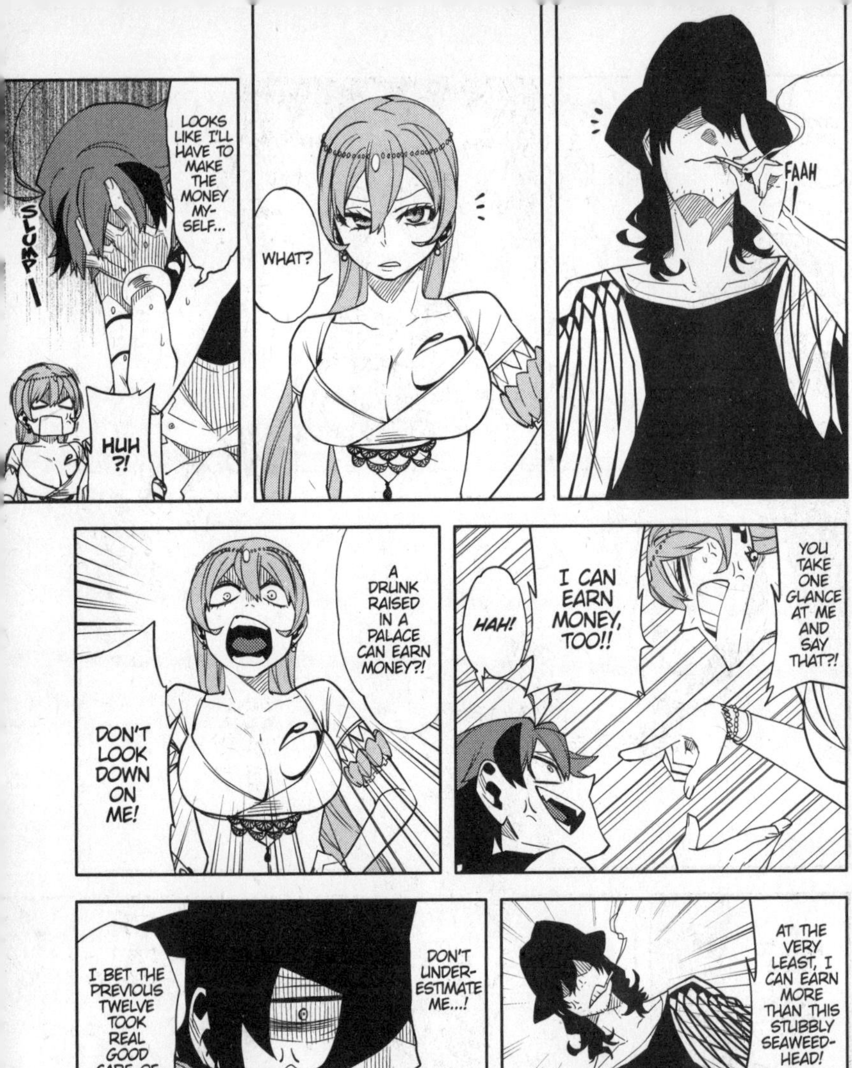
FAAH!
WHAT?
LOOKS LIKE I'LL HAVE TO MAKE THE MONEY MYSELF...
SLUMP!
HUH?!
YOU TAKE ONE GLANCE AT ME AND SAY THAT?!
I CAN EARN MONEY, TOO!!
HAH!
A DRUNK RAISED IN A PALACE CAN EARN MONEY?!
DON'T LOOK DOWN ON ME!
AT THE VERY LEAST, I CAN EARN MORE THAN THIS STUBBLY SEAWEED-HEAD!
HUUHHH?!
DON'T UNDERESTIMATE ME...!
I BET THE PREVIOUS TWELVE TOOK REAL GOOD CARE OF YOU!
I'VE BEEN RAMBLIN' LONGER'N EVERYONE HERE!
YOU BIG SEAWEED BABY!

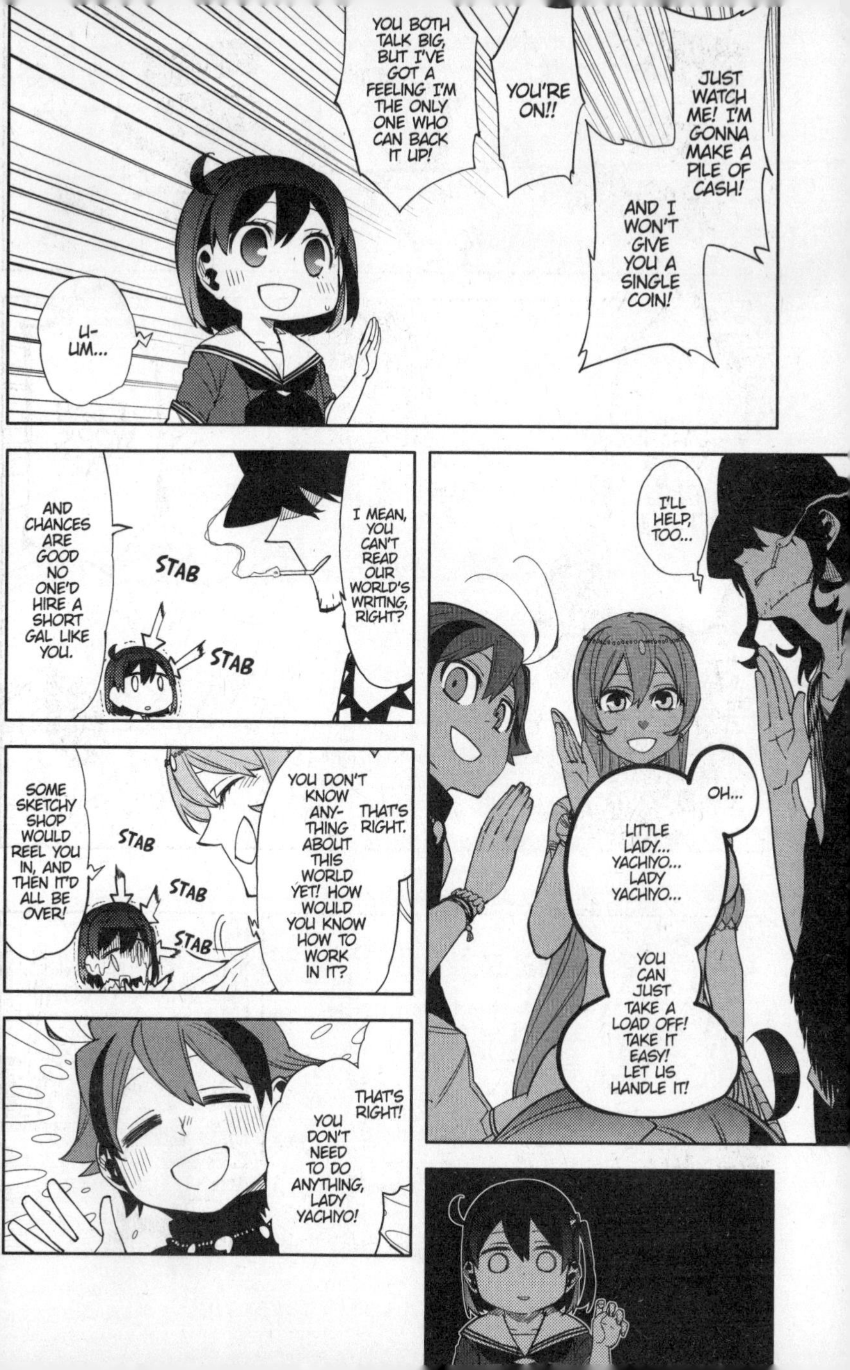
JUST WATCH ME! I'M GONNA MAKE A PILE OF CASH!
AND I WON'T GIVE YOU A SINGLE COIN!
YOU'RE ON!!
YOU BOTH TALK BIG, BUT I'VE GOT A FEELING I'M THE ONLY ONE WHO CAN BACK IT UP!
U-UM...
I'LL HELP, TOO...
OH...
LITTLE LADY... YACHIYO... LADY YACHIYO...
YOU CAN JUST TAKE A LOAD OFF! TAKE IT EASY! LET US HANDLE IT!
I MEAN, YOU CAN'T READ OUR WORLD'S WRITING, RIGHT?
STAB
AND CHANCES ARE GOOD NO ONE'D HIRE A SHORT GAL LIKE YOU.
STAB
THAT'S RIGHT.
YOU DON'T KNOW ANY-THING ABOUT THIS WORLD YET! HOW WOULD YOU KNOW HOW TO WORK IN IT?
STAB
STAB
STAB
SOME SKETCHY SHOP WOULD REEL YOU IN, AND THEN IT'D ALL BE OVER!
THAT'S RIGHT! YOU DON'T NEED TO DO ANYTHING, LADY YACHIYO!

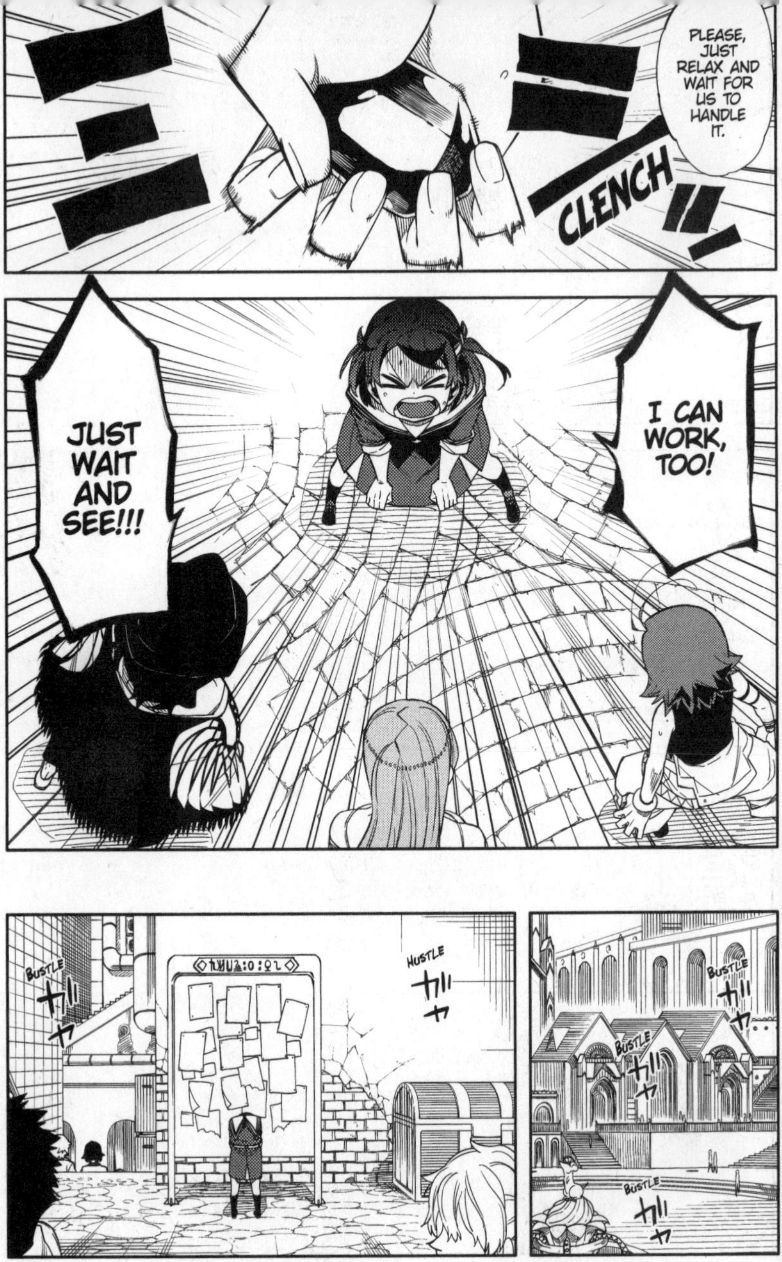
PLEASE, JUST RELAX AND WAIT FOR US TO HANDLE IT.
CLENCH
I CAN WORK, TOO!
JUST WAIT AND SEE!!!
BUSTLE
BUSTLE
BUSTLE
HUSTLE
BUSTLE

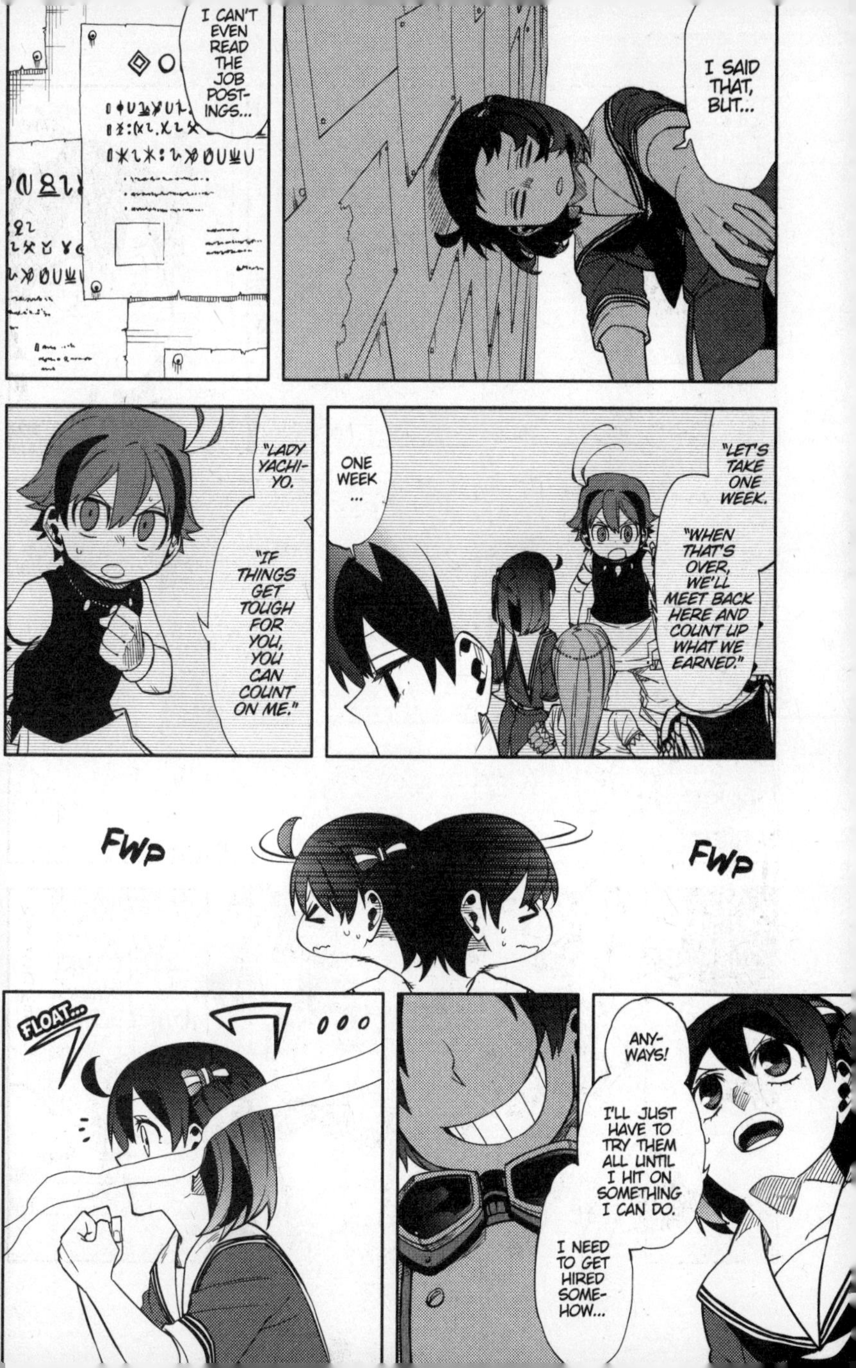
I SAID THAT, BUT...
I CAN'T EVEN READ THE JOB POST-INGS...
"LET'S TAKE ONE WEEK.
"WHEN THAT'S OVER, WE'LL MEET BACK HERE AND COUNT UP WHAT WE EARNED."
ONE WEEK ...
"LADY YACHI-YO.
"IF THINGS GET TOUGH FOR YOU, YOU CAN COUNT ON ME."
FWP
FWP
ANY-WAYS!
I'LL JUST HAVE TO TRY THEM ALL UNTIL I HIT ON SOMETHING I CAN DO.
I NEED TO GET HIRED SOME-HOW...
FLOAT...
ooo

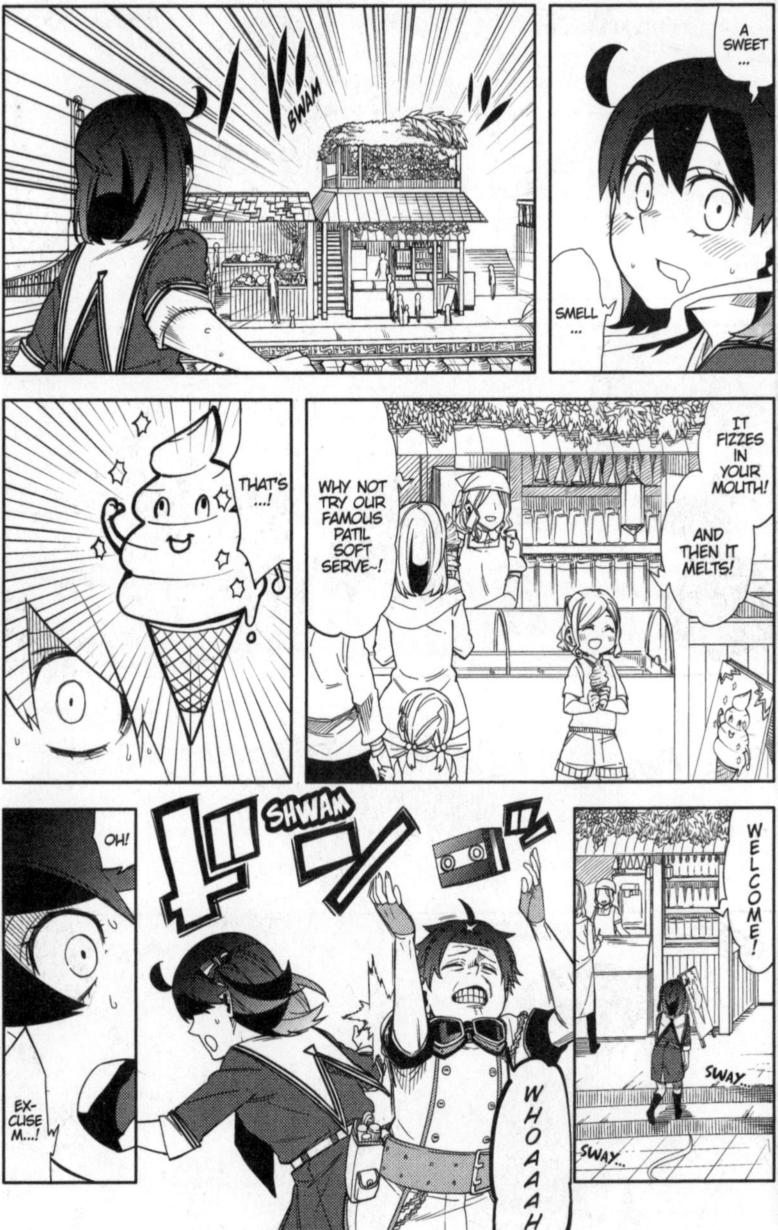
A SWEET ...
SMELL ...
BWAM
IT FIZZES IN YOUR MOUTH!
AND THEN IT MELTS!
WHY NOT TRY OUR FAMOUS PATIL SOFT SERVE~!
THAT'S ...!
WELCOME!
SWAY...
SWAY...
SHWAM
OH!
WHOAAAAH!
EX-CUSE M...!

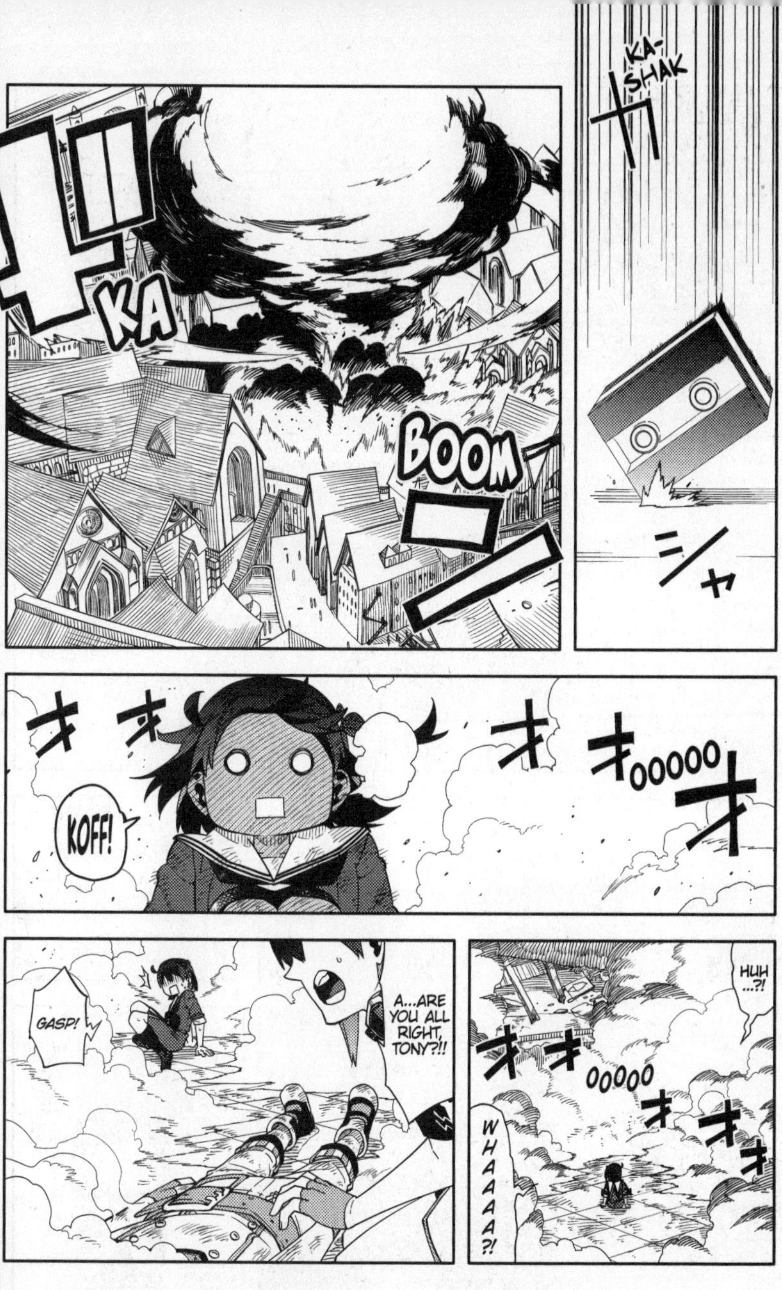
KA-SHAK
シャ
KA
BOOM
KOFF!
OOOOO
HUH...?!
OOOOO
WHAAAAA?!
A...ARE YOU ALL RIGHT, TONY?!!
GASP!

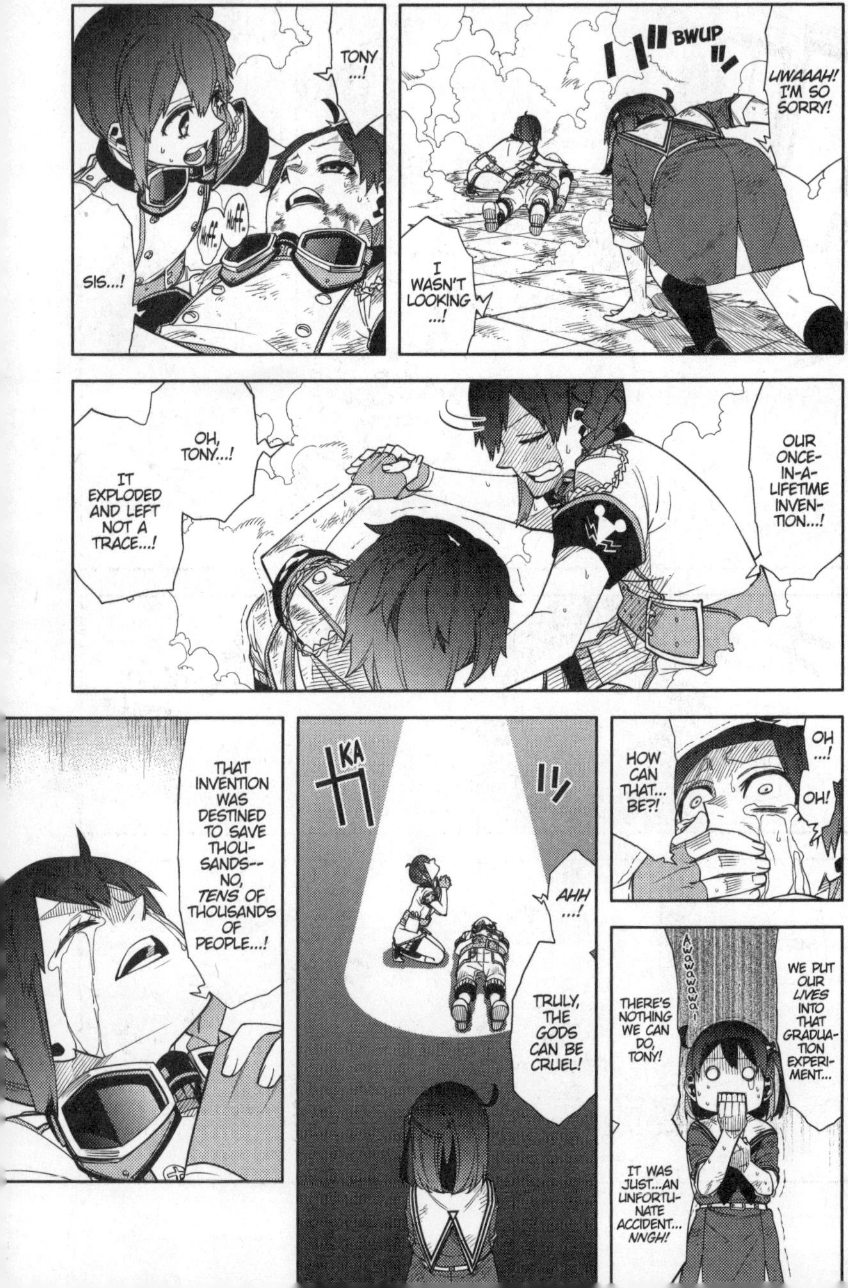
BWUP
UWAAAH! I'M SO SORRY!
I WASN'T LOOKING...!
TONY...!
Huff. Huff. Huff.
SIS...!
OUR ONCE-IN-A-LIFETIME INVENTION...!
OH, TONY...!
IT EXPLODED AND LEFT NOT A TRACE...!
OH...!
OH!
HOW CAN THAT... BE?!
AWAWAWAWA
WE PUT OUR *LIVES* INTO THAT GRADUATION EXPERIMENT...
THERE'S NOTHING WE CAN DO, TONY!
IT WAS JUST...AN UNFORTUNATE ACCIDENT... *NNGH!*
KA
AHH...!
TRULY, THE GODS CAN BE CRUEL!
THAT INVENTION WAS DESTINED TO SAVE THOUSANDS--NO, *TENS* OF THOUSANDS OF PEOPLE...!

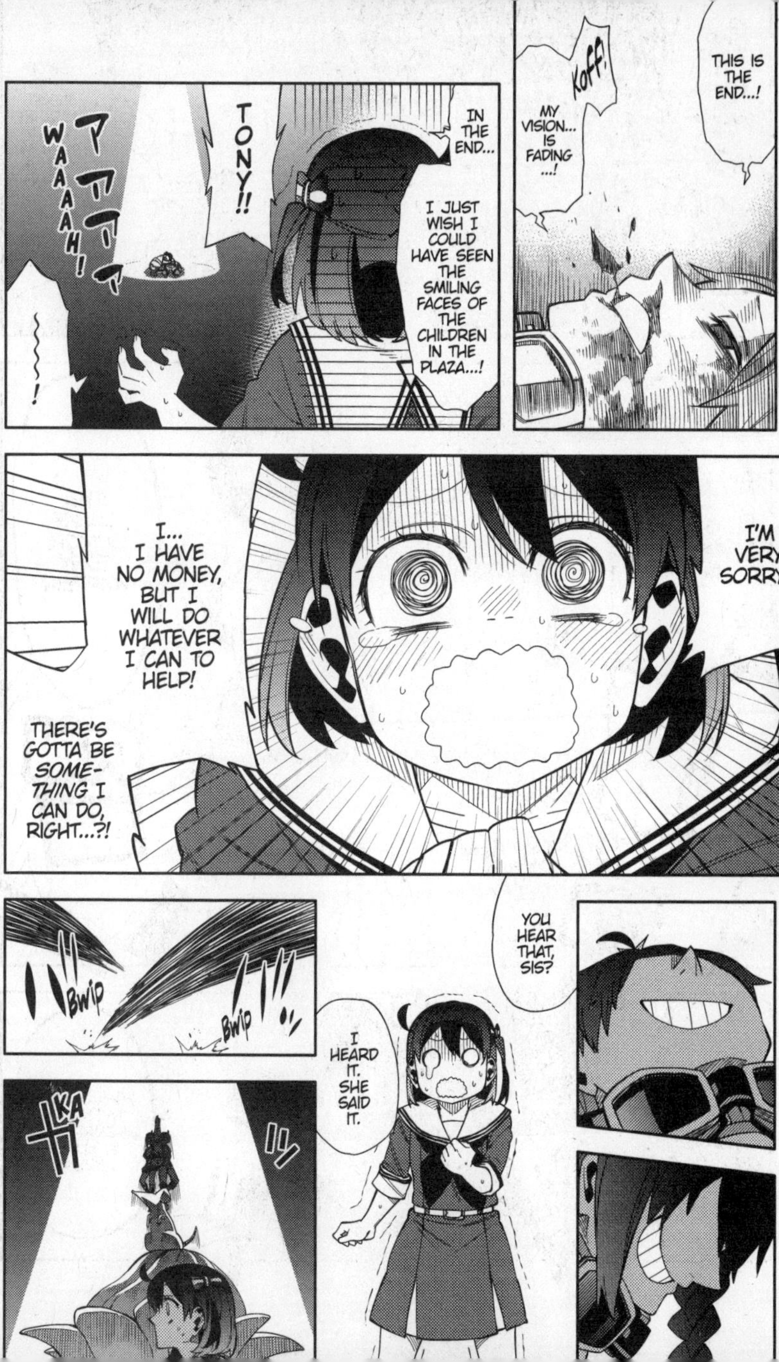
THIS IS THE END...!
Koff!
MY VISION... IS FADING...!
IN THE END...
I JUST WISH I COULD HAVE SEEN THE SMILING FACES OF THE CHILDREN IN THE PLAZA...!
TONY!!
WAAAAAH!
~~~~!
I'M VERY SORRY!!
I... I HAVE NO MONEY, BUT I WILL DO WHATEVER I CAN TO HELP!
THERE'S GOTTA BE *SOME-THING* I CAN DO, RIGHT...?!
YOU HEAR THAT, SIS?
I HEARD IT. SHE SAID IT.
Bwip
Bwip
KA
~~~~

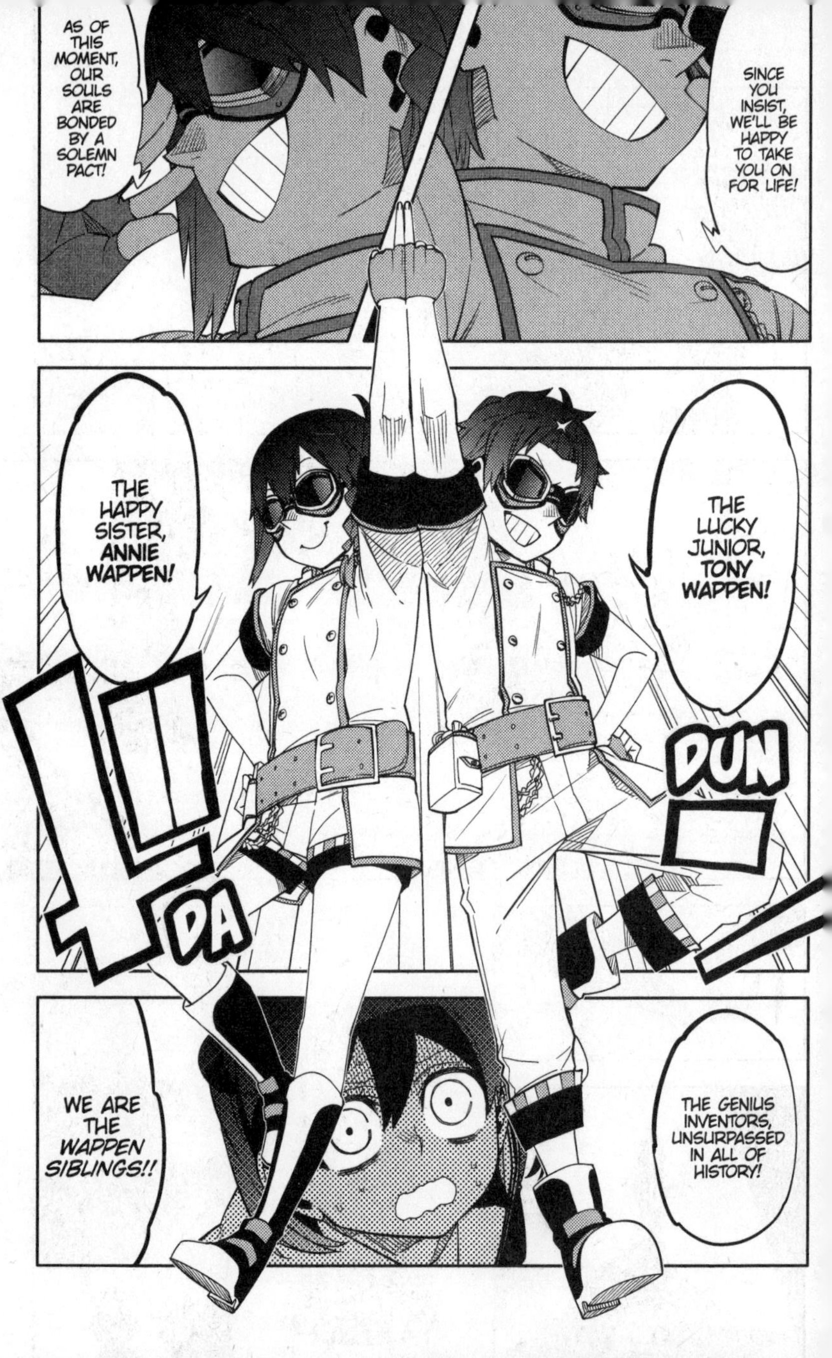
SINCE YOU INSIST, WE'LL BE HAPPY TO TAKE YOU ON FOR LIFE!
AS OF THIS MOMENT, OUR SOULS ARE BONDED BY A SOLEMN PACT!
THE LUCKY JUNIOR, TONY WAPPEN!
THE HAPPY SISTER, ANNIE WAPPEN!
DUN
DA
THE GENIUS INVENTORS, UNSURPASSED IN ALL OF HISTORY!
WE ARE THE WAPPEN SIBLINGS!!

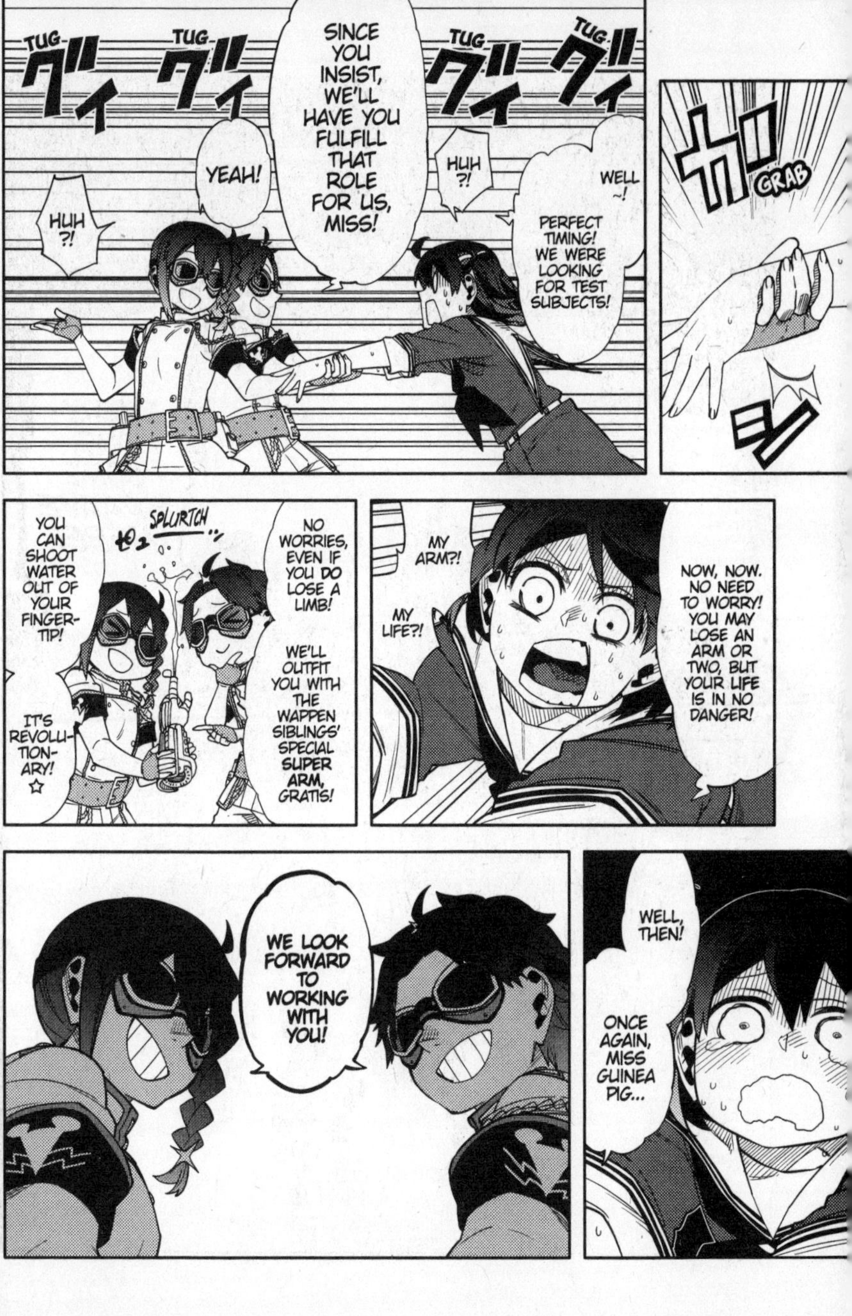
GRAB
TUG TUG
WELL ~!
PERFECT TIMING! WE WERE LOOKING FOR TEST SUBJECTS!
HUH ?!
SINCE YOU INSIST, WE'LL HAVE YOU FULFILL THAT ROLE FOR US, MISS!
YEAH!
HUH ?!
TUG TUG
NOW, NOW. NO NEED TO WORRY! YOU MAY LOSE AN ARM OR TWO, BUT YOUR LIFE IS IN NO DANGER!
MY ARM?!
MY LIFE?!
NO WORRIES, EVEN IF YOU DO LOSE A LIMB!
WE'LL OUTFIT YOU WITH THE WAPPEN SIBLINGS' SPECIAL SUPER ARM, GRATIS!
SPLURTCH
YOU CAN SHOOT WATER OUT OF YOUR FINGER-TIP!
IT'S REVOLU-TION-ARY! ☆
WELL, THEN!
ONCE AGAIN, MISS GUINEA PIG...
WE LOOK FORWARD TO WORKING WITH YOU!

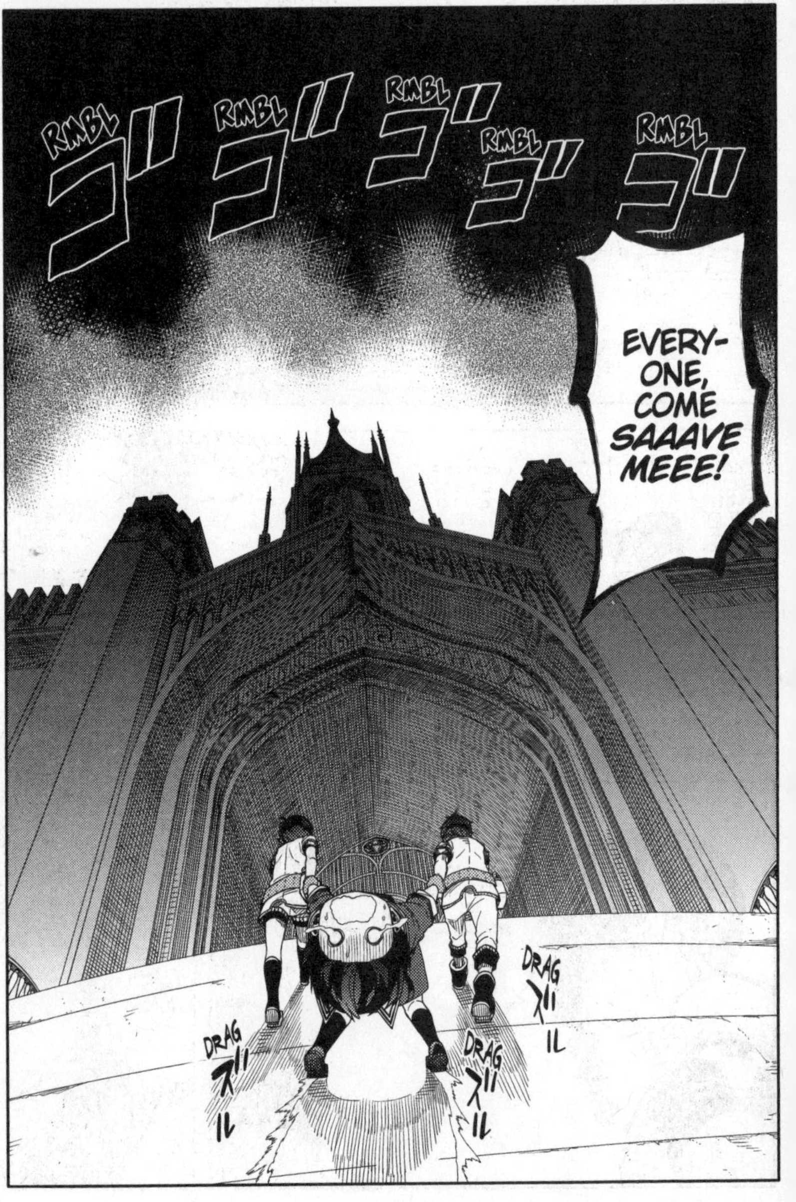
RMBL ゴ
RMBL ゴ
RMBL ゴ
RMBL ゴ
RMBL ゴ
EVERY-ONE, COME SAAAVE MEEE!
DRAG ズル
DRAG ズル
DRAG ズル

Character Introduction

Tenka Landgraf

- ◆ Birthday: 1/13
- ◆ Age: 21
- ◆ Height: 175cm
- ◆ Role/Job: God of "Domination"

  (Current Possessor of Diselveda)
- ◆ Hobbies: Creating new recipes
- ◆ Skill: Survival techniques
- ◆ Dislikes: Laughing
- ◆ Favorite Food: Seafood

  (but it's got to be fresh!)

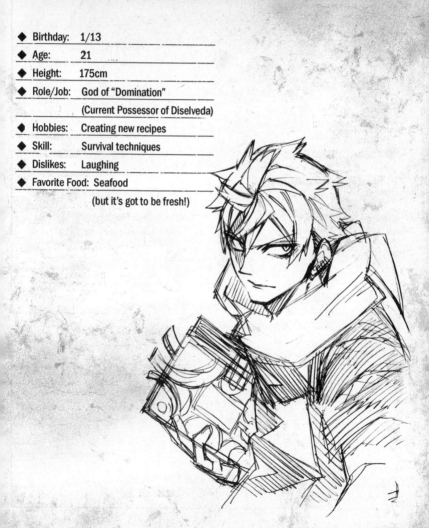

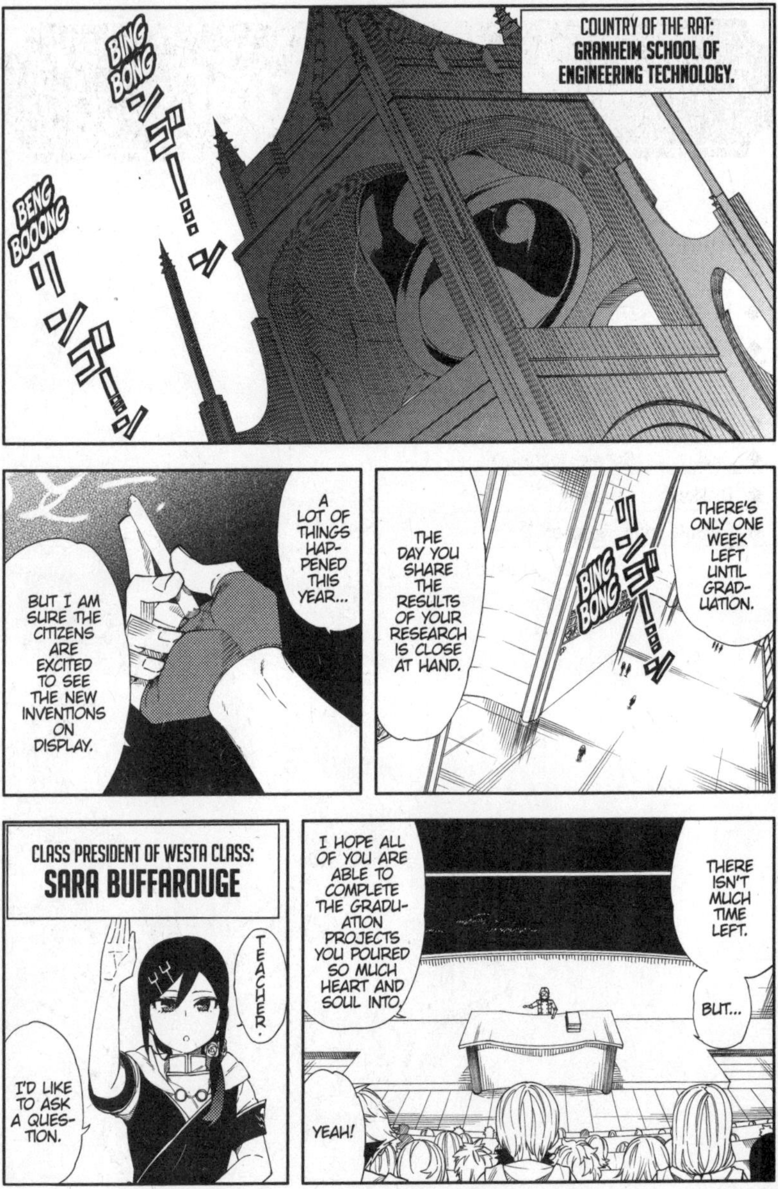
COUNTRY OF THE RAT: GRANHEIM SCHOOL OF ENGINEERING TECHNOLOGY.
BING BONG
BENG BOOONG
THERE'S ONLY ONE WEEK LEFT UNTIL GRAD-UATION.
BING BONG
THE DAY YOU SHARE THE RESULTS OF YOUR RESEARCH IS CLOSE AT HAND.
A LOT OF THINGS HAP-PENED THIS YEAR...
BUT I AM SURE THE CITIZENS ARE EXCITED TO SEE THE NEW INVENTIONS ON DISPLAY.
THERE ISN'T MUCH TIME LEFT.
BUT...
I HOPE ALL OF YOU ARE ABLE TO COMPLETE THE GRADU-ATION PROJECTS YOU POURED SO MUCH HEART AND SOUL INTO.
YEAH!
CLASS PRESIDENT OF WESTA CLASS:
SARA BUFFAROUGE
TEACHER.
I'D LIKE TO ASK A QUES-TION.

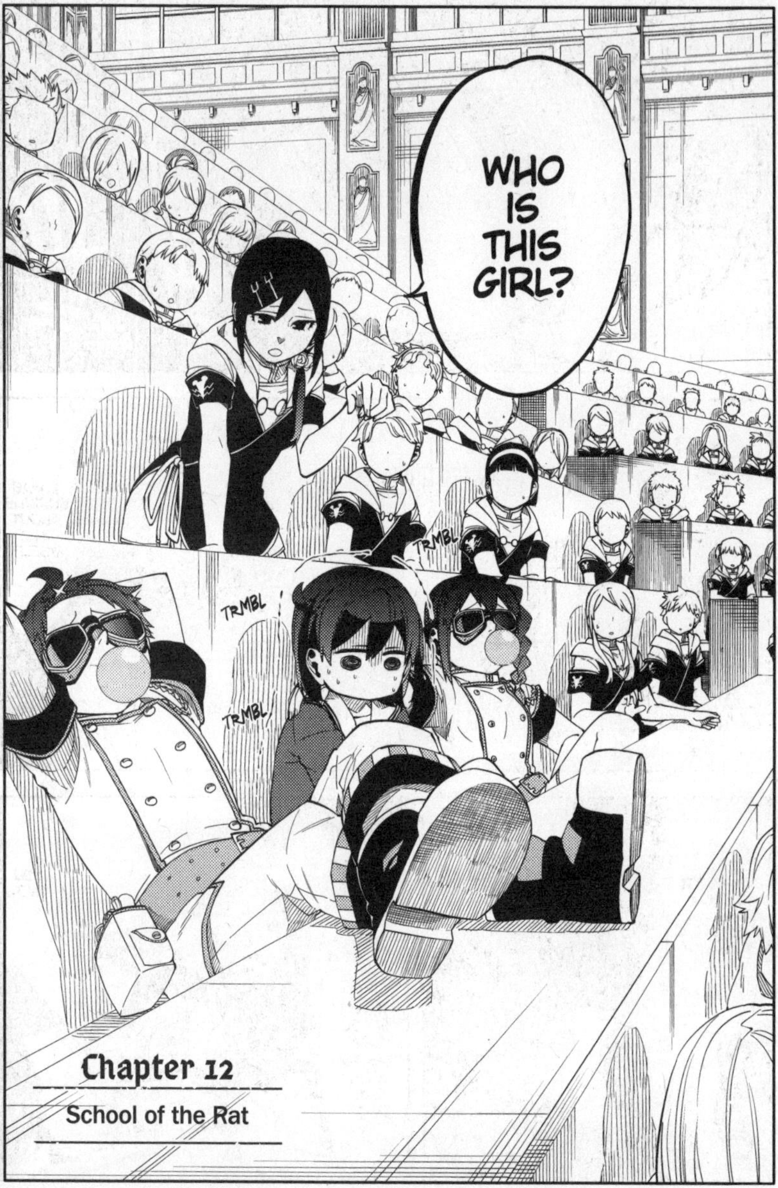
WHO IS THIS GIRL?
TRMBL
TRMBL
TRMBL

Chapter 12

School of the Rat

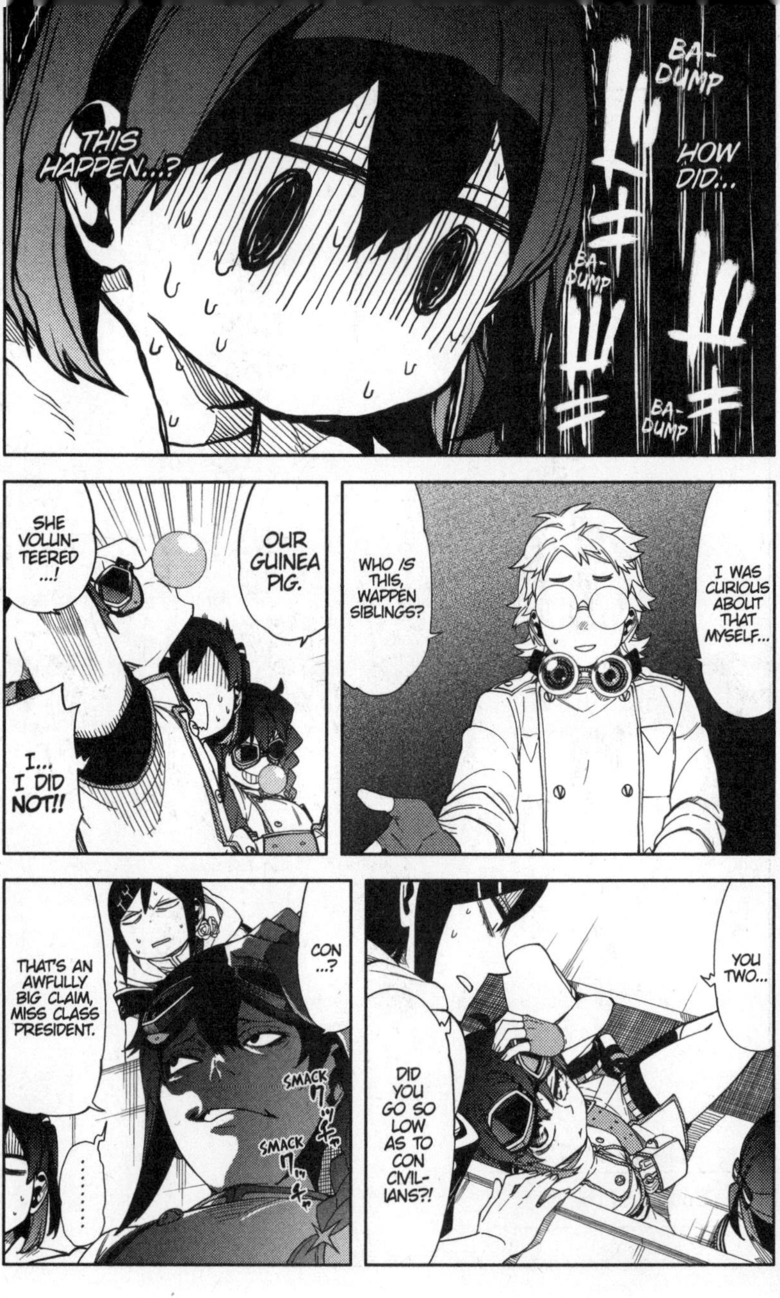
BA-DUMP
HOW DID...
THIS HAPPEN...?
BA-DUMP
BA-DUMP
I WAS CURIOUS ABOUT THAT MYSELF...
WHO IS THIS, WAPPEN SIBLINGS?
OUR GUINEA PIG.
SHE VOLUNTEERED ...!
I... I DID NOT!!
YOU TWO...
DID YOU GO SO LOW AS TO CON CIVILIANS?!
CON ...?
THAT'S AN AWFULLY BIG CLAIM, MISS CLASS PRESIDENT.
SMACK
SMACK
......

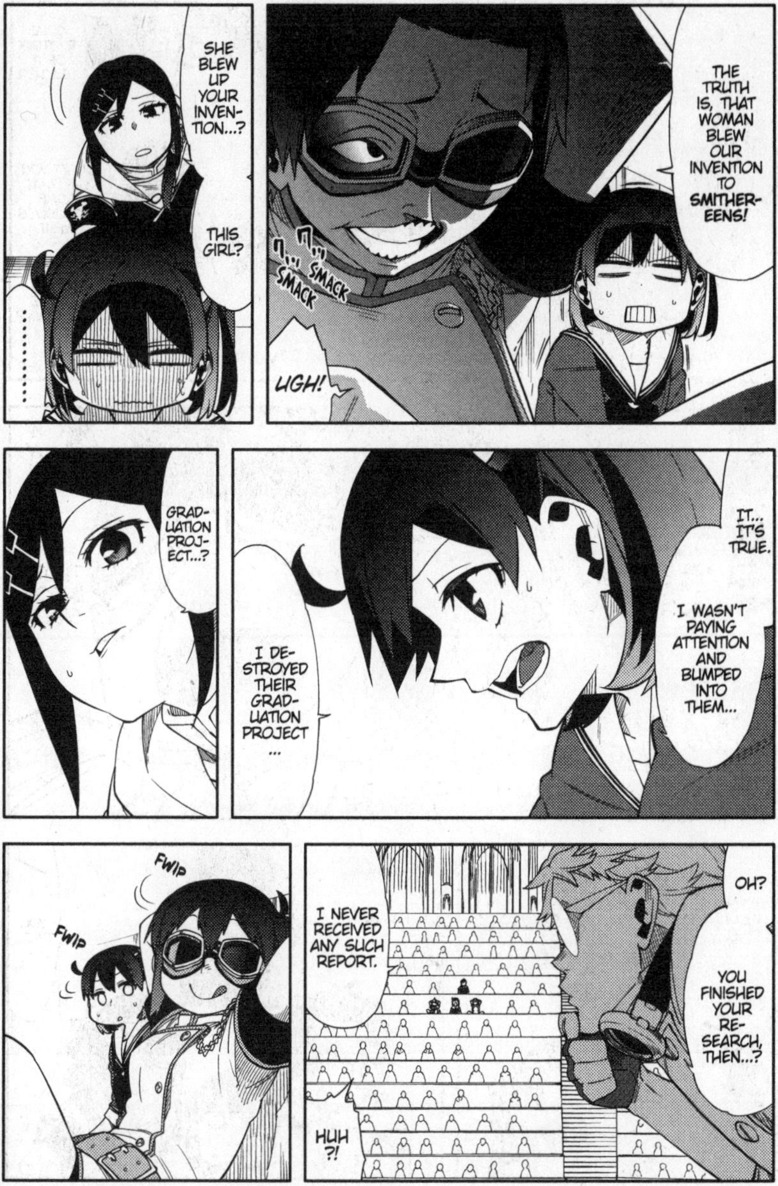
THE TRUTH IS, THAT WOMAN BLEW OUR INVENTION TO SMITHEREENS!
SMACK SMACK
UGH!
SHE BLEW UP YOUR INVENTION...?
THIS GIRL?
......
IT... IT'S TRUE.
I WASN'T PAYING ATTENTION AND BUMPED INTO THEM...
I DESTROYED THEIR GRADUATION PROJECT...
GRADUATION PROJECT...?
OH?
YOU FINISHED YOUR RESEARCH, THEN...?
I NEVER RECEIVED ANY SUCH REPORT.
HUH?!
FWIP
FWIP

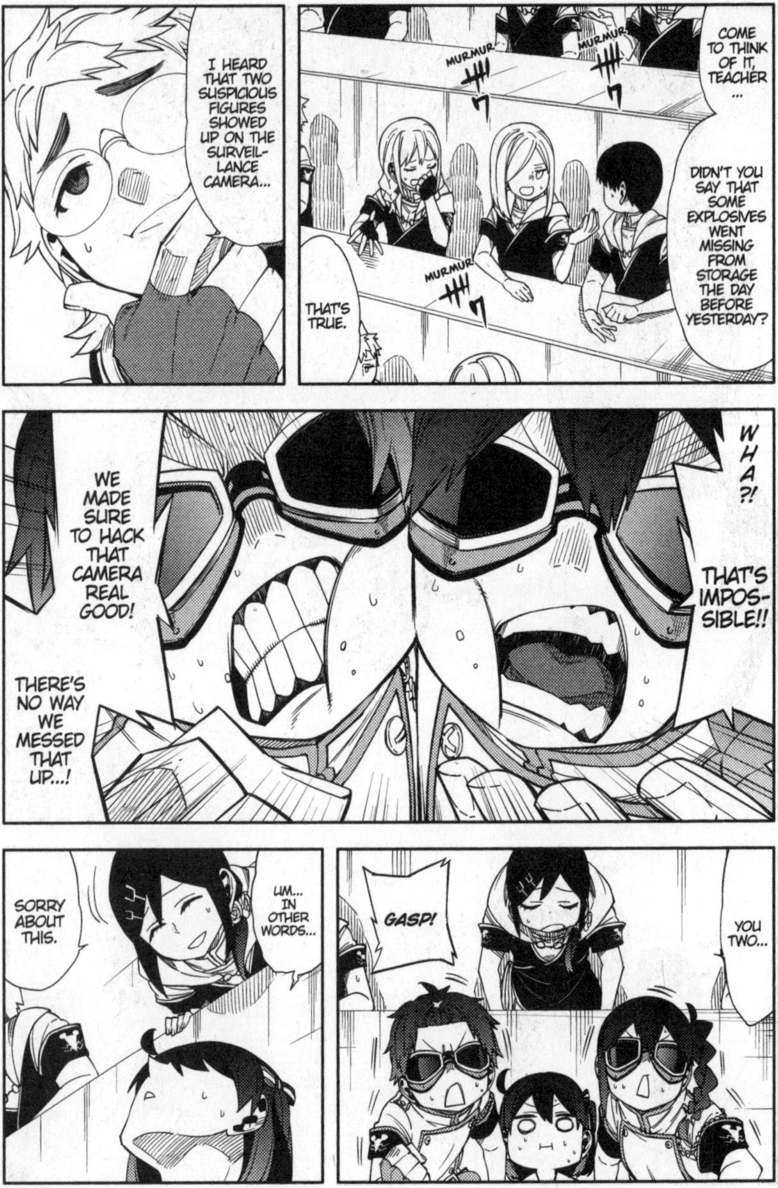
COME TO THINK OF IT, TEACHER...
DIDN'T YOU SAY THAT SOME EXPLOSIVES WENT MISSING FROM STORAGE THE DAY BEFORE YESTERDAY?
MURMUR
MURMUR
MURMUR
THAT'S TRUE.
I HEARD THAT TWO SUSPICIOUS FIGURES SHOWED UP ON THE SURVEIL-LANCE CAMERA...
WHA?!
THAT'S IMPOS-SIBLE!!
WE MADE SURE TO HACK THAT CAMERA REAL GOOD!
THERE'S NO WAY WE MESSED THAT UP...!
YOU TWO...
GASP!
UM... IN OTHER WORDS...
SORRY ABOUT THIS.

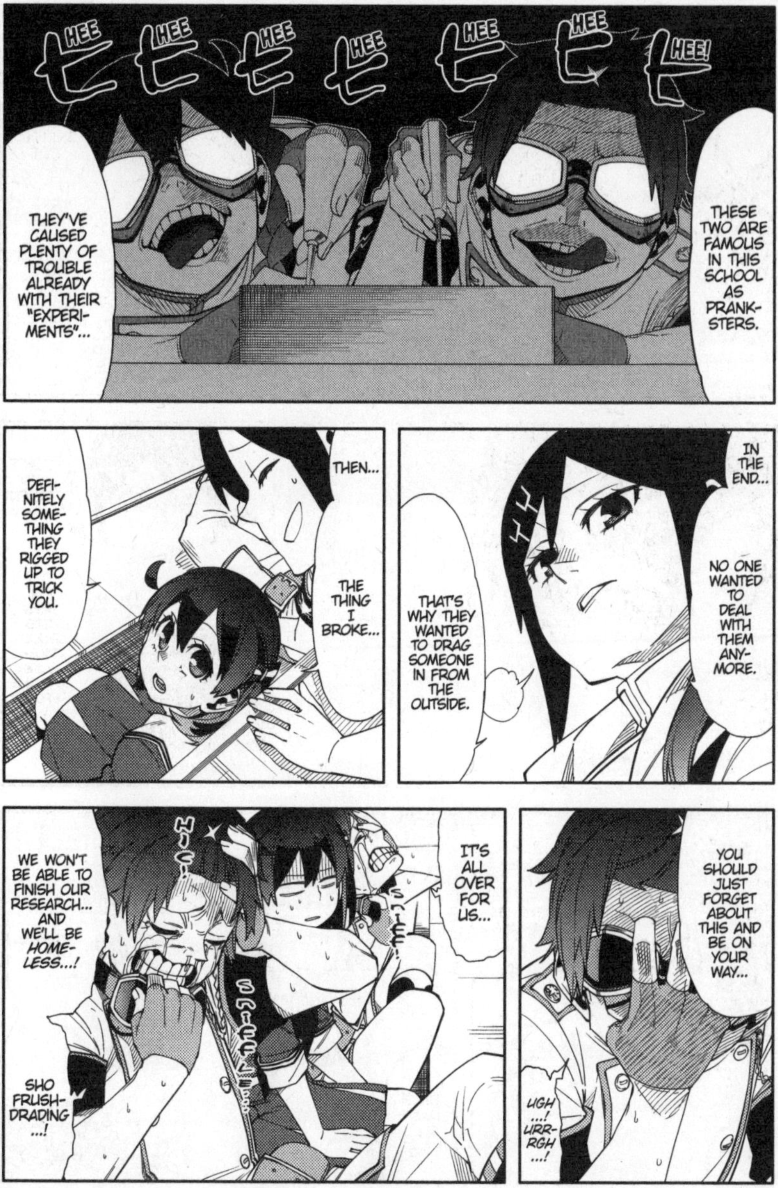
HEE HEE HEE HEE HEE HEE HEE!
THESE TWO ARE FAMOUS IN THIS SCHOOL AS PRANKSTERS.
THEY'VE CAUSED PLENTY OF TROUBLE ALREADY WITH THEIR "EXPERIMENTS"...
IN THE END...
NO ONE WANTED TO DEAL WITH THEM ANYMORE.
THAT'S WHY THEY WANTED TO DRAG SOMEONE IN FROM THE OUTSIDE.
THEN...
THE THING I BROKE...
DEFINITELY SOMETHING THEY RIGGED UP TO TRICK YOU.
YOU SHOULD JUST FORGET ABOUT THIS AND BE ON YOUR WAY...
UGH...! URRRGH...!
IT'S ALL OVER FOR US...
HIC
SNIFF...
WE WON'T BE ABLE TO FINISH OUR RESEARCH... AND WE'LL BE *HOMELESS*...!
SNIFFLE...
SHO FRUSHDRADING...!

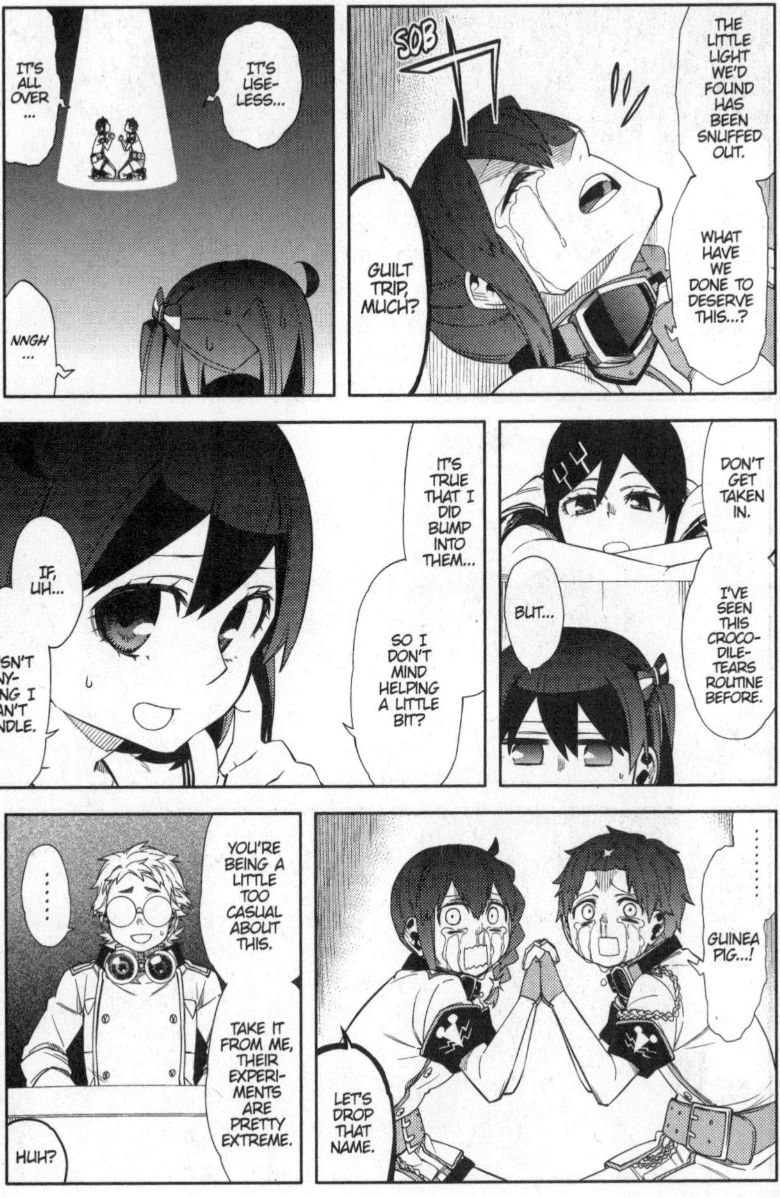
SOB
THE LITTLE LIGHT WE'D FOUND HAS BEEN SNUFFED OUT.
WHAT HAVE WE DONE TO DESERVE THIS...?
GUILT TRIP, MUCH?
IT'S USELESS...
IT'S ALL OVER...
NNGH...
DON'T GET TAKEN IN.
I'VE SEEN THIS CROCODILE-TEARS ROUTINE BEFORE.
BUT...
IT'S TRUE THAT I DID BUMP INTO THEM...
SO I DON'T MIND HELPING A LITTLE BIT?
IF, UH...
IT ISN'T ANYTHING I CAN'T HANDLE.
......
GUINEA PIG...!
LET'S DROP THAT NAME.
YOU'RE BEING A LITTLE TOO CASUAL ABOUT THIS.
TAKE IT FROM ME, THEIR EXPERIMENTS ARE PRETTY EXTREME.
......
HUH?

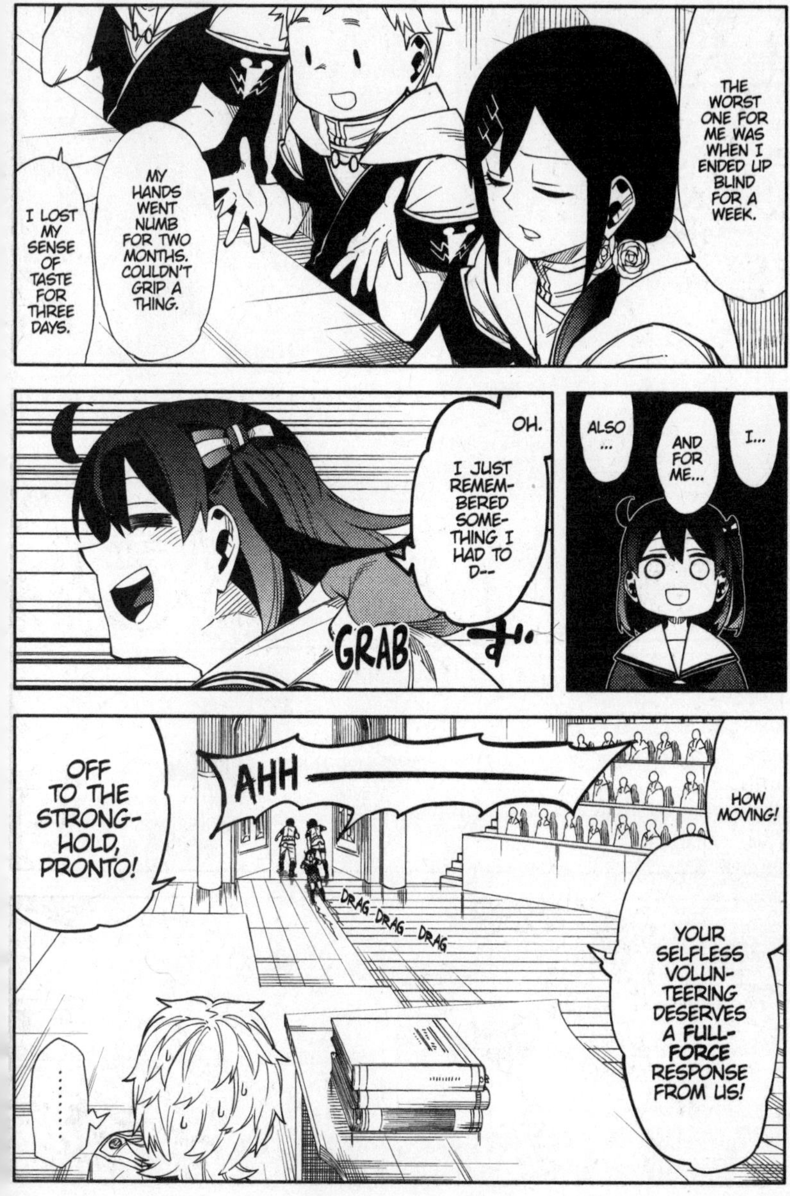
THE WORST ONE FOR ME WAS WHEN I ENDED UP BLIND FOR A WEEK.
MY HANDS WENT NUMB FOR TWO MONTHS. COULDN'T GRIP A THING.
I LOST MY SENSE OF TASTE FOR THREE DAYS.
I...
AND FOR ME...
ALSO...
OH.
I JUST REMEMBERED SOMETHING I HAD TO D--
GRAB
HOW MOVING!
AHH——
OFF TO THE STRONGHOLD, PRONTO!
YOUR SELFLESS VOLUNTEERING DESERVES A FULL-FORCE RESPONSE FROM US!
DRAG-DRAG-DRAG
......

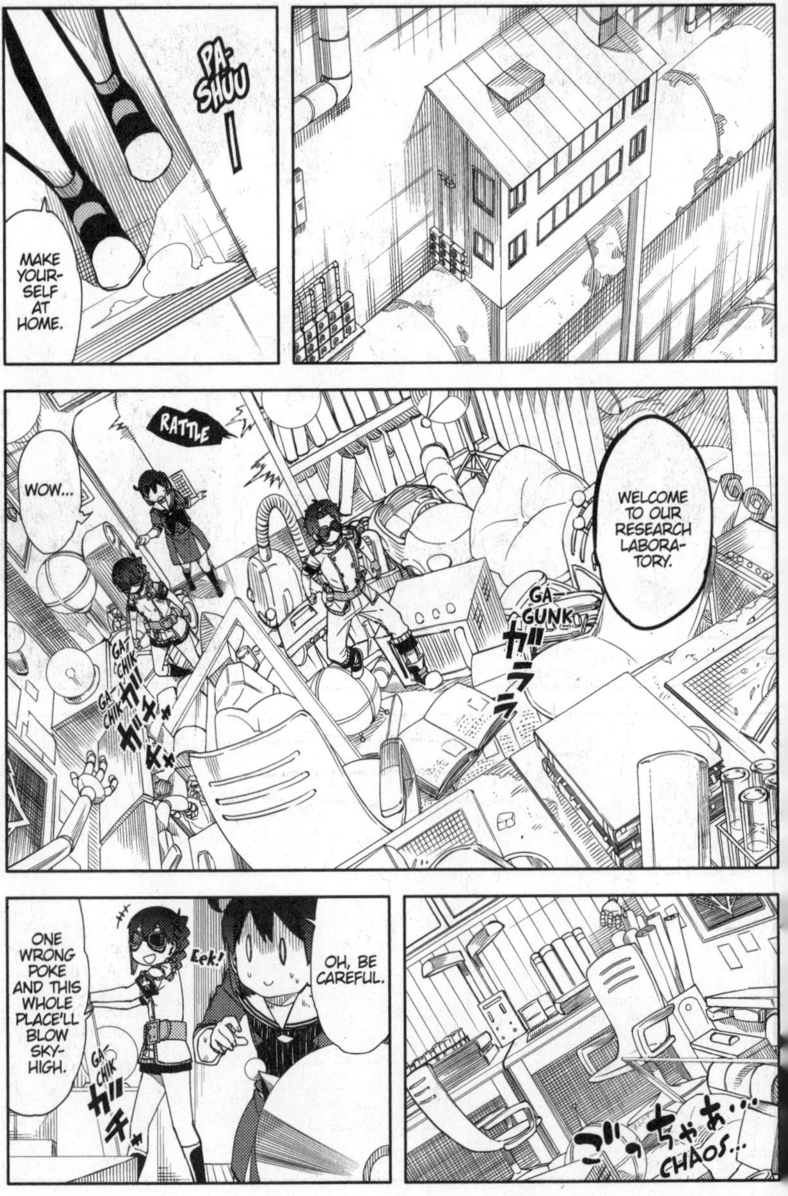
PA-SHUU
MAKE YOURSELF AT HOME.
WELCOME TO OUR RESEARCH LABORATORY.
GA-GUNK
ガラララ
RATTLE
WOW...
GA-CHIK GA-CHIK
ガチャガチャ
ごっちゃあ…
CHAOS...
OH, BE CAREFUL.
Eek!
ONE WRONG POKE AND THIS WHOLE PLACE'LL BLOW SKY-HIGH.
GA-CHIK
ガチャ

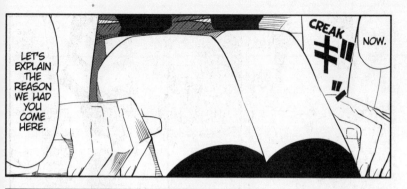

CREAK
NOW.
LET'S EXPLAIN THE REASON WE HAD YOU COME HERE.
WE ONLY HAVE ONE OBJECTIVE...
WE WISH TO PRESENT THE ULTIMATE INVENTION IN THE UPCOMING CEREMONY...
AND BECOME THE SUCCESSORS TO THE NIDANA OF LIGHTNING!
THEY SAY THAT THE NIDANA OF LIGHTNING CHOOSES TO DWELL WITHIN THE MOST TALENTED OF ENGINEERS.
AS THERE IS CURRENTLY NO RAT OF THE TWELVE, THIS IS THE PERFECT CHANCE!
WHAT?!
THERE'S NO RAT AT ALL RIGHT NOW?!
RIGHT.
AND IT'S BEEN FIFTEEN YEARS SINCE THE PREVIOUS ONE DIED.

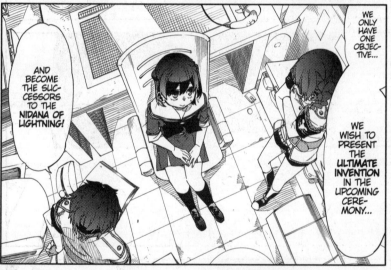

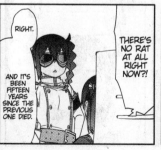

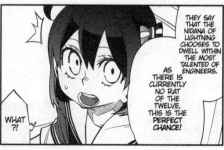

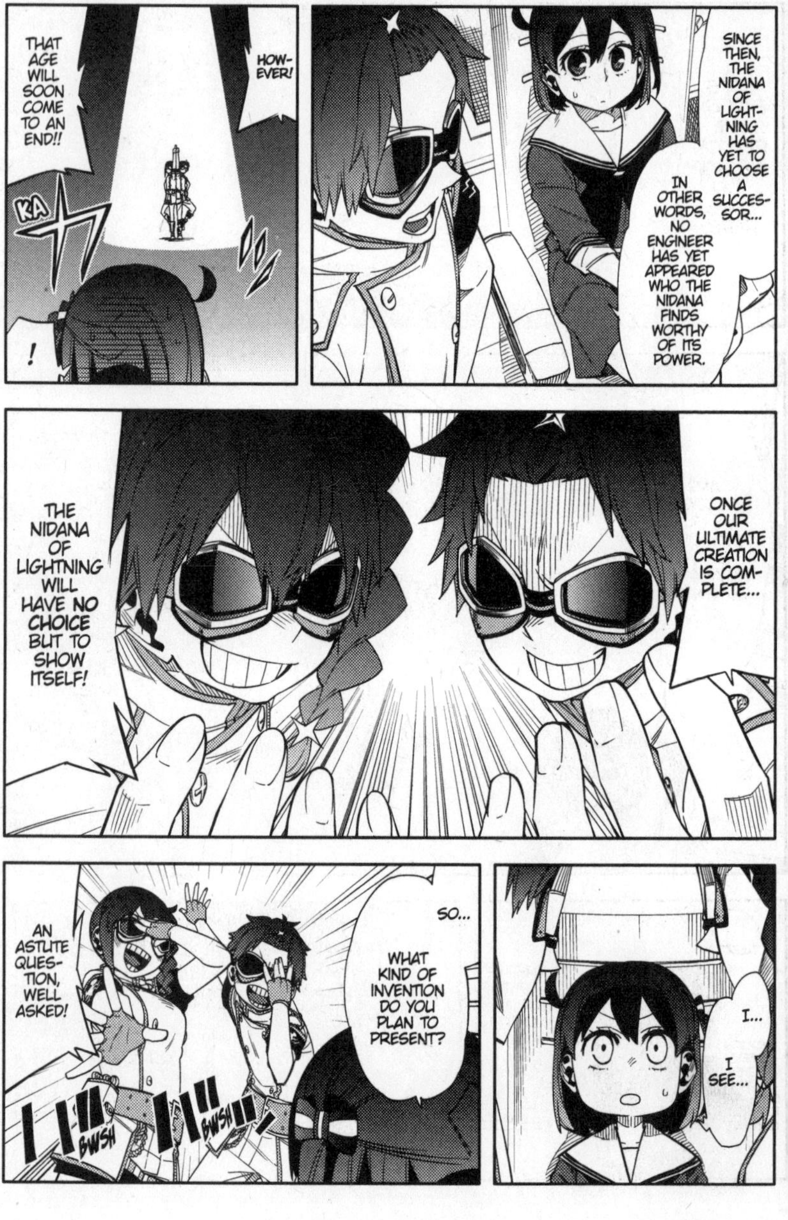
SINCE THEN, THE NIDANA OF LIGHT-NING HAS YET TO CHOOSE A SUCCES-SOR...
IN OTHER WORDS, NO ENGINEER HAS YET APPEARED WHO THE NIDANA FINDS WORTHY OF ITS POWER.
HOW-EVER!
THAT AGE WILL SOON COME TO AN END!!
KA
!
ONCE OUR ULTIMATE CREATION IS COM-PLETE...
THE NIDANA OF LIGHTNING WILL HAVE NO CHOICE BUT TO SHOW ITSELF!
I...
I SEE...
SO...
WHAT KIND OF INVENTION DO YOU PLAN TO PRESENT?
AN ASTUTE QUES-TION, WELL ASKED!
BWSH
BWSH

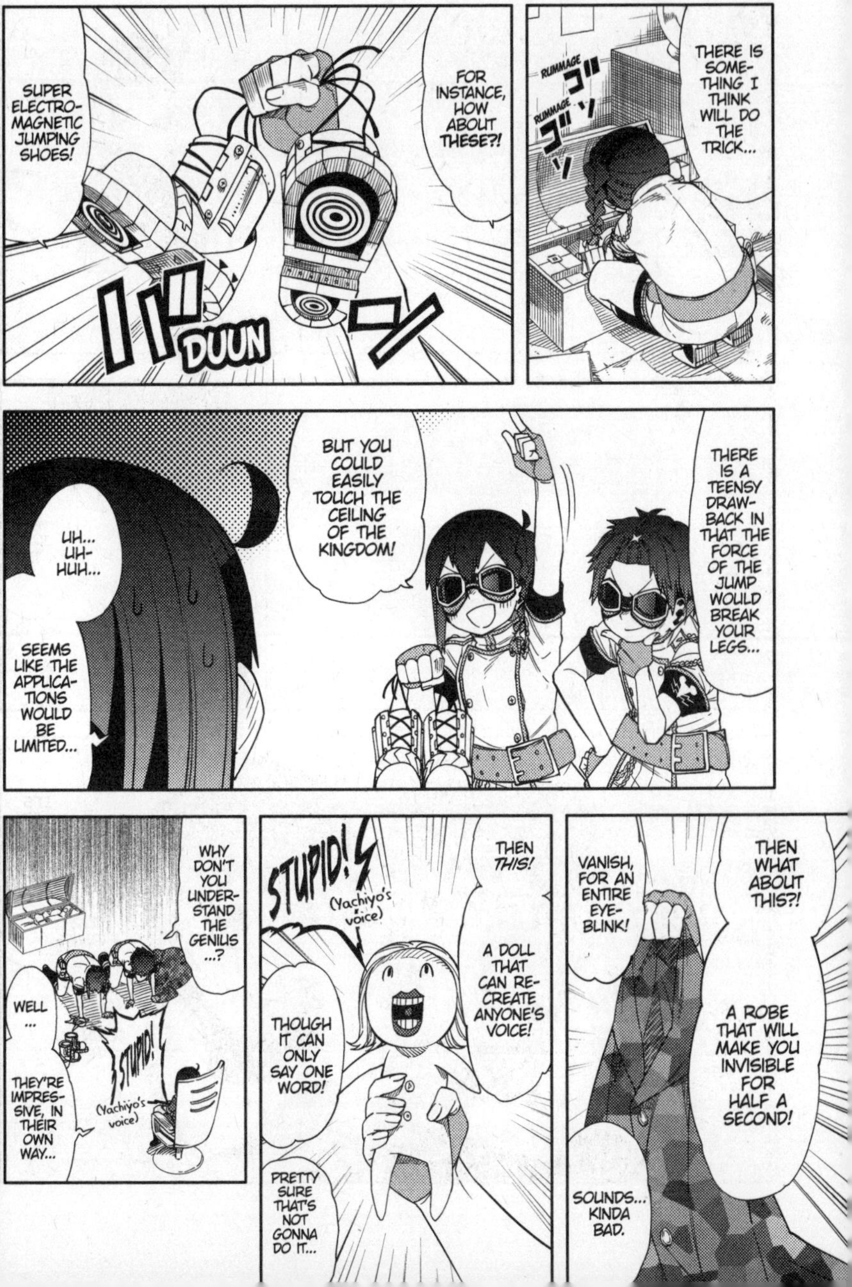
RUMMAGE
RUMMAGE
THERE IS SOME-THING I THINK WILL DO THE TRICK...
FOR INSTANCE, HOW ABOUT THESE?!
SUPER ELECTRO-MAGNETIC JUMPING SHOES!
DUUN
THERE IS A TEENSY DRAW-BACK IN THAT THE FORCE OF THE JUMP WOULD BREAK YOUR LEGS...
BUT YOU COULD EASILY TOUCH THE CEILING OF THE KINGDOM!
UH... UH-HUH...
SEEMS LIKE THE APPLICA-TIONS WOULD BE LIMITED...
THEN WHAT ABOUT THIS?!
A ROBE THAT WILL MAKE YOU INVISIBLE FOR HALF A SECOND!
VANISH, FOR AN ENTIRE EYE-BLINK!
SOUNDS... KINDA BAD.
THEN *THIS!*
A DOLL THAT CAN RE-CREATE ANYONE'S VOICE!
STUPID!
(Yachiyo's voice)
THOUGH IT CAN ONLY SAY ONE WORD!
PRETTY SURE THAT'S NOT GONNA DO IT...
WHY DON'T YOU UNDER-STAND THE GENIUS ...?
STUPID!
(Yachiyo's voice)
WELL ...
THEY'RE IMPRES-SIVE, IN THEIR OWN WAY...

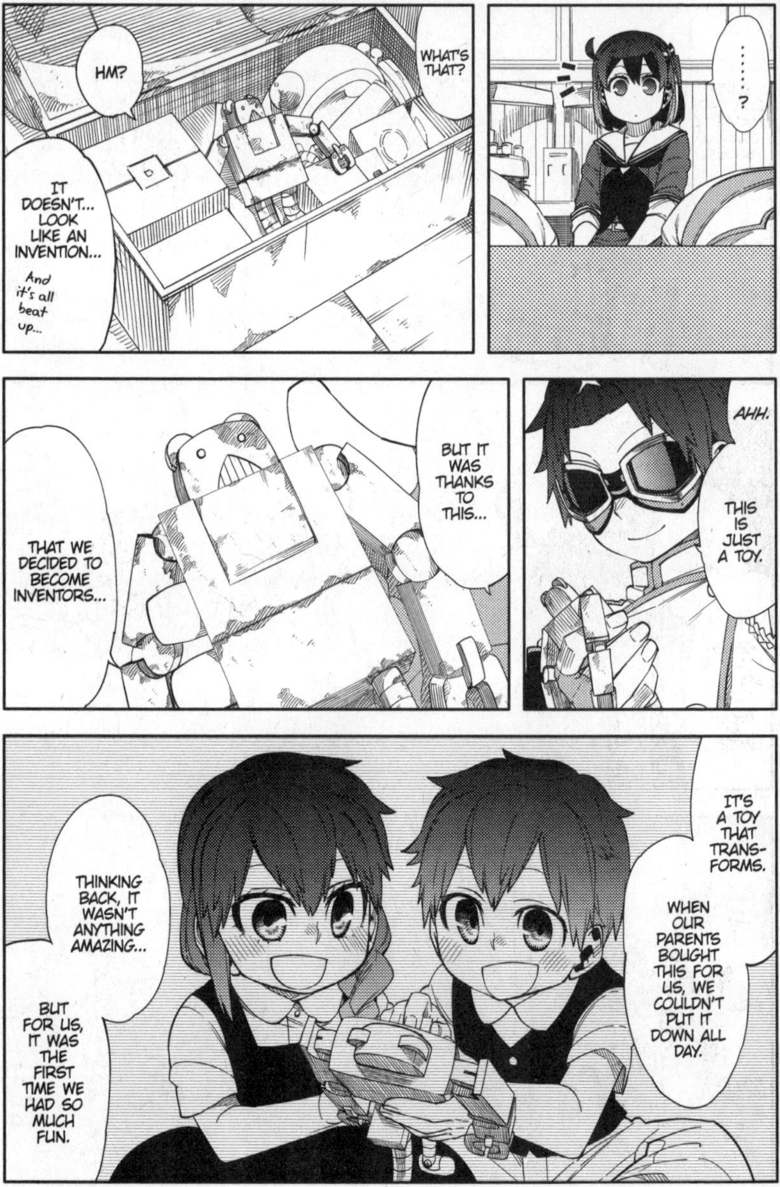
......?
WHAT'S THAT?
HM?
IT DOESN'T... LOOK LIKE AN INVENTION...
And it's all beat up...
AHH.
THIS IS JUST A TOY.
BUT IT WAS THANKS TO THIS...
THAT WE DECIDED TO BECOME INVENTORS...
IT'S A TOY THAT TRANS-FORMS.
WHEN OUR PARENTS BOUGHT THIS FOR US, WE COULDN'T PUT IT DOWN ALL DAY.
THINKING BACK, IT WASN'T ANYTHING AMAZING...
BUT FOR US, IT WAS THE FIRST TIME WE HAD SO MUCH FUN.

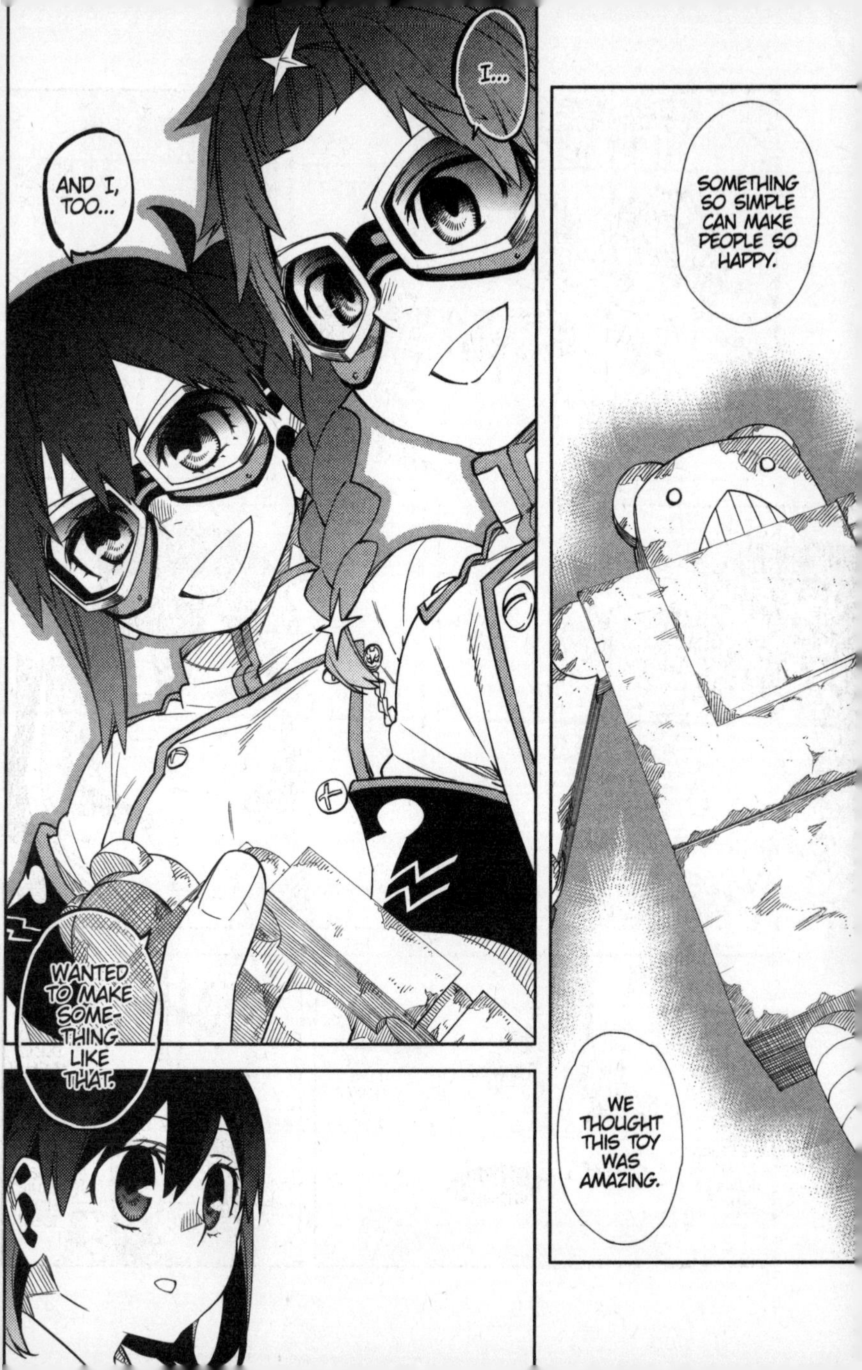
SOMETHING SO SIMPLE CAN MAKE PEOPLE SO HAPPY.
WE THOUGHT THIS TOY WAS AMAZING.
I...
AND I, TOO...
WANTED TO MAKE SOME-THING LIKE THAT.

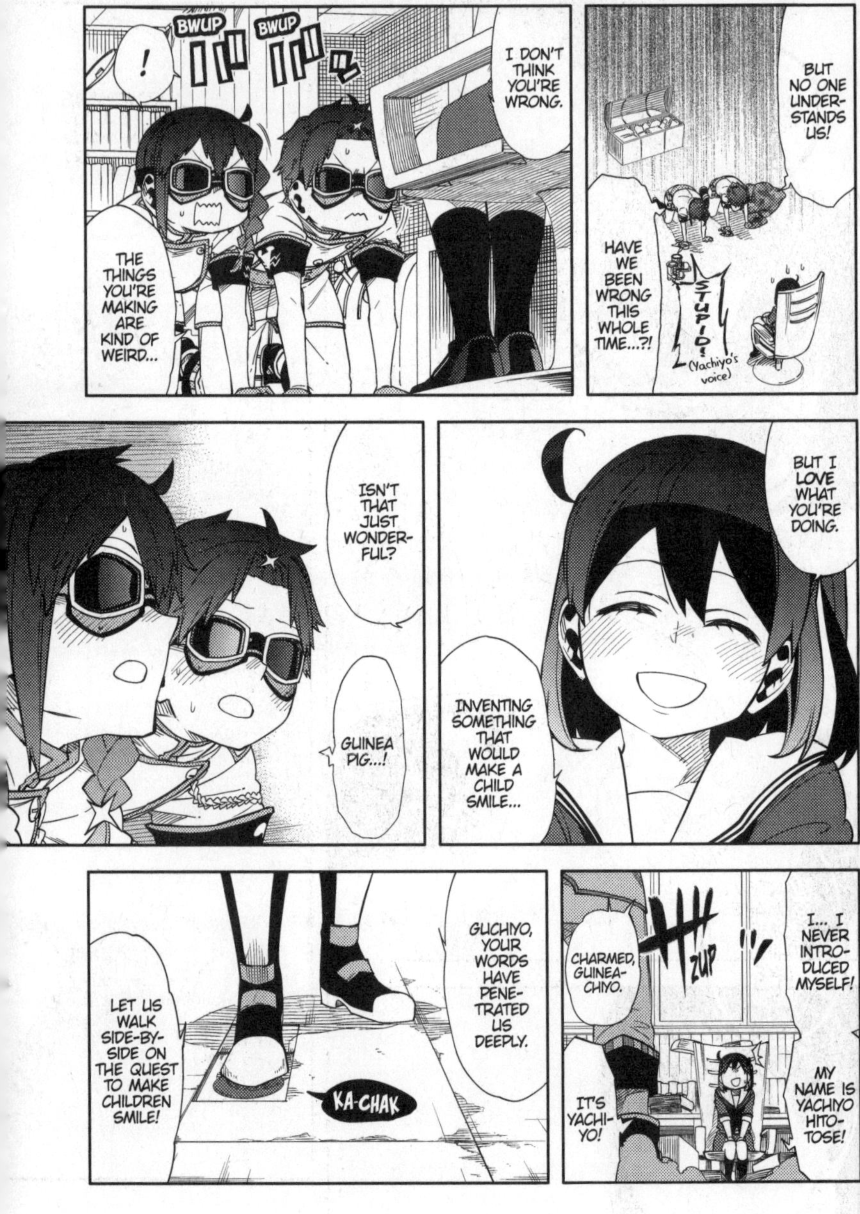
BUT NO ONE UNDER-STANDS US!
HAVE WE BEEN WRONG THIS WHOLE TIME...?!
STUPID!
(Yachiyo's voice)
I DON'T THINK YOU'RE WRONG.
BWUP
BWUP
!
THE THINGS YOU'RE MAKING ARE KIND OF WEIRD...
BUT I LOVE WHAT YOU'RE DOING.
INVENTING SOMETHING THAT WOULD MAKE A CHILD SMILE...
ISN'T THAT JUST WONDER-FUL?
GUINEA PIG...!
I... I NEVER INTRO-DUCED MYSELF!
MY NAME IS YACHIYO HITO-TOSE!
ZUP
CHARMED, GUINEA-CHIYO.
IT'S YACHI-YO!
GUCHIYO, YOUR WORDS HAVE PENE-TRATED US DEEPLY.
KA-CHAK
LET US WALK SIDE-BY-SIDE ON THE QUEST TO MAKE CHILDREN SMILE!

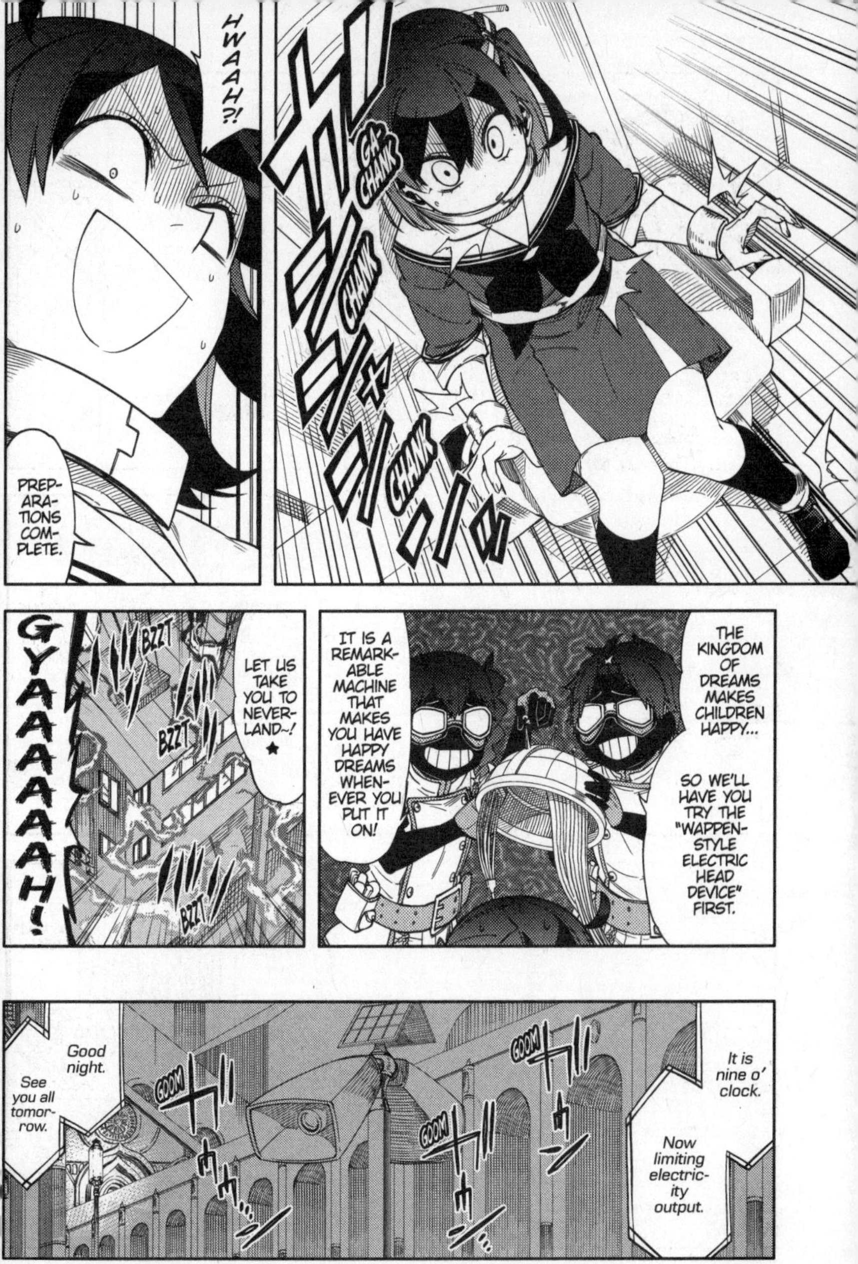
CA-CHANK
CHANK
CHANK
HWAAAH?!
PREP-ARA-TIONS COM-PLETE.
THE KINGDOM OF DREAMS MAKES CHILDREN HAPPY...
SO WE'LL HAVE YOU TRY THE "WAPPEN-STYLE ELECTRIC HEAD DEVICE" FIRST.
IT IS A REMARK-ABLE MACHINE THAT MAKES YOU HAVE HAPPY DREAMS WHEN-EVER YOU PUT IT ON!
LET US TAKE YOU TO NEVER-LAND~! ★
BZZT
BZZT
BZZT
GYAAAAAAAAH!
It is nine o' clock.
Now limiting electric-ity output.
GOOM
GOOM
GOOM
Good night.
See you all tomor-row.

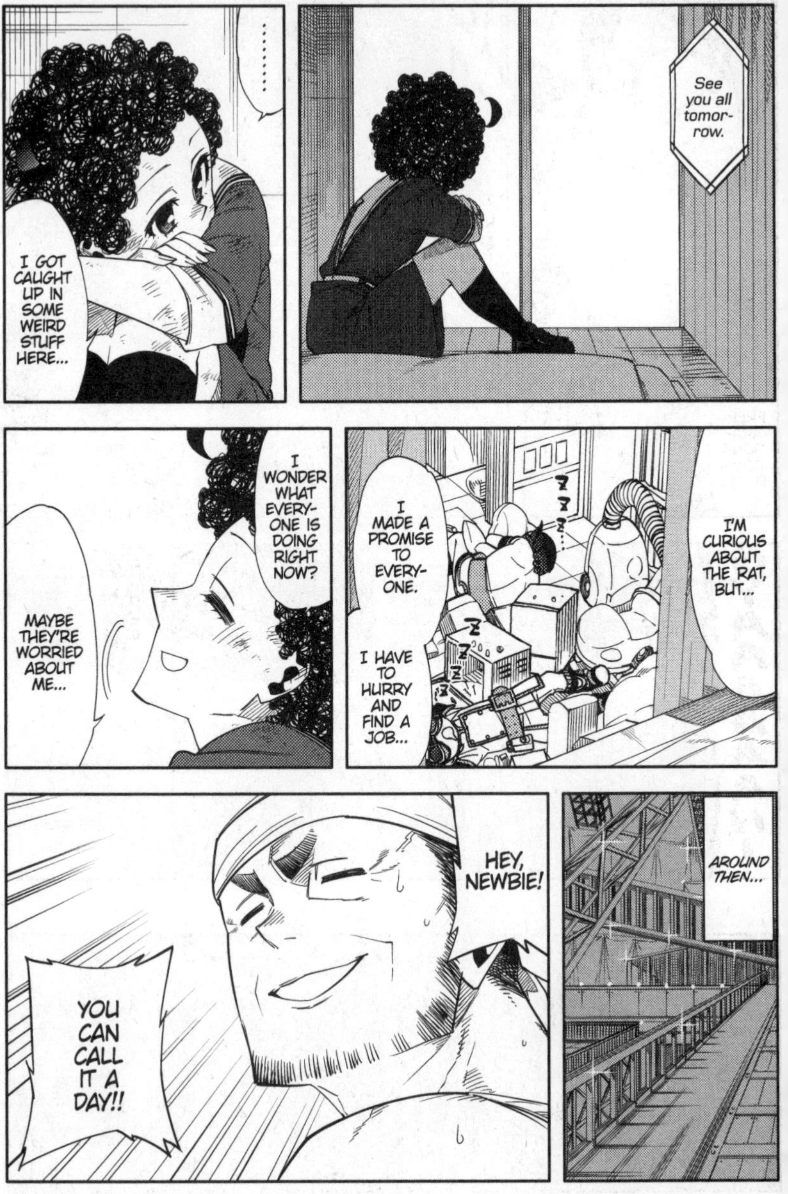
See you all tomorrow.
......
I GOT CAUGHT UP IN SOME WEIRD STUFF HERE...
I'M CURIOUS ABOUT THE RAT, BUT...
I MADE A PROMISE TO EVERYONE.
I HAVE TO HURRY AND FIND A JOB...
I WONDER WHAT EVERYONE IS DOING RIGHT NOW?
MAYBE THEY'RE WORRIED ABOUT ME...
AROUND THEN...
HEY, NEWBIE!
YOU CAN CALL IT A DAY!!

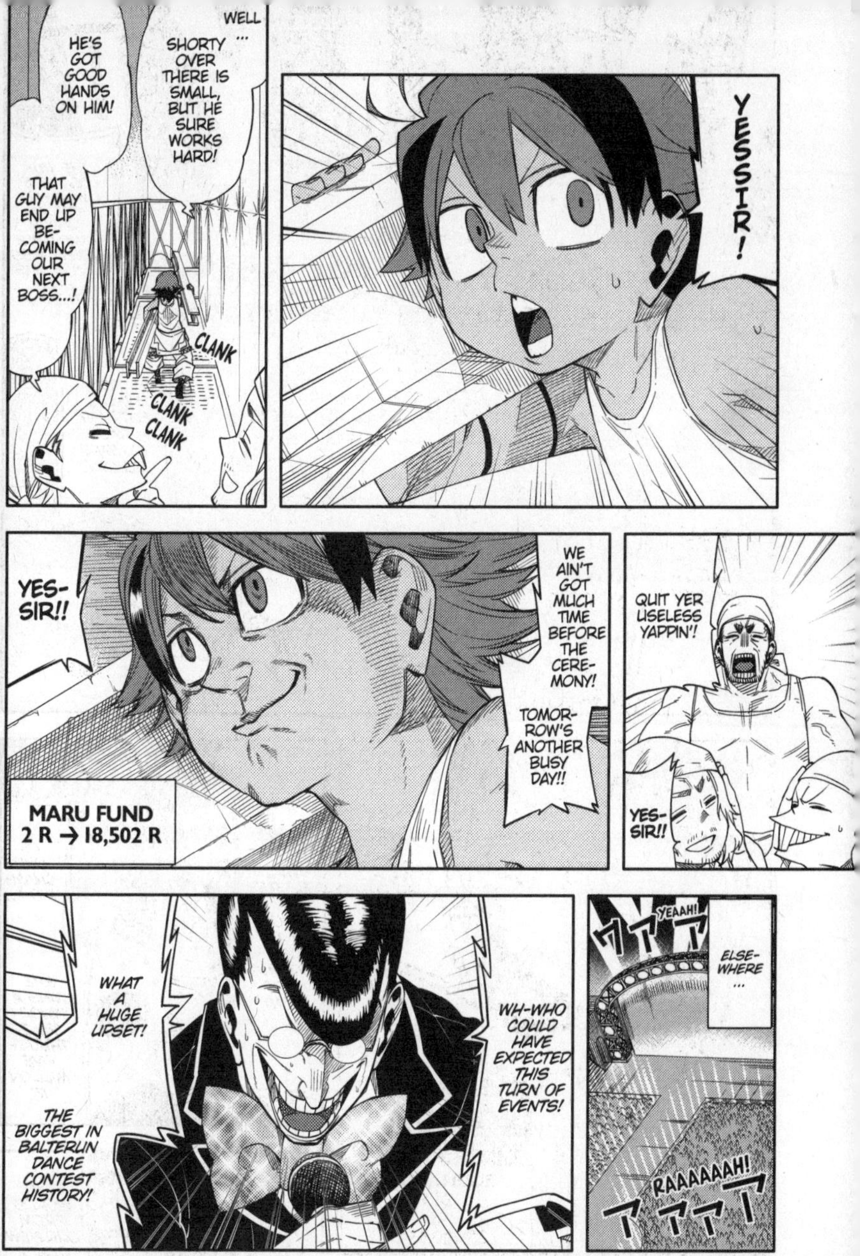
YESSIR!
WELL ...
SHORTY OVER THERE IS SMALL, BUT HE SURE WORKS HARD!
HE'S GOT GOOD HANDS ON HIM!
THAT GUY MAY END UP BE-COMING OUR NEXT BOSS...!
CLANK
CLANK CLANK
QUIT YER USELESS YAPPIN'!
YES-SIR!!
WE AIN'T GOT MUCH TIME BEFORE THE CERE-MONY!
TOMOR-ROW'S ANOTHER BUSY DAY!!
YES-SIR!!
MARU FUND
2 R → 18,502 R
YEAAH!
ELSE-WHERE ...
RAAAAAAH!
WH-WHO COULD HAVE EXPECTED THIS TURN OF EVENTS!
WHAT A HUGE UPSET!
THE BIGGEST IN BALTERUN DANCE CONTEST HISTORY!

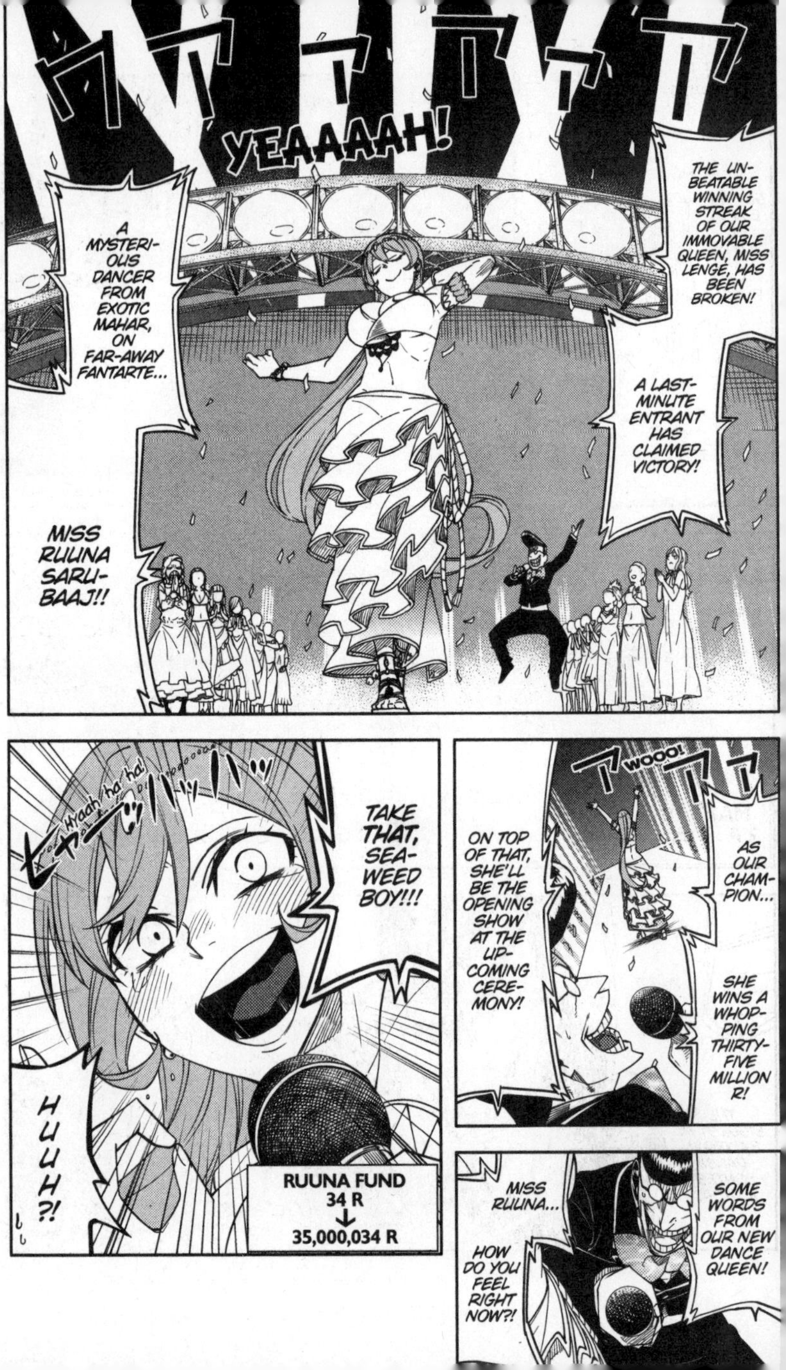
YEAAAAH!
THE UNBEATABLE WINNING STREAK OF OUR IMMOVABLE QUEEN, MISS LENGE, HAS BEEN BROKEN!
A LAST-MINUTE ENTRANT HAS CLAIMED VICTORY!
A MYSTERIOUS DANCER FROM EXOTIC MAHAR, ON FAR-AWAY FANTARTE...
MISS RUUNA SARUBAAJ!!
WOOO!
AS OUR CHAMPION...
SHE WINS A WHOPPING THIRTY-FIVE MILLION R!
ON TOP OF THAT, SHE'LL BE THE OPENING SHOW AT THE UPCOMING CEREMONY!
SOME WORDS FROM OUR NEW DANCE QUEEN!
MISS RUUNA...
HOW DO YOU FEEL RIGHT NOW?!
TAKE THAT, SEAWEED BOY!!!
Hyaah ha ha!
HUUUH?!
RUUNA FUND
34 R
↓
35,000,034 R

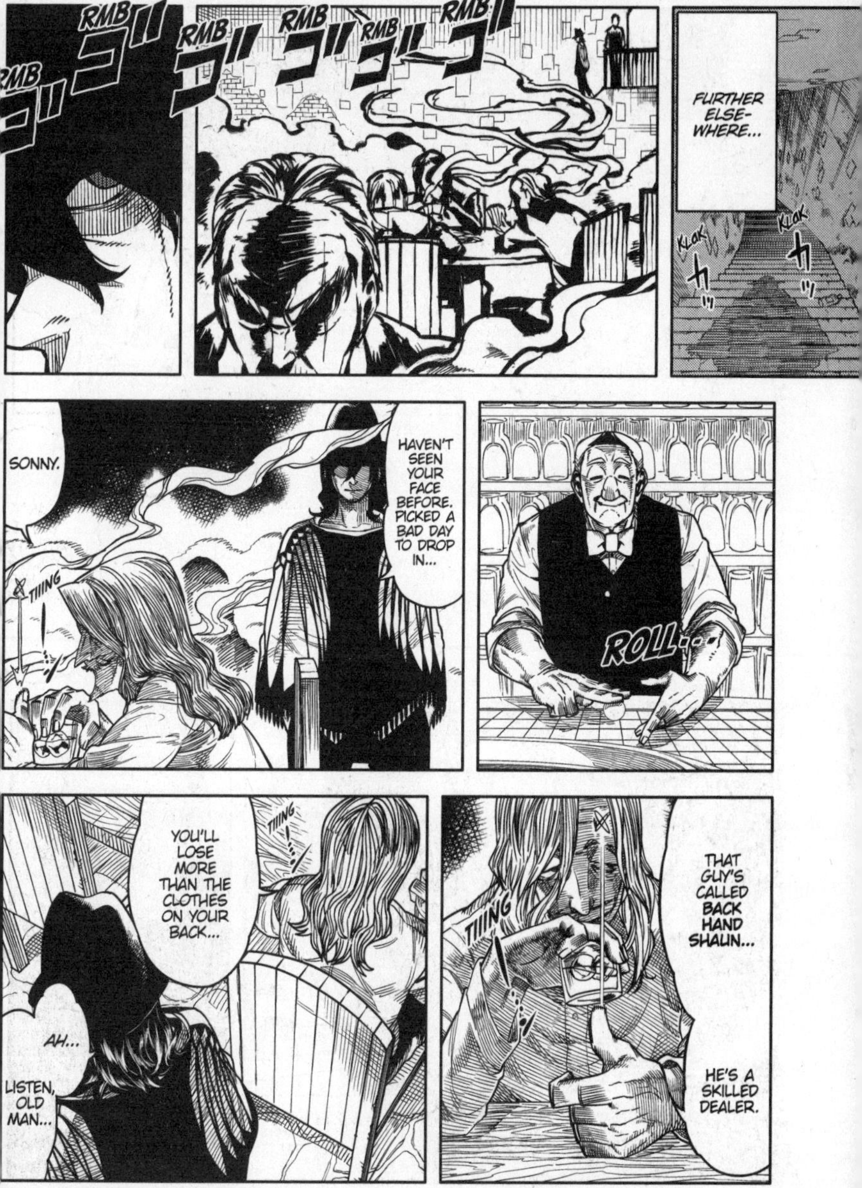
FURTHER ELSE-WHERE...
KLAK
KLAK
RMB
RMB
RMB
RMB
RMB
RMB
ROLL...
HAVEN'T SEEN YOUR FACE BEFORE. PICKED A BAD DAY TO DROP IN...
SONNY.
TIIING
THAT GUY'S CALLED BACK HAND SHAUN...
TIIING
HE'S A SKILLED DEALER.
TIIING
YOU'LL LOSE MORE THAN THE CLOTHES ON YOUR BACK...
AH...
LISTEN, OLD MAN...

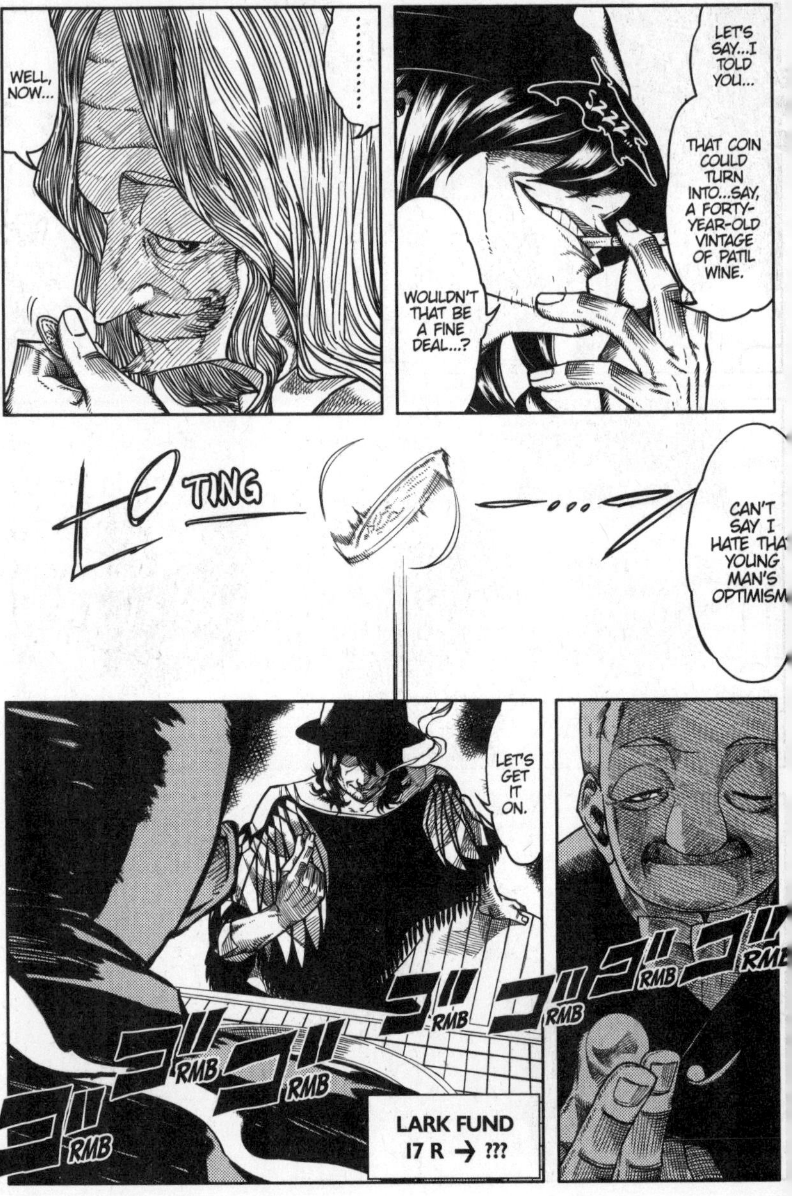
LET'S SAY...I TOLD YOU...
THAT COIN COULD TURN INTO...SAY, A FORTY-YEAR-OLD VINTAGE OF PATIL WINE.
WOULDN'T THAT BE A FINE DEAL...?
WELL, NOW...
TING
CAN'T SAY I HATE THA YOUNG MAN'S OPTIMISM
RMB
RMB
LET'S GET IT ON.
RMB
RMB
RMB
RMB
RMB
RMB
LARK FUND
17 R → ???

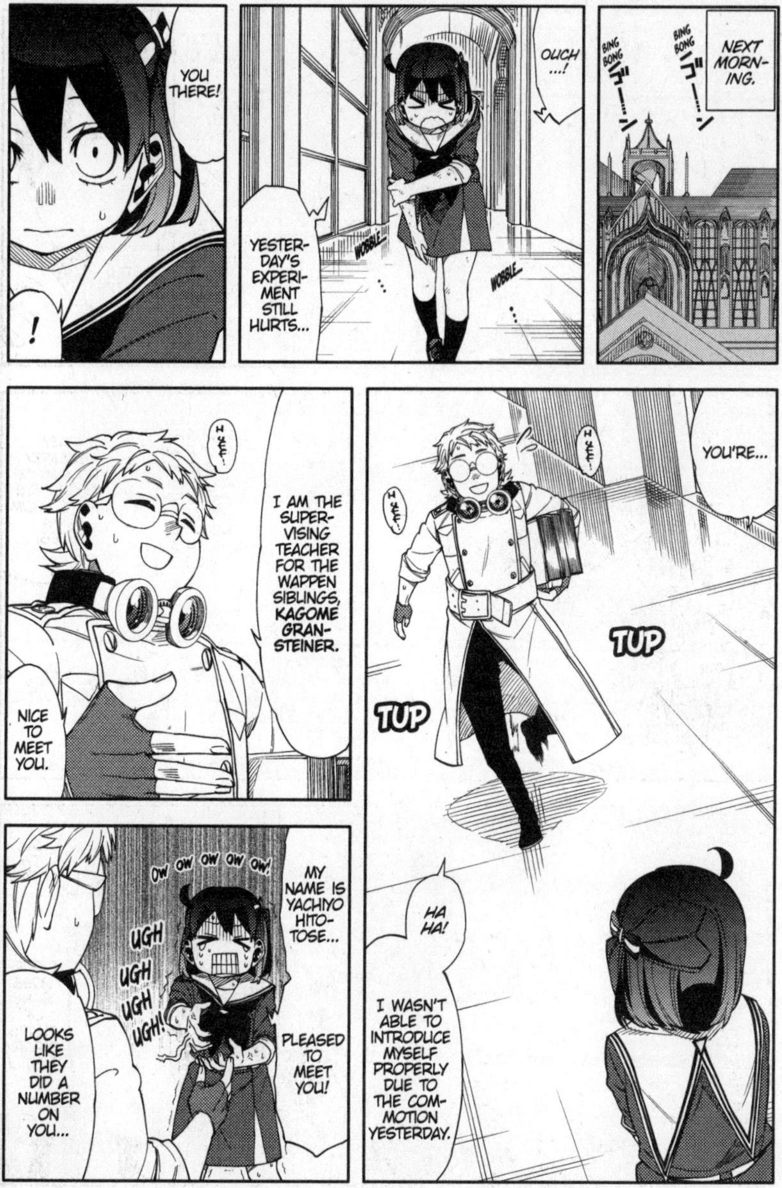
NEXT MORNING.
BING BONG
BING BONG
OUCH ...!
YESTER-DAY'S EXPERI-MENT STILL HURTS...
WOBBLE ...
WOBBLE ...
YOU THERE!
!
YOU'RE...
TUP
TUP
HA HA!
I WASN'T ABLE TO INTRODUCE MYSELF PROPERLY DUE TO THE COM-MOTION YESTERDAY.
I AM THE SUPER-VISING TEACHER FOR THE WAPPEN SIBLINGS, KAGOME GRAN-STEINER.
NICE TO MEET YOU.
MY NAME IS YACHIYO HITO-TOSE...
OW OW OW OW OW!
PLEASED TO MEET YOU!
UGH UGH UGH UGH!
LOOKS LIKE THEY DID A NUMBER ON YOU...

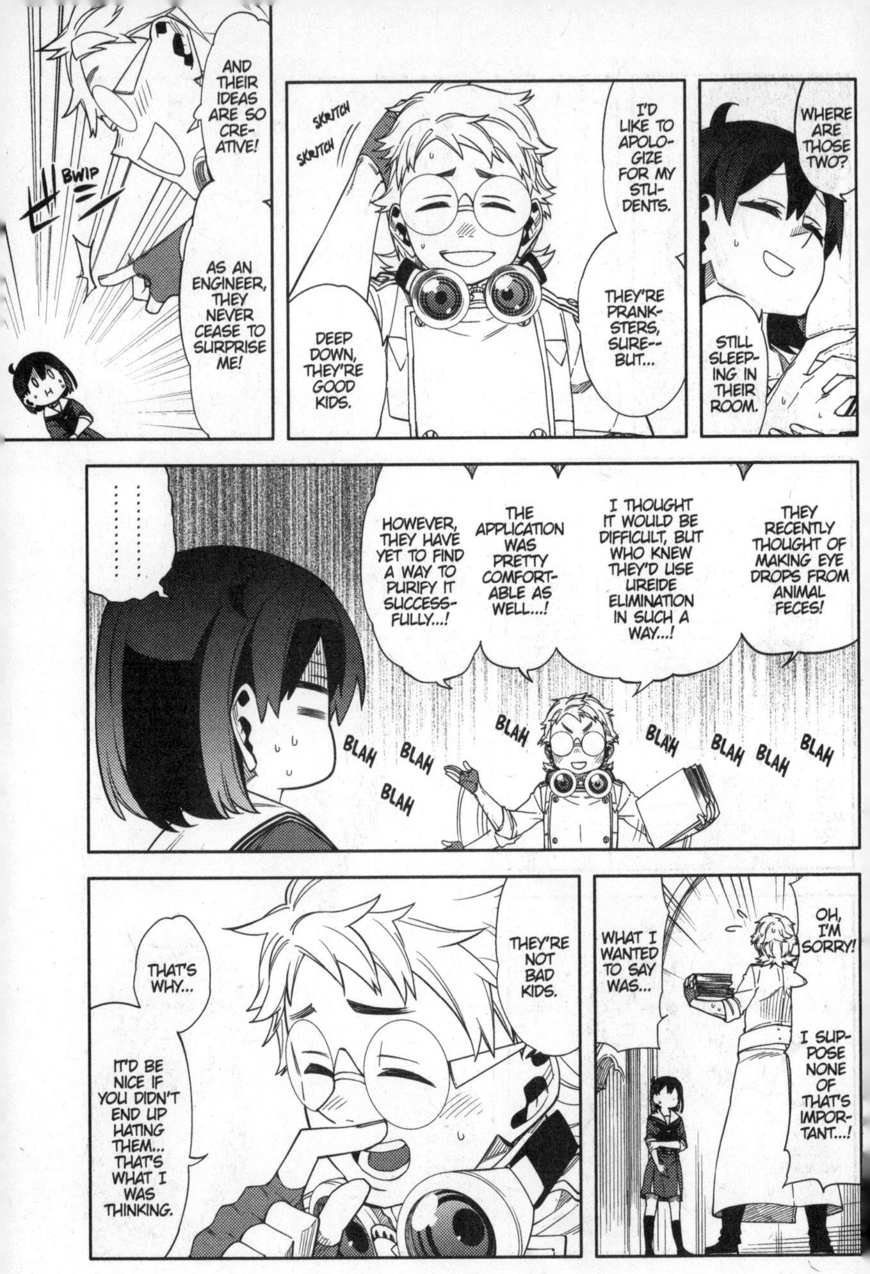
WHERE ARE THOSE TWO?
STILL SLEEPING IN THEIR ROOM.
SKRITCH
SKRITCH
I'D LIKE TO APOLOGIZE FOR MY STUDENTS.
THEY'RE PRANKSTERS, SURE--BUT...
DEEP DOWN, THEY'RE GOOD KIDS.
AND THEIR IDEAS ARE SO CREATIVE!
BWIP
AS AN ENGINEER, THEY NEVER CEASE TO SURPRISE ME!
THEY RECENTLY THOUGHT OF MAKING EYE DROPS FROM ANIMAL FECES!
I THOUGHT IT WOULD BE DIFFICULT, BUT WHO KNEW THEY'D USE UREIDE ELIMINATION IN SUCH A WAY...!
THE APPLICATION WAS PRETTY COMFORTABLE AS WELL...!
HOWEVER, THEY HAVE YET TO FIND A WAY TO PURIFY IT SUCCESSFULLY...!
BLAH BLAH BLAH BLAH
BLAH
BLAH BLAH BLAH
......
OH, I'M SORRY!
I SUPPOSE NONE OF THAT'S IMPORTANT...!
WHAT I WANTED TO SAY WAS...
THEY'RE NOT BAD KIDS.
THAT'S WHY...
IT'D BE NICE IF YOU DIDN'T END UP HATING THEM... THAT'S WHAT I WAS THINKING.

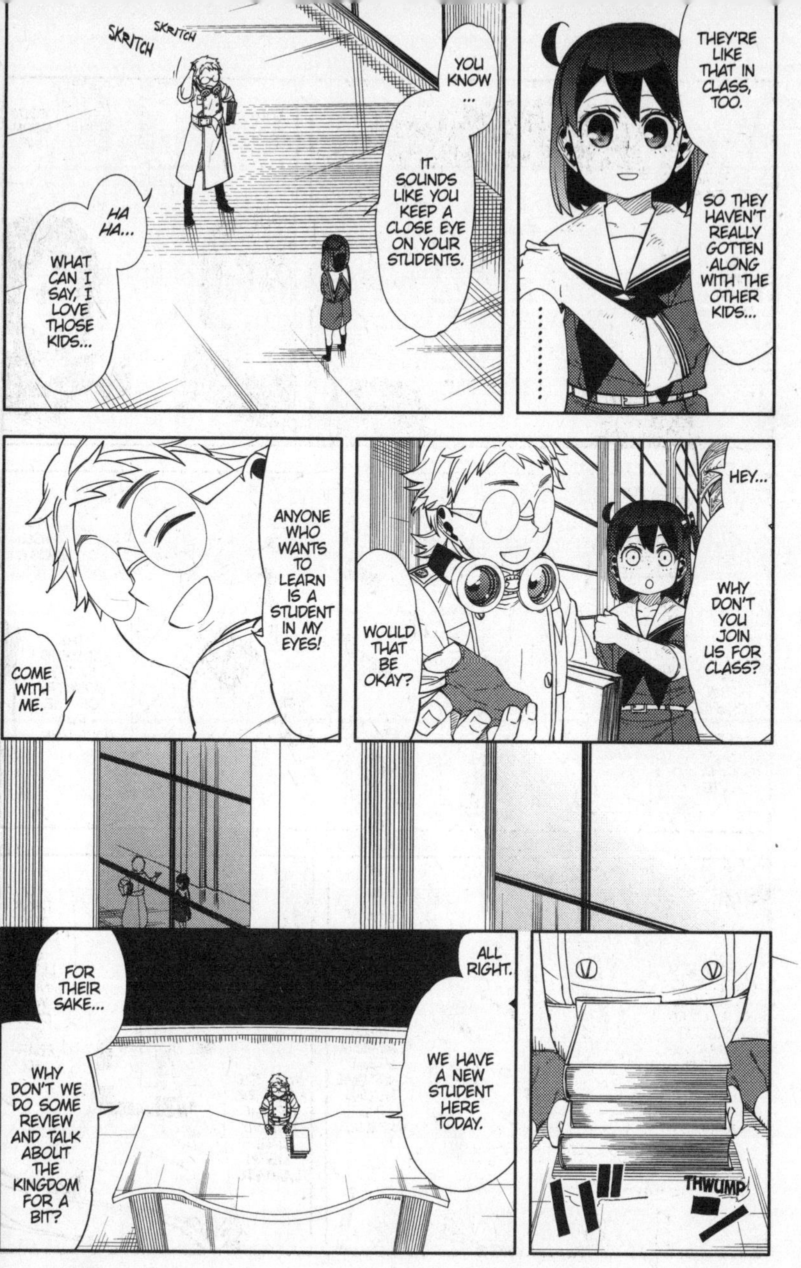
THEY'RE LIKE THAT IN CLASS, TOO.
SO THEY HAVEN'T REALLY GOTTEN ALONG WITH THE OTHER KIDS...
......
YOU KNOW...
IT SOUNDS LIKE YOU KEEP A CLOSE EYE ON YOUR STUDENTS.
SKRITCH
SKRITCH
HA HA...
WHAT CAN I SAY, I LOVE THOSE KIDS...
HEY...
WHY DON'T YOU JOIN US FOR CLASS?
WOULD THAT BE OKAY?
ANYONE WHO WANTS TO LEARN IS A STUDENT IN MY EYES!
COME WITH ME.
THWUMP
ALL RIGHT.
WE HAVE A NEW STUDENT HERE TODAY.
FOR THEIR SAKE...
WHY DON'T WE DO SOME REVIEW AND TALK ABOUT THE KINGDOM FOR A BIT?

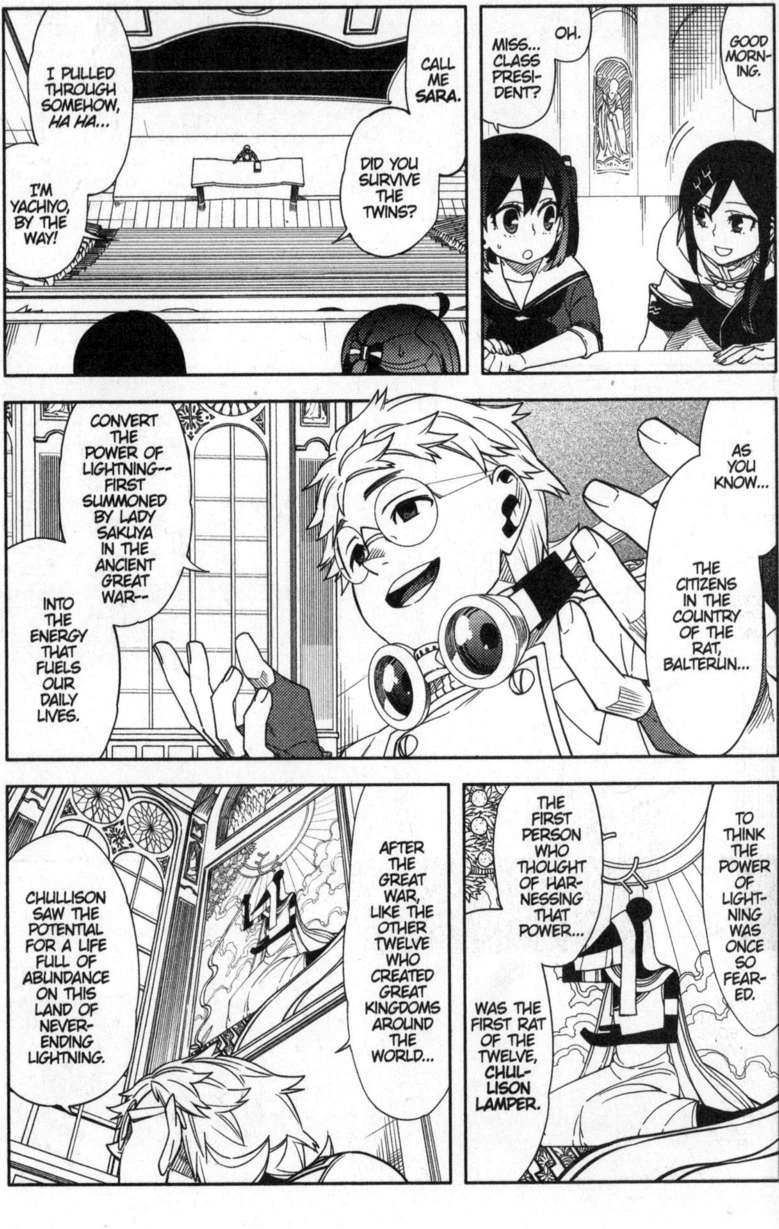
GOOD MORNING.
OH.
MISS... CLASS PRESIDENT?
CALL ME SARA.
DID YOU SURVIVE THE TWINS?
I PULLED THROUGH SOMEHOW, HA HA...
I'M YACHIYO, BY THE WAY!
AS YOU KNOW...
THE CITIZENS IN THE COUNTRY OF THE RAT, BALTERUN...
CONVERT THE POWER OF LIGHTNING--FIRST SUMMONED BY LADY SAKUYA IN THE ANCIENT GREAT WAR--
INTO THE ENERGY THAT FUELS OUR DAILY LIVES.
TO THINK THE POWER OF LIGHTNING WAS ONCE SO FEARED.
THE FIRST PERSON WHO THOUGHT OF HARNESSING THAT POWER...
WAS THE FIRST RAT OF THE TWELVE, CHULLISON LAMPER.
AFTER THE GREAT WAR, LIKE THE OTHER TWELVE WHO CREATED GREAT KINGDOMS AROUND THE WORLD...
CHULLISON SAW THE POTENTIAL FOR A LIFE FULL OF ABUNDANCE ON THIS LAND OF NEVER-ENDING LIGHTNING.

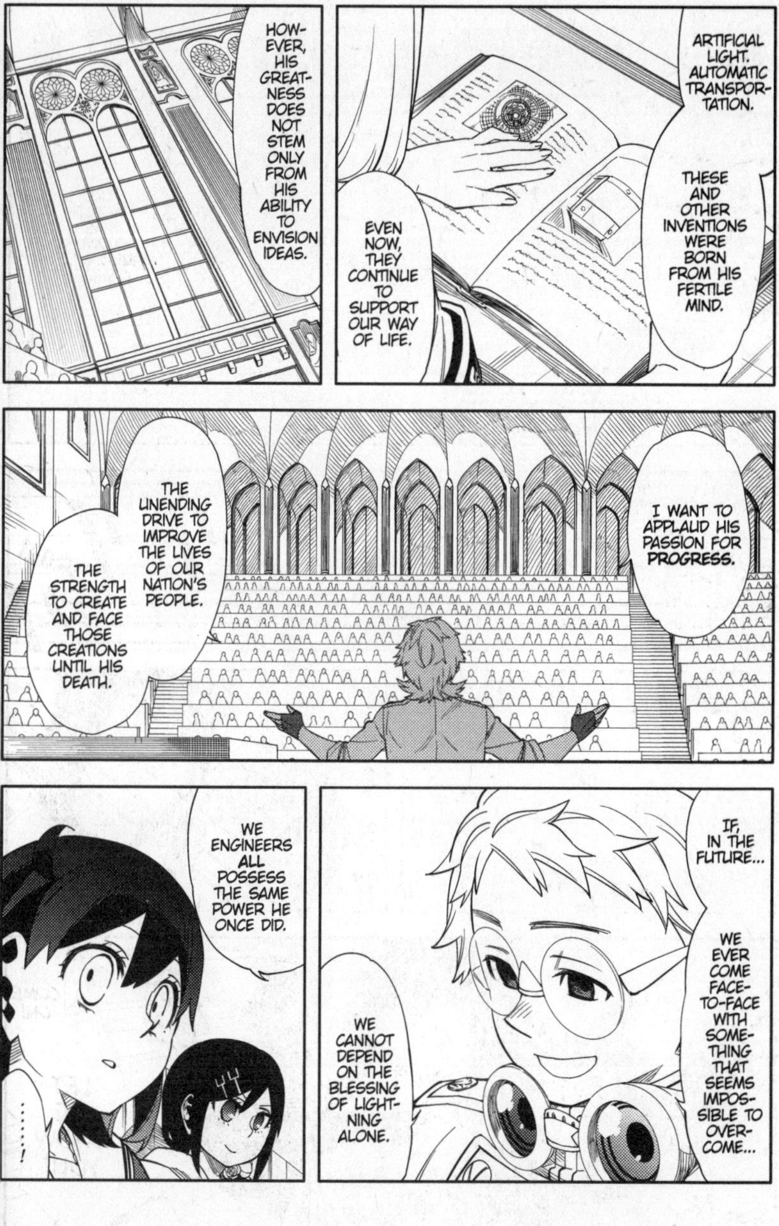
ARTIFICIAL LIGHT. AUTOMATIC TRANSPORTATION.
THESE AND OTHER INVENTIONS WERE BORN FROM HIS FERTILE MIND.
EVEN NOW, THEY CONTINUE TO SUPPORT OUR WAY OF LIFE.
HOWEVER, HIS GREATNESS DOES NOT STEM ONLY FROM HIS ABILITY TO ENVISION IDEAS.
I WANT TO APPLAUD HIS PASSION FOR **PROGRESS.**
THE UNENDING DRIVE TO IMPROVE THE LIVES OF OUR NATION'S PEOPLE.
THE STRENGTH TO CREATE AND FACE THOSE CREATIONS UNTIL HIS DEATH.
IF, IN THE FUTURE...
WE EVER COME FACE-TO-FACE WITH SOMETHING THAT SEEMS IMPOSSIBLE TO OVERCOME...
WE CANNOT DEPEND ON THE BLESSING OF LIGHTNING ALONE.
WE ENGINEERS ALL POSSESS THE SAME POWER HE ONCE DID.
......!

AS YOU CAN SEE, SINCE THAT DAY FIFTEEN YEARS AGO...

THE WORLD HAS SLOWLY BEGUN TO CHANGE.

EVEN OUR KINGDOM HAS....

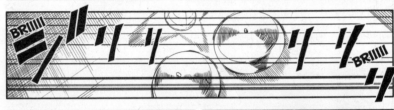

BRIIIII

BRIIIII

RIIIII

BLAU ...?!

LOOKS LIKE IT!

RIII

Westa area representative...

please head to your station.

Blau attack.

!

RIIIII

?!

RIIIII

Blau attack.

CLOP

COME ON!

LET ME SHOW YOU!

HUH ?!

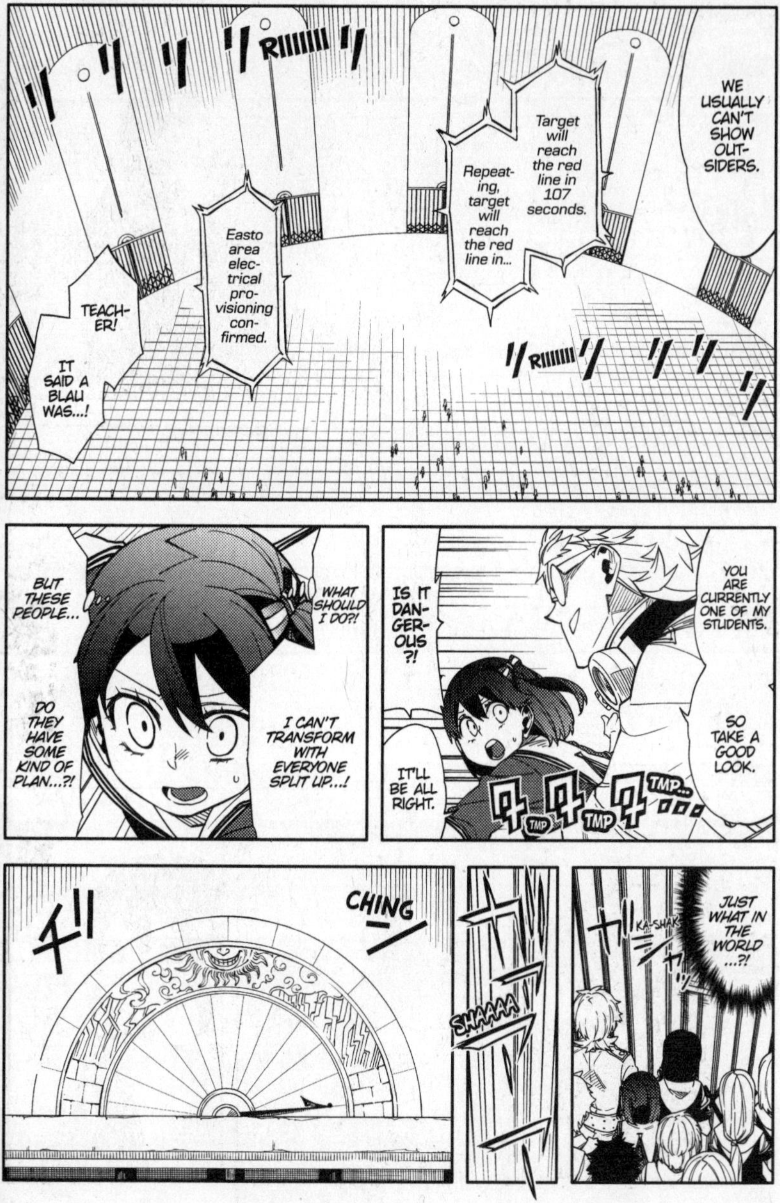
RIIIIIII
WE USUALLY CAN'T SHOW OUTSIDERS.
Target will reach the red line in 107 seconds.
Repeating, target will reach the red line in...
RIIIIIII
Easto area electrical provisioning confirmed.
TEACHER!
IT SAID A BLAU WAS...!
YOU ARE CURRENTLY ONE OF MY STUDENTS.
IS IT DANGEROUS?!
SO TAKE A GOOD LOOK.
IT'LL BE ALL RIGHT.
TMP TMP TMP...
WHAT SHOULD I DO?!
BUT THESE PEOPLE...
I CAN'T TRANSFORM WITH EVERYONE SPLIT UP...!
DO THEY HAVE SOME KIND OF PLAN...?!
JUST WHAT IN THE WORLD...?!
KA-SHAK
SHAAAA
CHING

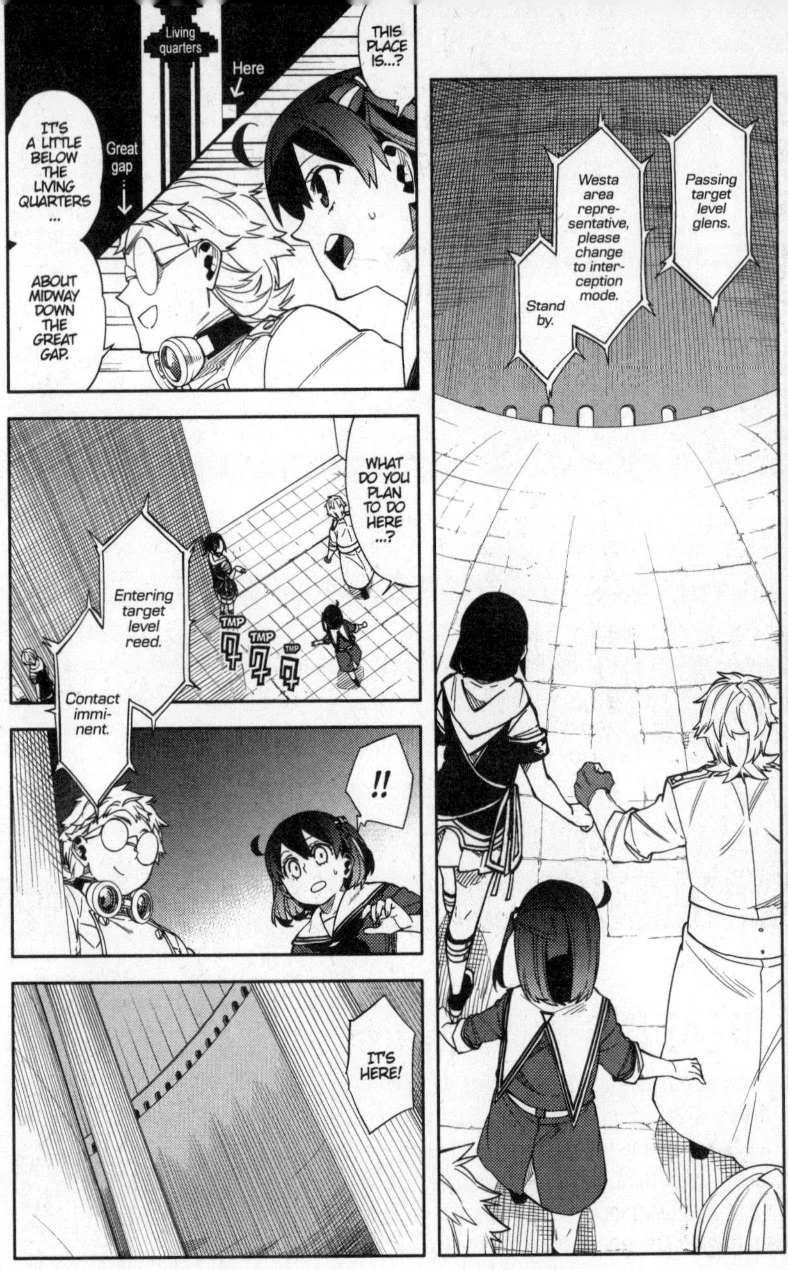
THIS PLACE IS...?
Living quarters
Here
Great gap
IT'S A LITTLE BELOW THE LIVING QUARTERS ...
ABOUT MIDWAY DOWN THE GREAT GAP.
Passing target level glens.
Westa area representative, please change to interception mode.
Stand by.
WHAT DO YOU PLAN TO DO HERE ...?
Entering target level reed.
Contact imminent.
TMP
TMP
TMP
!!
IT'S HERE!

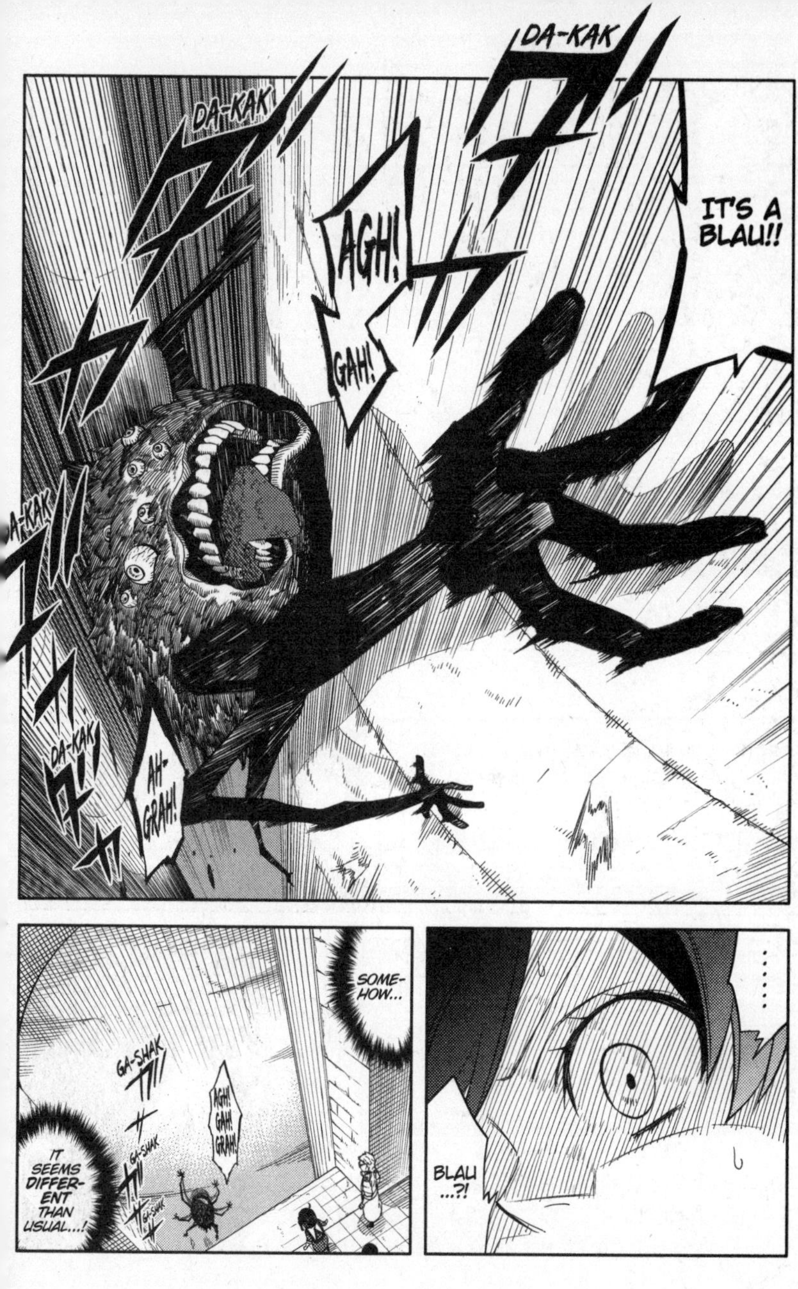
DA-KAK
IT'S A BLAU!!
AGH!
GAH!
DA-KAK
DA-KAK
AH-GRAH!
......
BLAU ...?!
SOME-HOW...
GA-SHAK
AGH! GAH! GRAH!
IT SEEMS DIFFER-ENT THAN USUAL...!
GA-SHAK
GA-SHAK

Target locked.

GASHAK

KA CHAK CHAK CHAK CHAK

All hands--

set.

Charge is... eighty percent.

WATCH CLOSELY, MISS YACHIYO.

MISS SARA ...?!

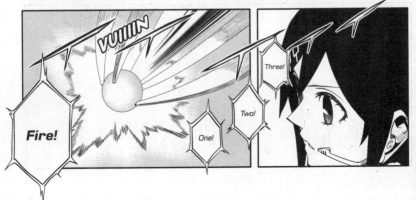

VUIIIIN

Three!

Two!

One!

Fire!

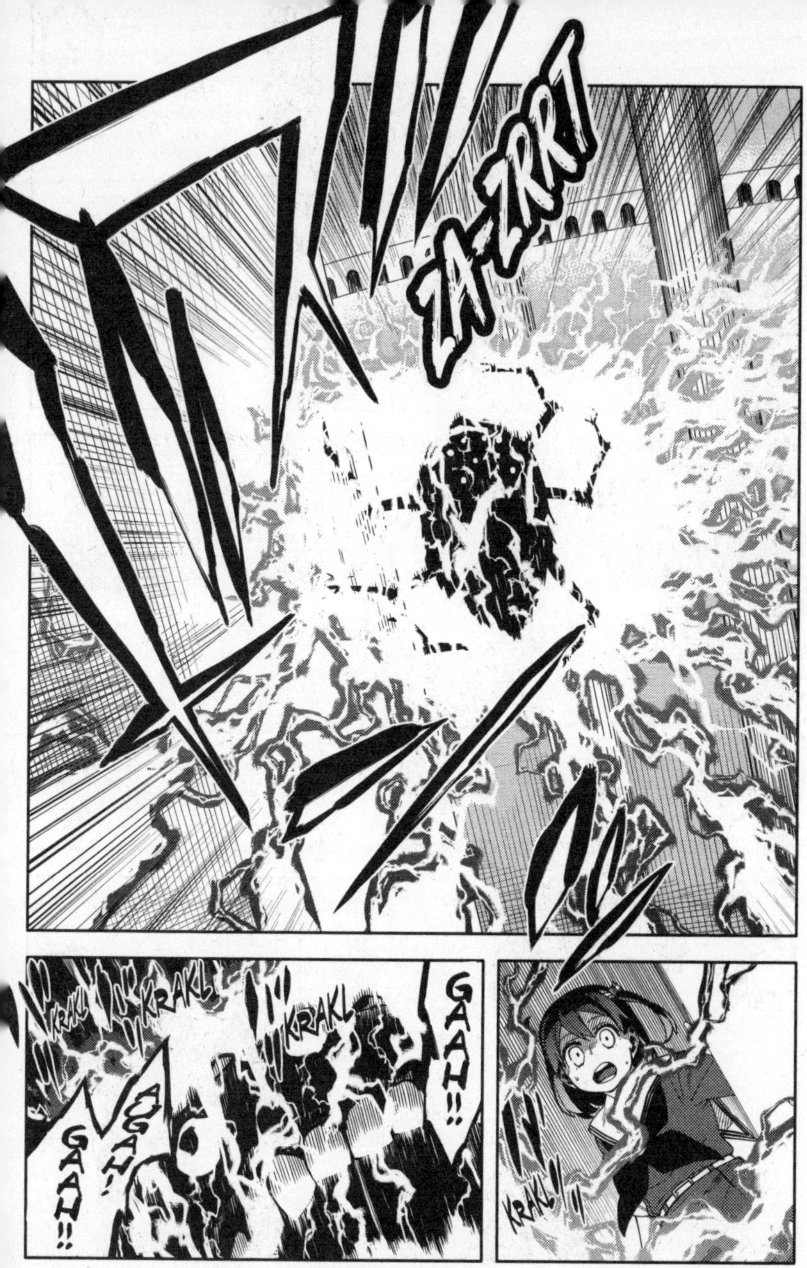
ZA-ZRRT
KRAKL
GAAH!!
KRAKL
KRAKL
KRAKL
GAAH! GAAH!!

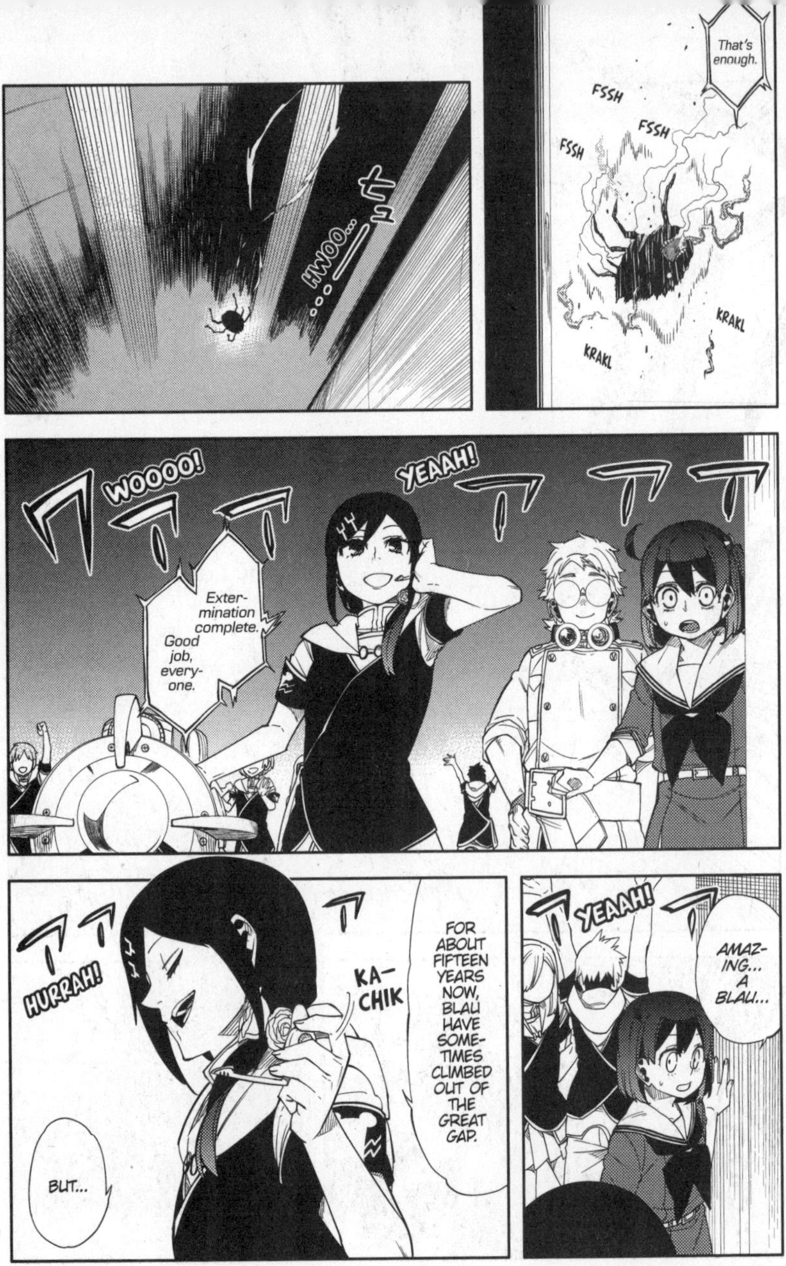
That's enough.
FSSH
FSSH
FSSH
KRAKL
KRAKL
HWOO...
WOOOO!
YEAAH!
Extermination complete. Good job, everyone.
YEAAH!
AMAZING... A BLAU...
HURRAH!
KA-CHIK
FOR ABOUT FIFTEEN YEARS NOW, BLAU HAVE SOMETIMES CLIMBED OUT OF THE GREAT GAP.
BUT...

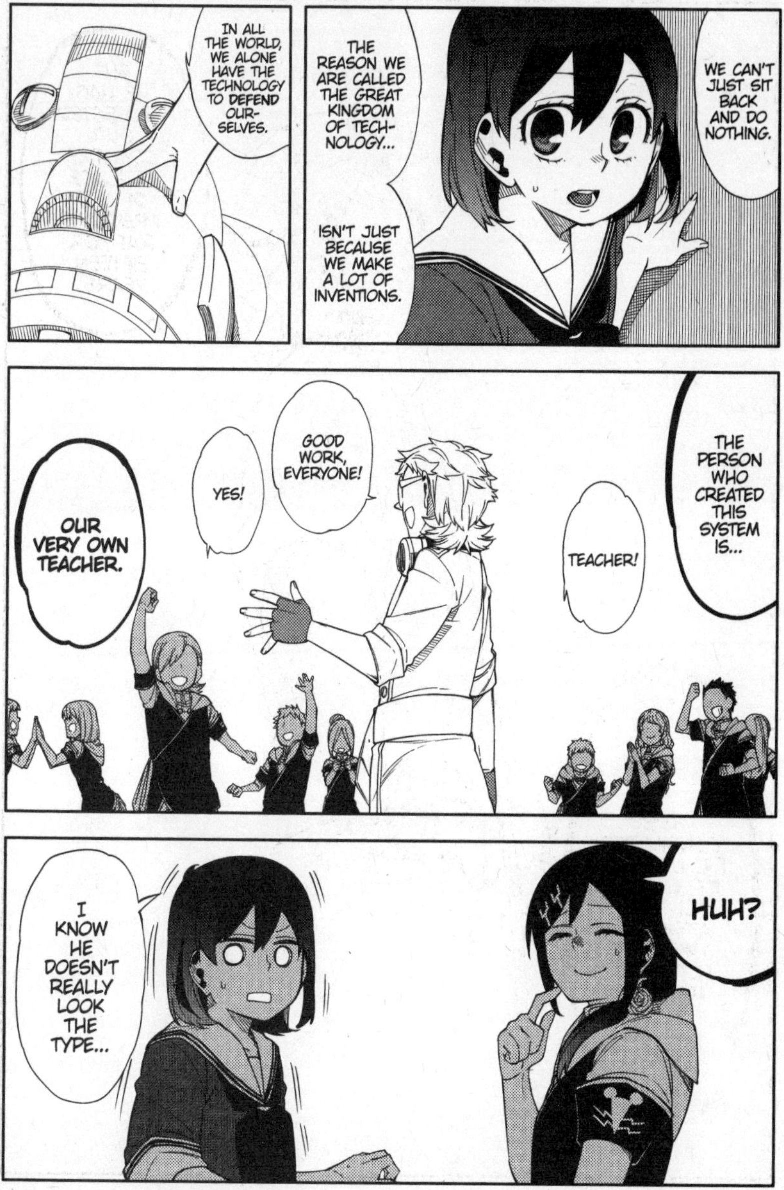
WE CAN'T JUST SIT BACK AND DO NOTHING.
THE REASON WE ARE CALLED THE GREAT KINGDOM OF TECHNOLOGY...
ISN'T JUST BECAUSE WE MAKE A LOT OF INVENTIONS.
IN ALL THE WORLD, WE ALONE HAVE THE TECHNOLOGY TO DEFEND OURSELVES.
THE PERSON WHO CREATED THIS SYSTEM IS...
TEACHER!
GOOD WORK, EVERYONE!
YES!
OUR VERY OWN TEACHER.
HUH?
I KNOW HE DOESN'T REALLY LOOK THE TYPE...

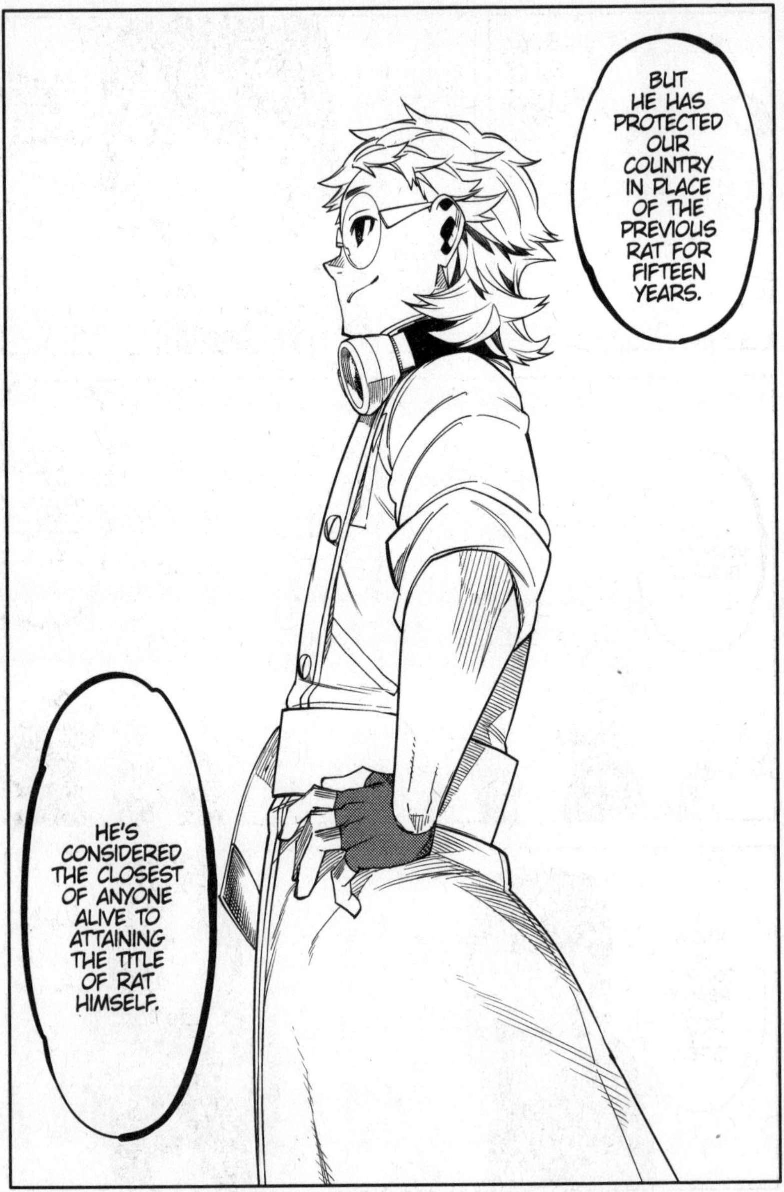
BUT HE HAS PROTECTED OUR COUNTRY IN PLACE OF THE PREVIOUS RAT FOR FIFTEEN YEARS.
HE'S CONSIDERED THE CLOSEST OF ANYONE ALIVE TO ATTAINING THE TITLE OF RAT HIMSELF.

NIRVANA

ニルヴァーナ

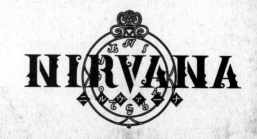

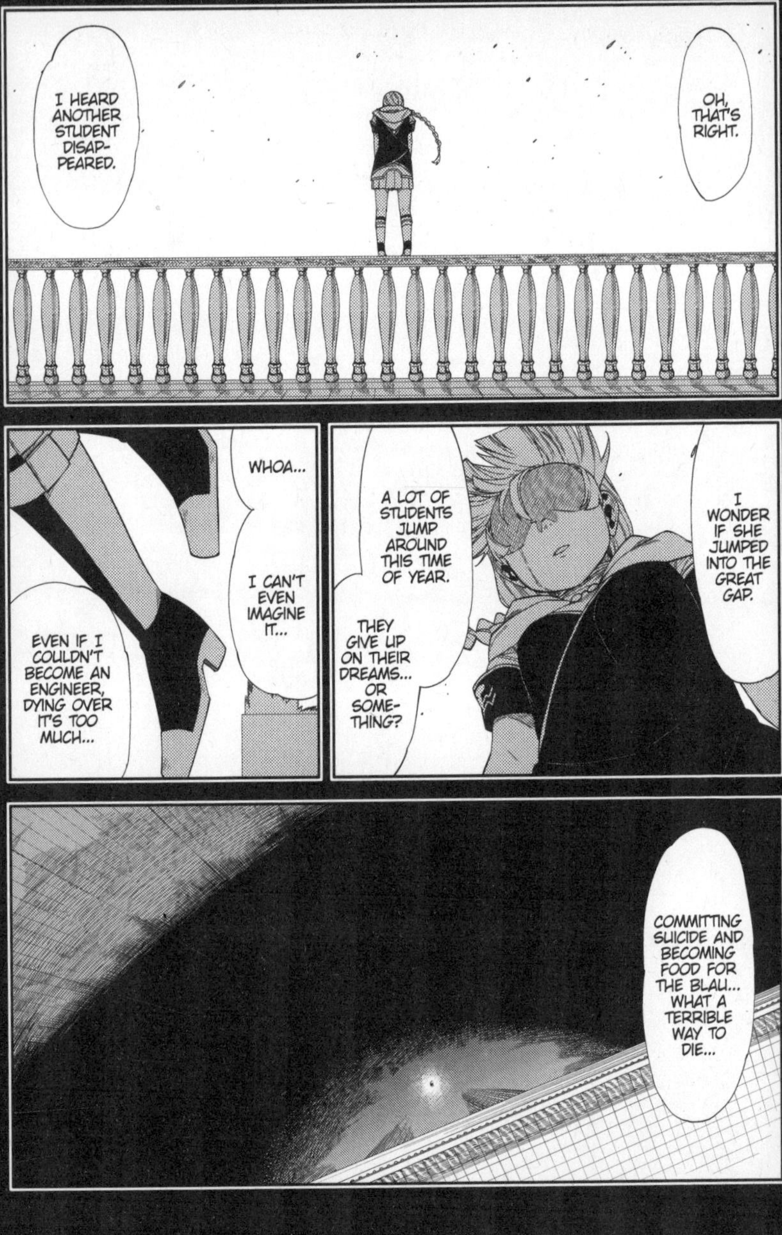
OH, THAT'S RIGHT.
I HEARD ANOTHER STUDENT DISAPPEARED.
I WONDER IF SHE JUMPED INTO THE GREAT GAP.
A LOT OF STUDENTS JUMP AROUND THIS TIME OF YEAR.
THEY GIVE UP ON THEIR DREAMS... OR SOMETHING?
WHOA...
I CAN'T EVEN IMAGINE IT...
EVEN IF I COULDN'T BECOME AN ENGINEER, DYING OVER IT'S TOO MUCH...
COMMITTING SUICIDE AND BECOMING FOOD FOR THE BLAU... WHAT A TERRIBLE WAY TO DIE...

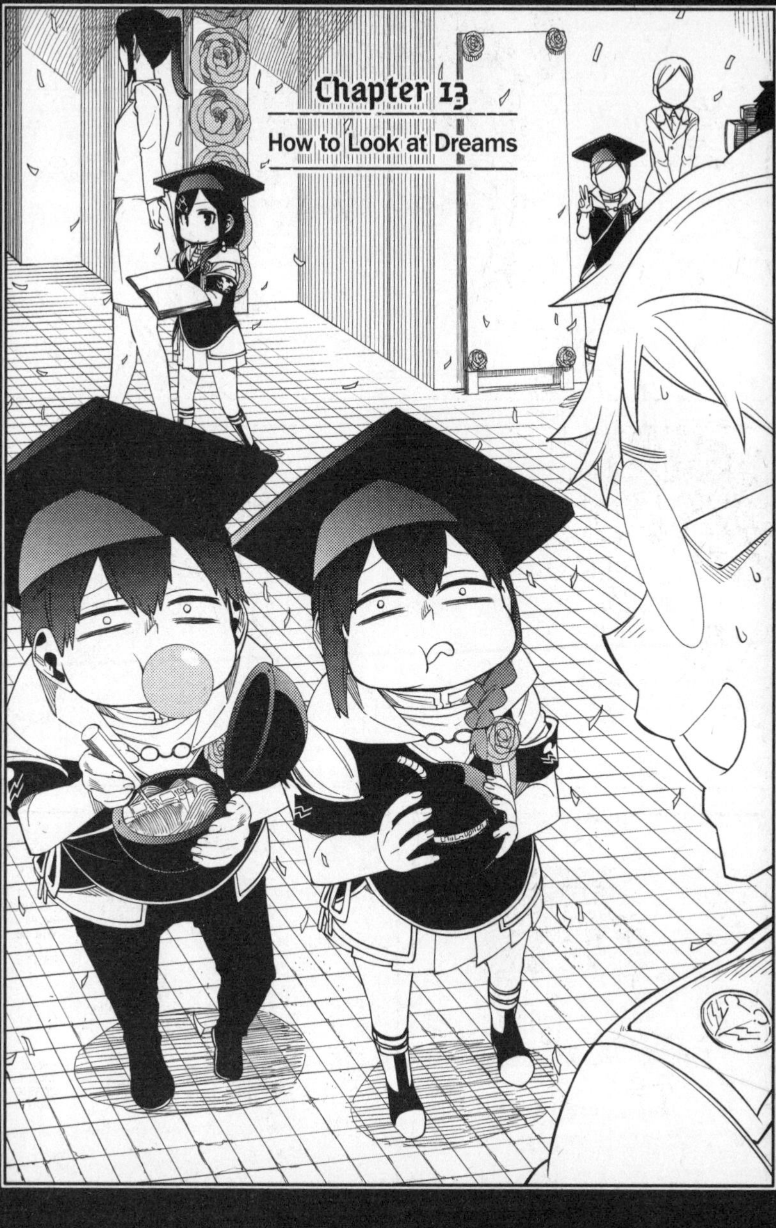
Chapter 13
How to Look at Dreams

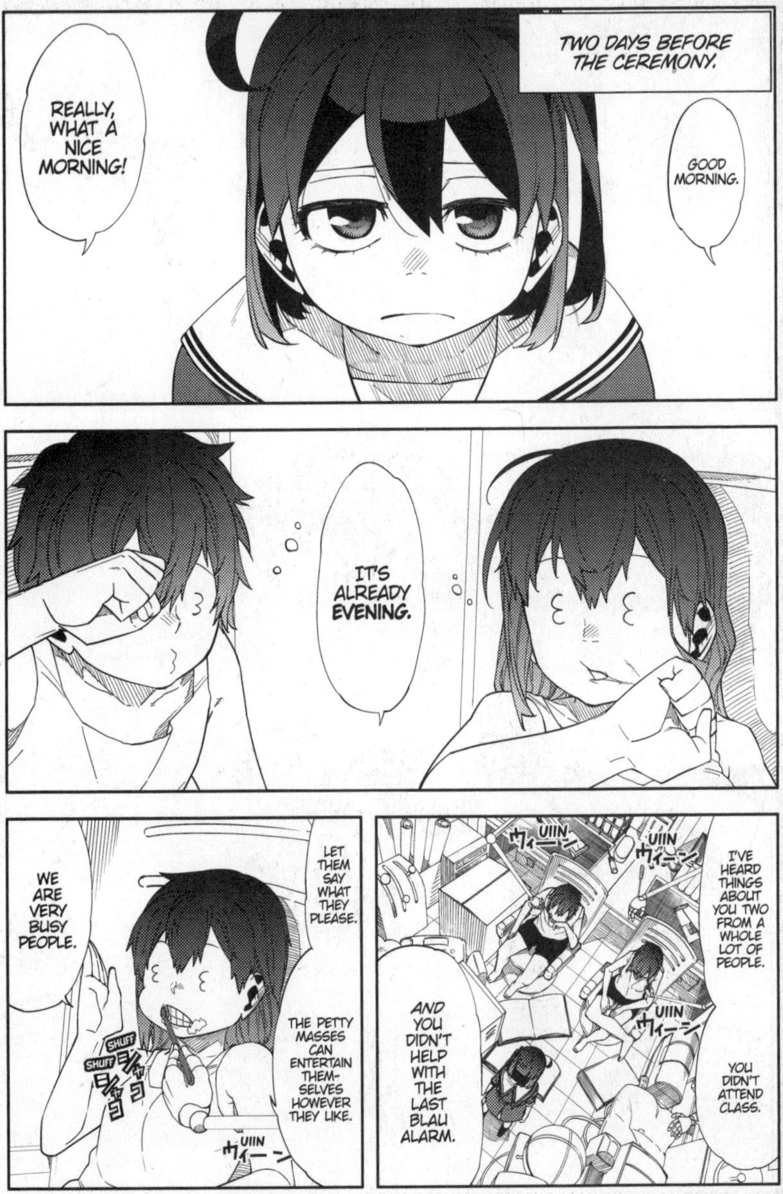
TWO DAYS BEFORE THE CEREMONY.
GOOD MORNING.
REALLY, WHAT A NICE MORNING!
IT'S ALREADY EVENING.
UIIN ウィーン
UIIN ウィーン
I'VE HEARD THINGS ABOUT YOU TWO FROM A WHOLE LOT OF PEOPLE.
UIIN ウィーン
YOU DIDN'T ATTEND CLASS.
AND YOU DIDN'T HELP WITH THE LAST BLAU ALARM.
LET THEM SAY WHAT THEY PLEASE.
THE PETTY MASSES CAN ENTERTAIN THEMSELVES HOWEVER THEY LIKE.
WE ARE VERY BUSY PEOPLE.
SHUFF
SHUFF
UIIN ウィーン

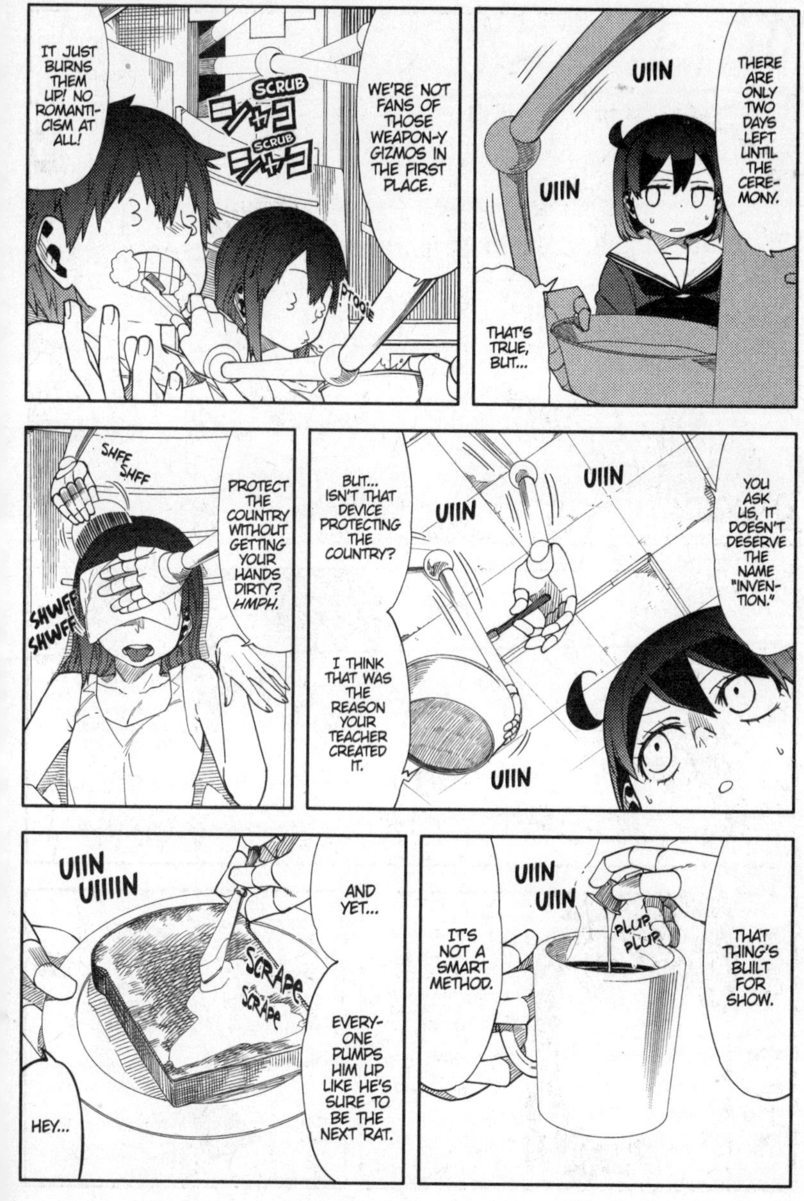
UIIN
THERE ARE ONLY TWO DAYS LEFT UNTIL THE CEREMONY.
UIIN
THAT'S TRUE, BUT...
WE'RE NOT FANS OF THOSE WEAPON-Y GIZMOS IN THE FIRST PLACE.
SCRUB
SCRUB
IT JUST BURNS THEM UP! NO ROMANTICISM AT ALL!
PTOOIE
YOU ASK US, IT DOESN'T DESERVE THE NAME "INVENTION."
UIIN
UIIN
BUT... ISN'T THAT DEVICE PROTECTING THE COUNTRY?
I THINK THAT WAS THE REASON YOUR TEACHER CREATED IT.
UIIN
PROTECT THE COUNTRY WITHOUT GETTING YOUR HANDS DIRTY? *HMPH.*
SHFF SHFF
SHWFF SHWFF
UIIN
UIIN
PLUP PLUP
THAT THING'S BUILT FOR SHOW.
IT'S NOT A SMART METHOD.
AND YET...
UIIN
UIIIIN
SCRAPE SCRAPE
EVERYONE PUMPS HIM UP LIKE HE'S SURE TO BE THE NEXT RAT.
HEY...

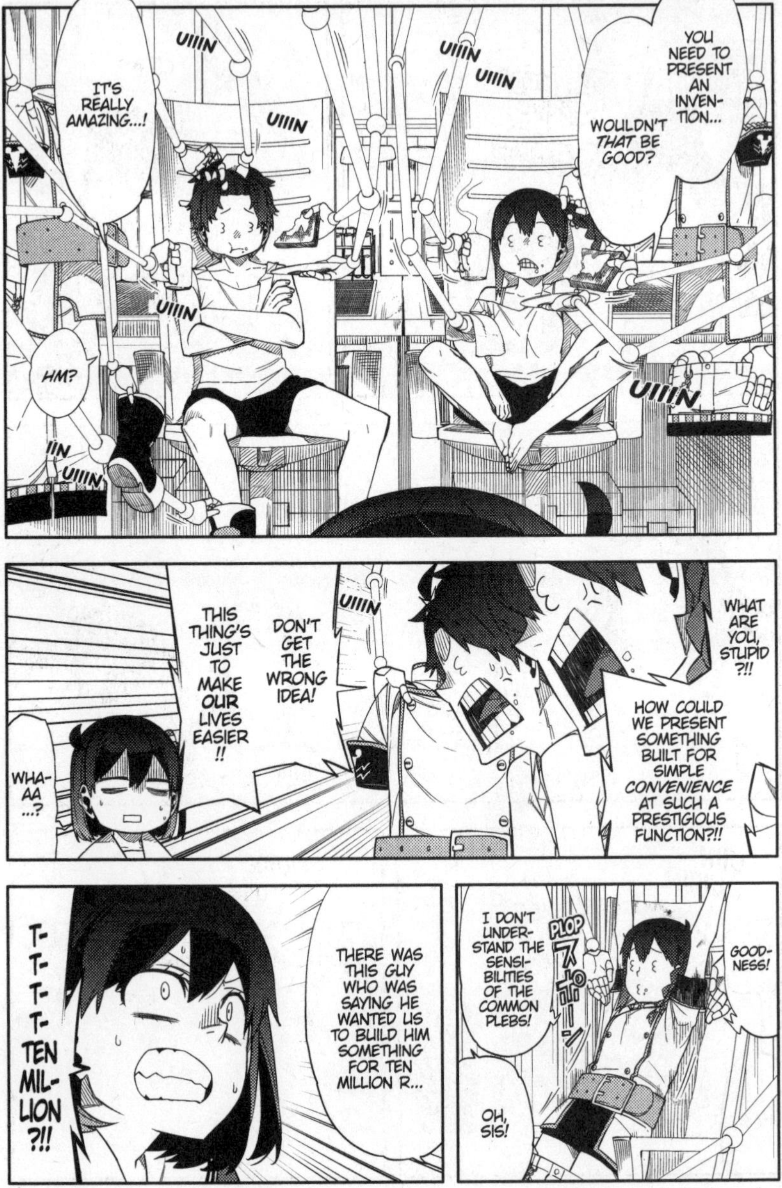
UIIIN
UIIIN
YOU NEED TO PRESENT AN INVENTION...
WOULDN'T THAT BE GOOD?
UIIIN
IT'S REALLY AMAZING...!
UIIIN
UIIIN
UIIIN
HM?
IIN
UIIIN
WHAT ARE YOU, STUPID?!!
HOW COULD WE PRESENT SOMETHING BUILT FOR SIMPLE CONVENIENCE AT SUCH A PRESTIGIOUS FUNCTION?!!
UIIIN
DON'T GET THE WRONG IDEA!
THIS THING'S JUST TO MAKE OUR LIVES EASIER!!
WHAA-AA...?
GOOD-NESS!
PLOP
I DON'T UNDER-STAND THE SENSI-BILITIES OF THE COMMON PLEBS!
OH, SIS!
THERE WAS THIS GUY WHO WAS SAYING HE WANTED US TO BUILD HIM SOMETHING FOR TEN MILLION R...
T-T-T-T-TEN MIL-LION?!!

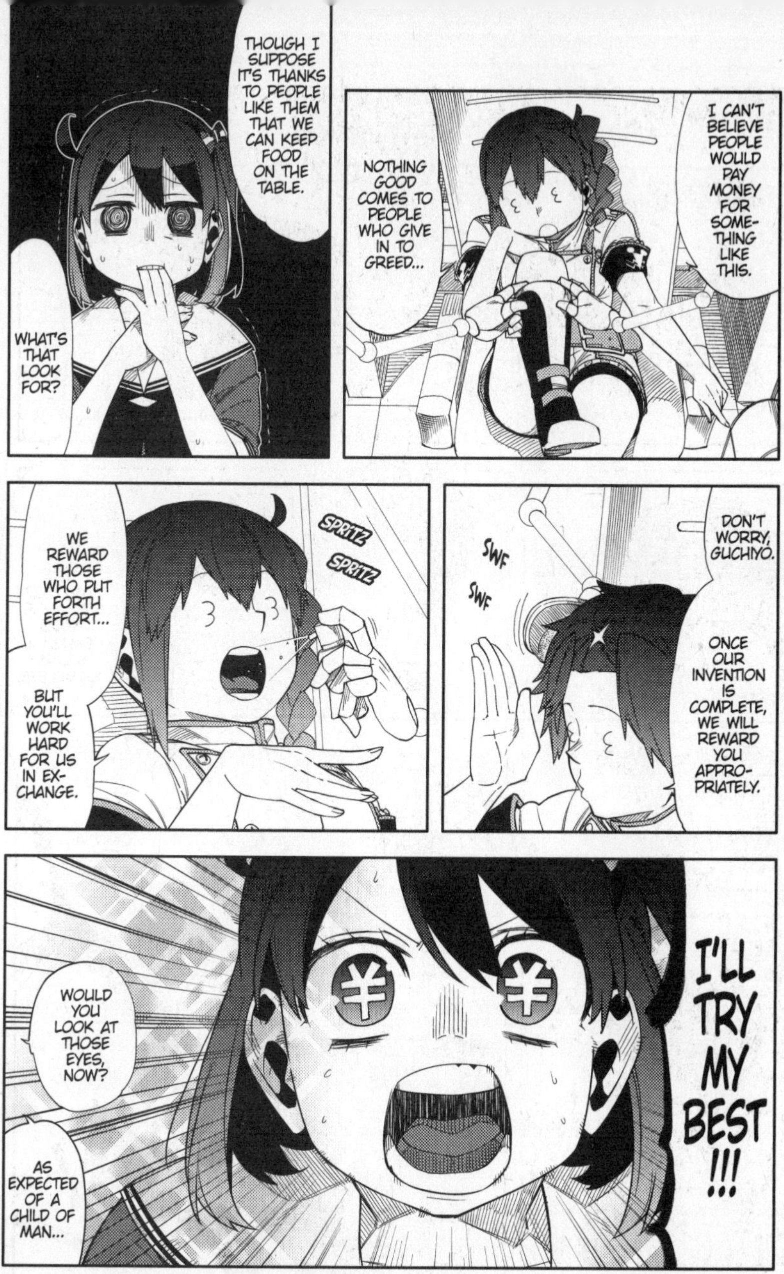
I CAN'T BELIEVE PEOPLE WOULD PAY MONEY FOR SOMETHING LIKE THIS.
NOTHING GOOD COMES TO PEOPLE WHO GIVE IN TO GREED...
THOUGH I SUPPOSE IT'S THANKS TO PEOPLE LIKE THEM THAT WE CAN KEEP FOOD ON THE TABLE.
WHAT'S THAT LOOK FOR?
DON'T WORRY, GUCHIYO.
SWF
SWF
ONCE OUR INVENTION IS COMPLETE, WE WILL REWARD YOU APPROPRIATELY.
SPRITZ
SPRITZ
WE REWARD THOSE WHO PUT FORTH EFFORT...
BUT YOU'LL WORK HARD FOR US IN EXCHANGE.
I'LL TRY MY BEST!!!
WOULD YOU LOOK AT THOSE EYES, NOW?
AS EXPECTED OF A CHILD OF MAN...

Eyes: Yen Symbols

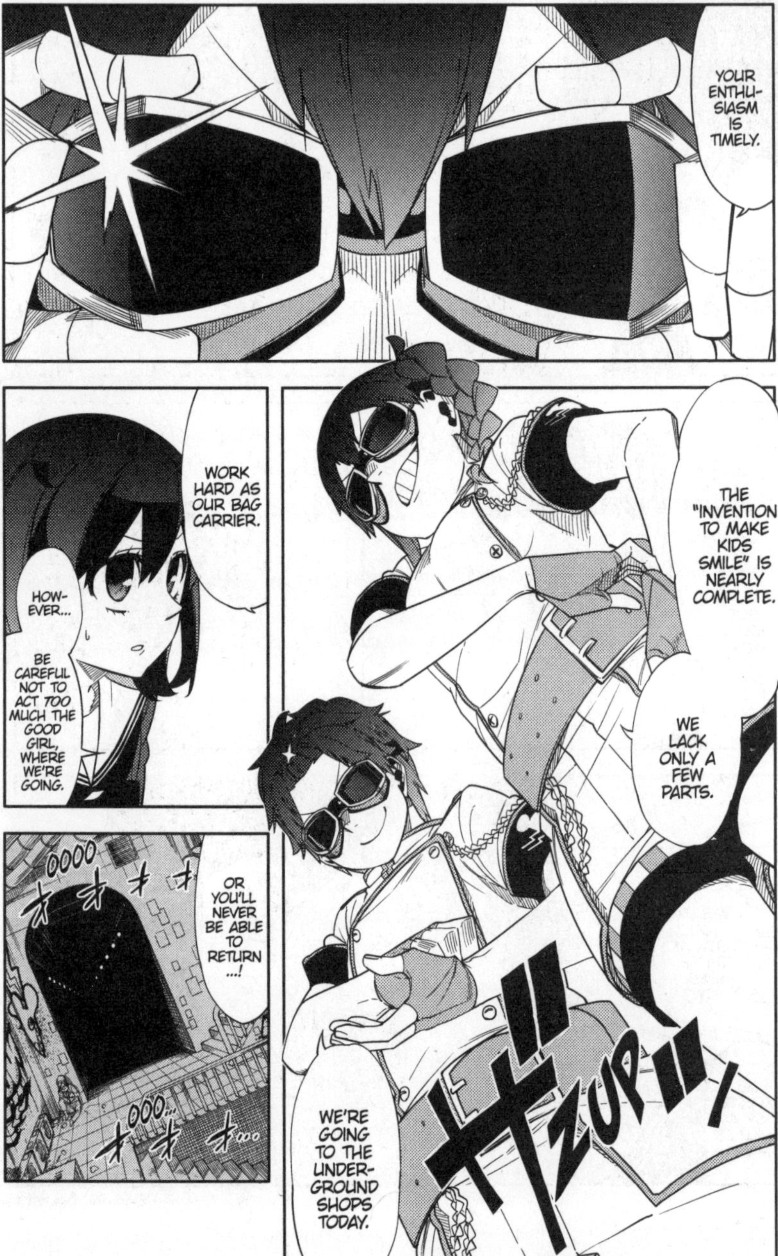
YOUR ENTHUSIASM IS TIMELY.
THE "INVENTION TO MAKE KIDS SMILE" IS NEARLY COMPLETE.
WE LACK ONLY A FEW PARTS.
WE'RE GOING TO THE UNDERGROUND SHOPS TODAY.
ZUP!!
WORK HARD AS OUR BAG CARRIER.
HOWEVER...
BE CAREFUL NOT TO ACT *TOO* MUCH THE GOOD GIRL, WHERE WE'RE GOING.
OR YOU'LL NEVER BE ABLE TO RETURN...!
OOOO
OOO...

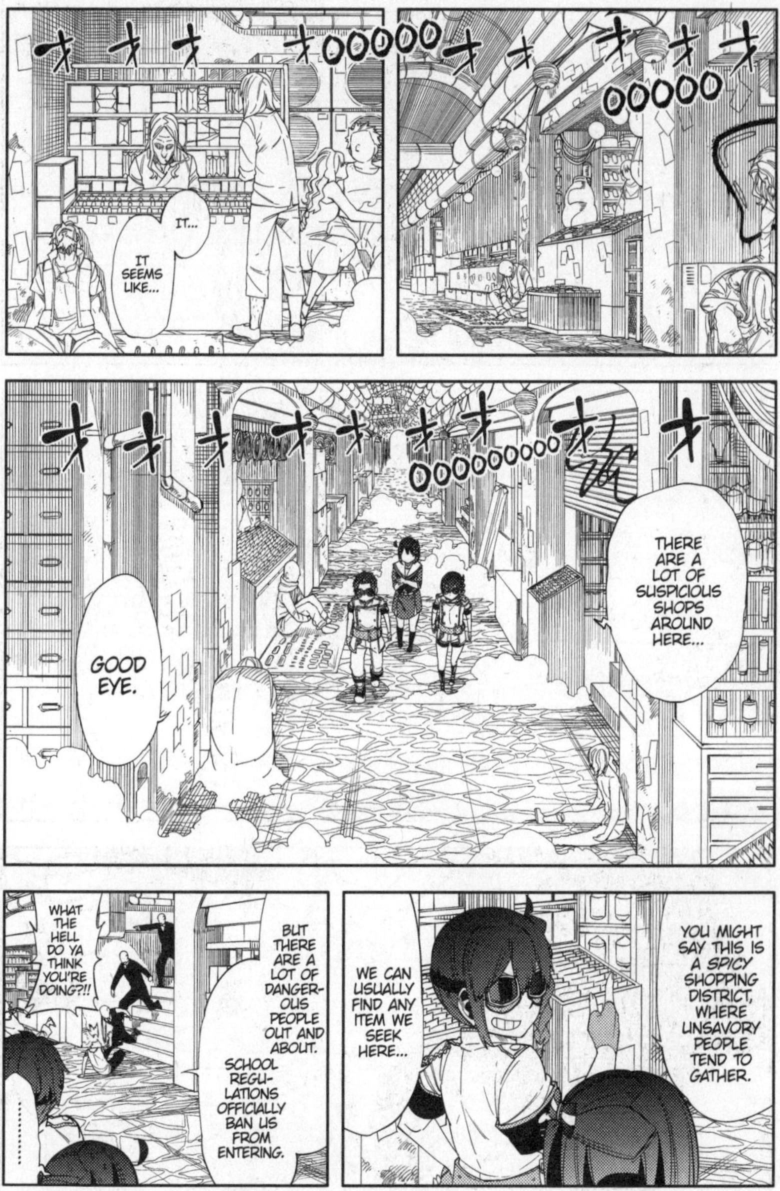
OOOOO
OOOOO
IT...
IT SEEMS LIKE...
OOOOOOOOO
THERE ARE A LOT OF SUSPICIOUS SHOPS AROUND HERE...
GOOD EYE.
YOU MIGHT SAY THIS IS A *SPICY* SHOPPING DISTRICT, WHERE UNSAVORY PEOPLE TEND TO GATHER.
WE CAN USUALLY FIND ANY ITEM WE SEEK HERE...
BUT THERE ARE A LOT OF DANGER-OUS PEOPLE OUT AND ABOUT.
SCHOOL REGU-LATIONS OFFICIALLY BAN US FROM ENTERING.
WHAT THE HELL DO YA THINK YOU'RE DOING?!!
......

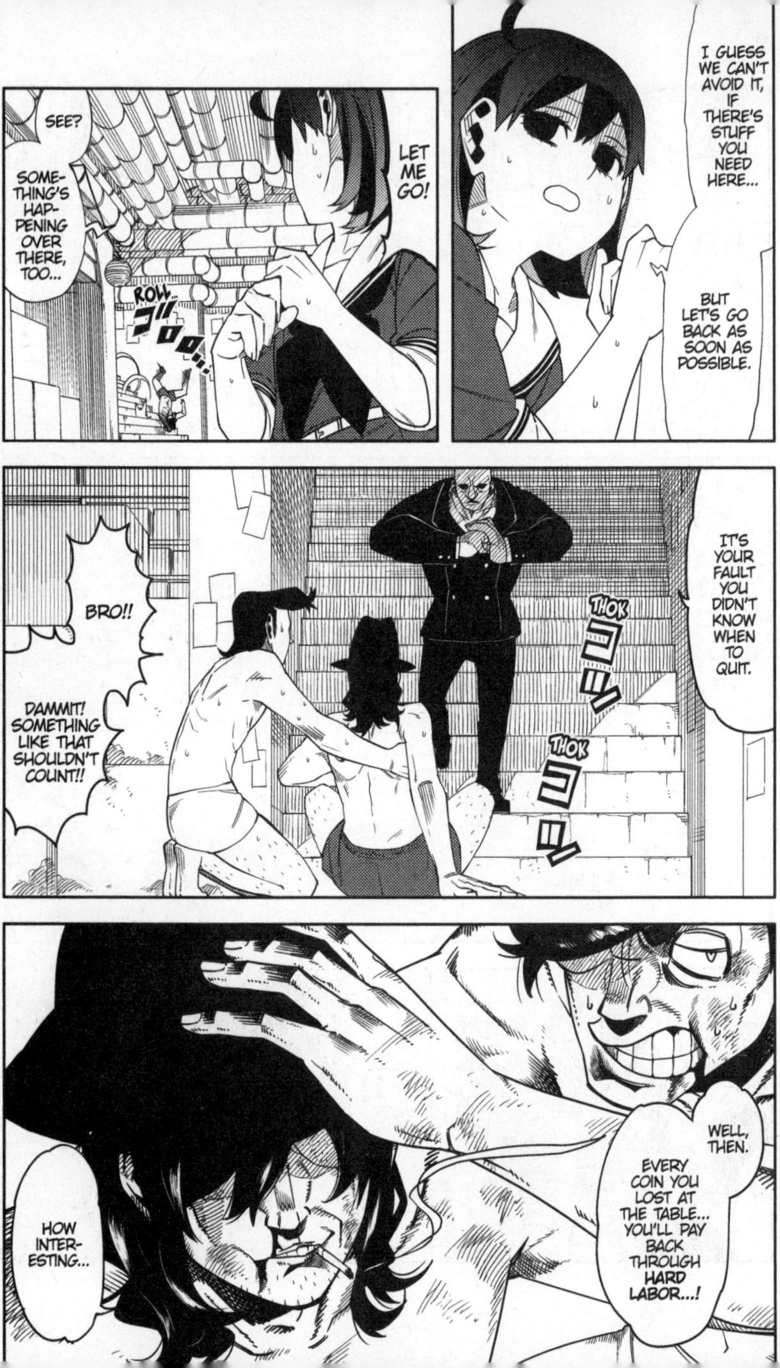
I GUESS WE CAN'T AVOID IT, IF THERE'S STUFF YOU NEED HERE...
BUT LET'S GO BACK AS SOON AS POSSIBLE.
LET ME GO!
SEE?
SOMETHING'S HAPPENING OVER THERE, TOO...
ROLL...
IT'S YOUR FAULT YOU DIDN'T KNOW WHEN TO QUIT.
THOK
THOK
BRO!!
DAMMIT! SOMETHING LIKE THAT SHOULDN'T COUNT!!
WELL, THEN.
EVERY COIN YOU LOST AT THE TABLE... YOU'LL PAY BACK THROUGH HARD LABOR...!
HOW INTERESTING...

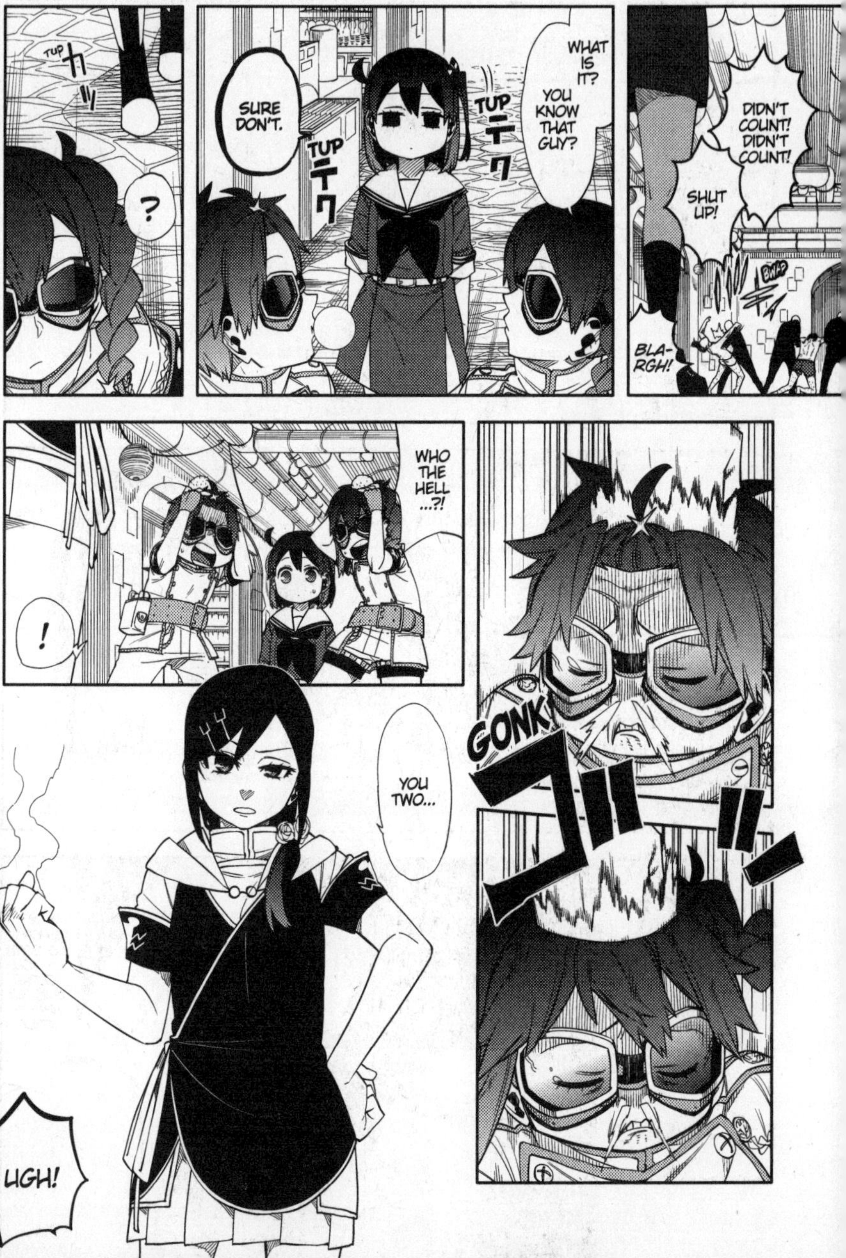
DIDN'T COUNT! DIDN'T COUNT!
SHUT UP!
BWAP
BLA-RGH!
WHAT IS IT? YOU KNOW THAT GUY?
TUP テク
SURE DON'T.
TUP テク
TUP カツ
?
GONK ゴッ
WHO THE HELL ...?!
!
YOU TWO...
UGH!

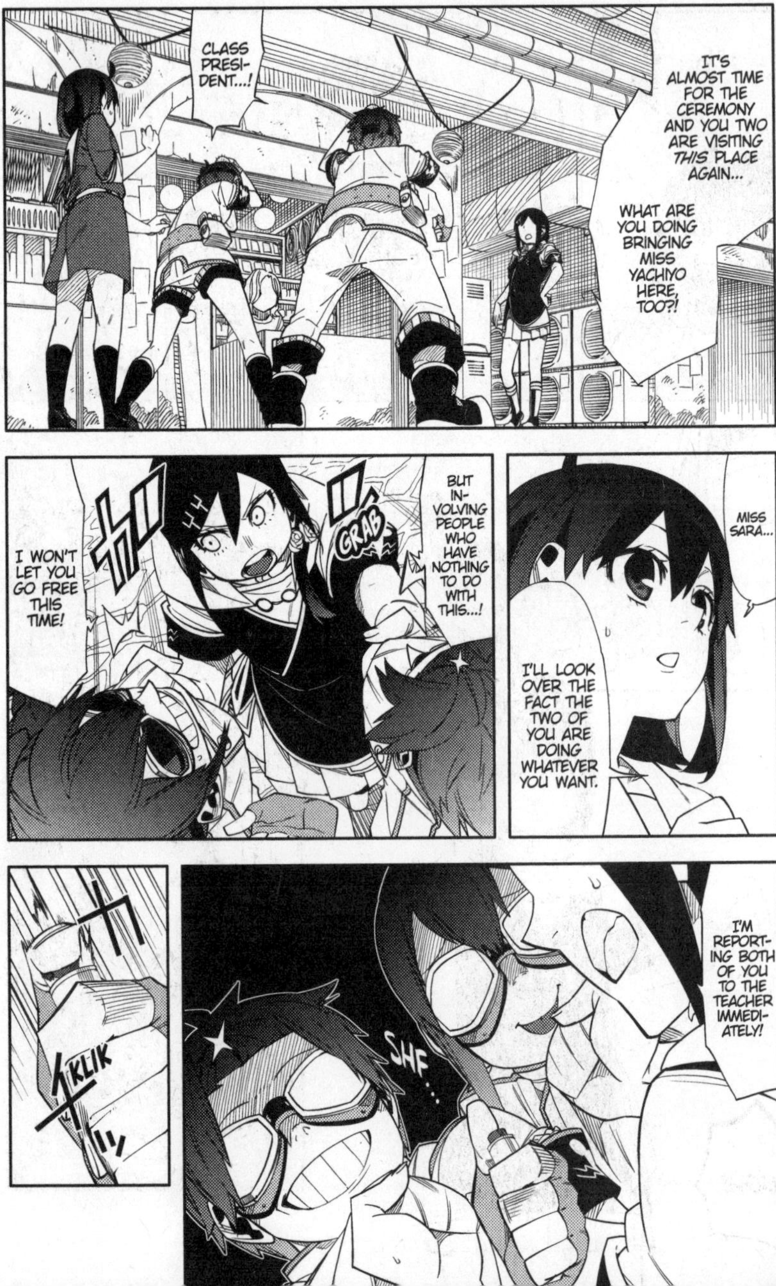
CLASS PRESI-DENT...!
IT'S ALMOST TIME FOR THE CEREMONY AND YOU TWO ARE VISITING *THIS* PLACE AGAIN...
WHAT ARE YOU DOING BRINGING MISS YACHIYO HERE, TOO?!
MISS SARA...
I'LL LOOK OVER THE FACT THE TWO OF YOU ARE DOING WHATEVER YOU WANT.
BUT IN-VOLVING PEOPLE WHO HAVE NOTHING TO DO WITH THIS...!
GRAB
I WON'T LET YOU GO FREE THIS TIME!
I'M REPORT-ING BOTH OF YOU TO THE TEACHER IMMEDI-ATELY!
SHF...
KLIK

HA HA HA! YOU UNDER- ESTIMATED US, CLASS PRESI- DENT!

KOFF! KOFF!

WHAT IS THIS?! IT STINKS!

!!

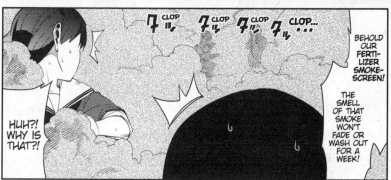

CLOP CLOP CLOP CLOP...

BEHOLD OUR FERTI- LIZER SMOKE- SCREEN!

THE SMELL OF THAT SMOKE WON'T FADE OR WASH OUT FOR A WEEK!

HUH?! WHY IS THAT?!

KERTHUD

BLUH!

SKSH

DASH

HEY, YOU TWO...!

WAIT --!

TMP

ARE YOU OKAY?! MISS YACHIYO...?!

IT HURTS... IT STINKS...

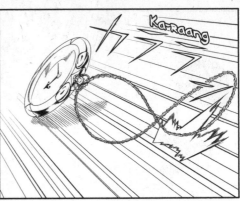
Ka-raang

WHAT...

CHING...

IS THIS...?

They sold me out...

THOSE TWO...!

MISS YACHIYO...

YES?

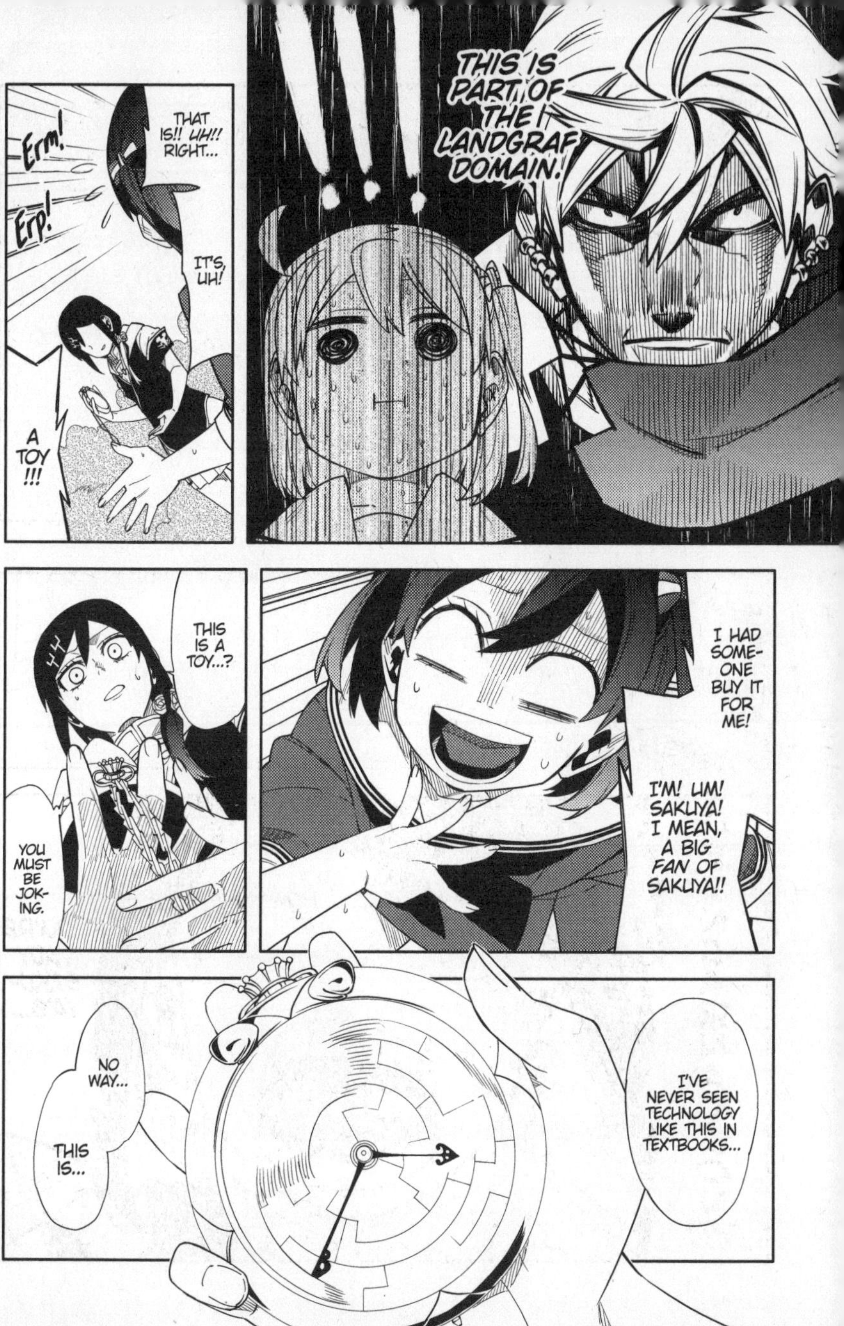
THIS IS PART OF THE LANDGRAF DOMAIN!
THAT IS!! UH!! RIGHT...
Erm!
Erp!
IT'S, UH!
A TOY!!!
I HAD SOMEONE BUY IT FOR ME!
I'M! UM! SAKUYA! I MEAN, A BIG FAN OF SAKUYA!!
THIS IS A TOY...?
YOU MUST BE JOKING.
I'VE NEVER SEEN TECHNOLOGY LIKE THIS IN TEXTBOOKS...
NO WAY...
THIS IS...

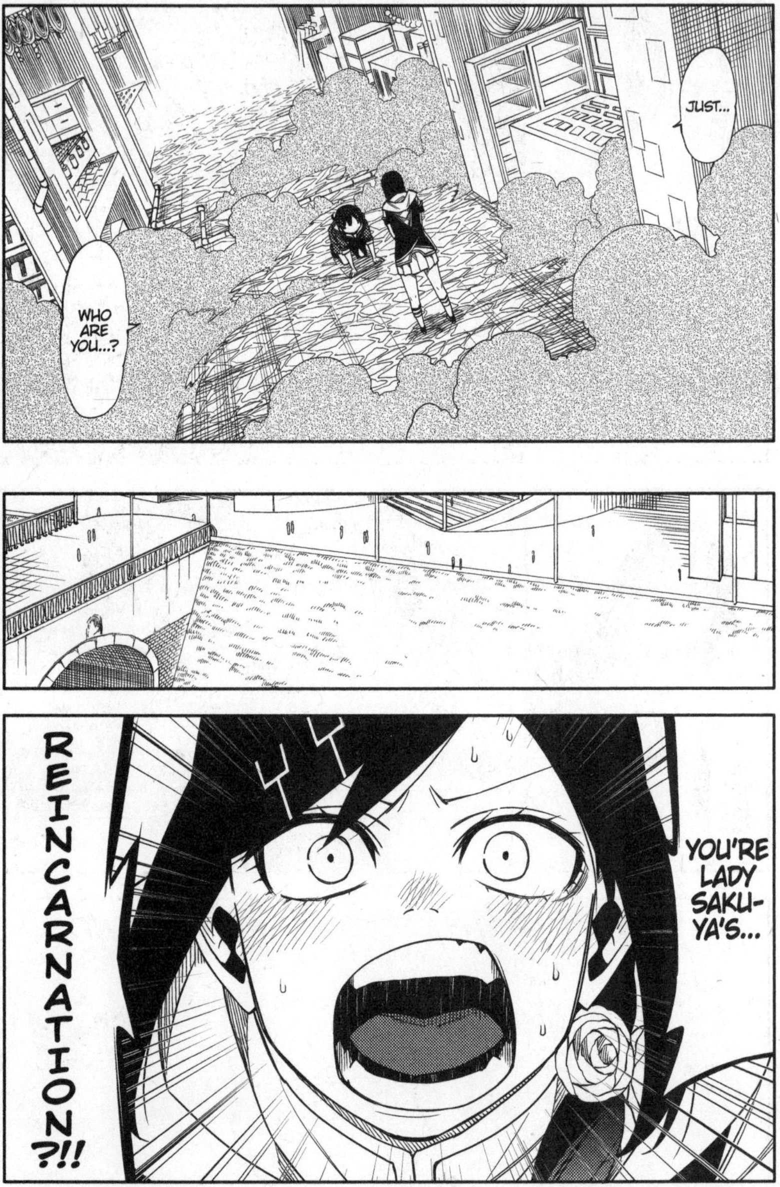
JUST...
WHO ARE YOU...?
YOU'RE LADY SAKU-YA'S...
REINCARNATION?!!

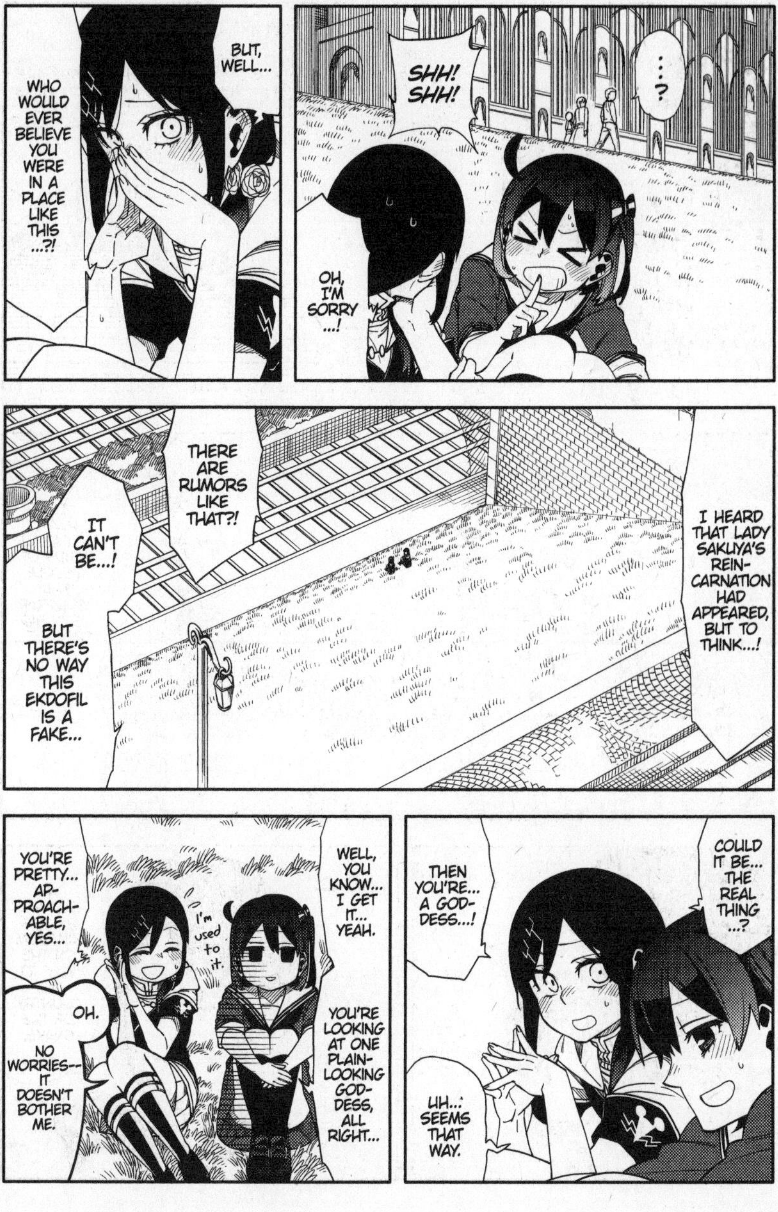
SHH! SHH!
...?
OH, I'M SORRY ...!
BUT, WELL...
WHO WOULD EVER BELIEVE YOU WERE IN A PLACE LIKE THIS ...?!
I HEARD THAT LADY SAKUYA'S REINCARNATION HAD APPEARED, BUT TO THINK...!
THERE ARE RUMORS LIKE THAT?!
IT CAN'T BE...!
BUT THERE'S NO WAY THIS EKDOFIL IS A FAKE...
COULD IT BE... THE REAL THING ...?
THEN YOU'RE... A GODDESS...!
UH... SEEMS THAT WAY.
WELL, YOU KNOW... I GET IT... YEAH.
YOU'RE PRETTY... APPROACHABLE, YES...
I'm used to it.
YOU'RE LOOKING AT ONE PLAIN-LOOKING GODDESS, ALL RIGHT...
OH.
NO WORRIES--IT DOESN'T BOTHER ME.

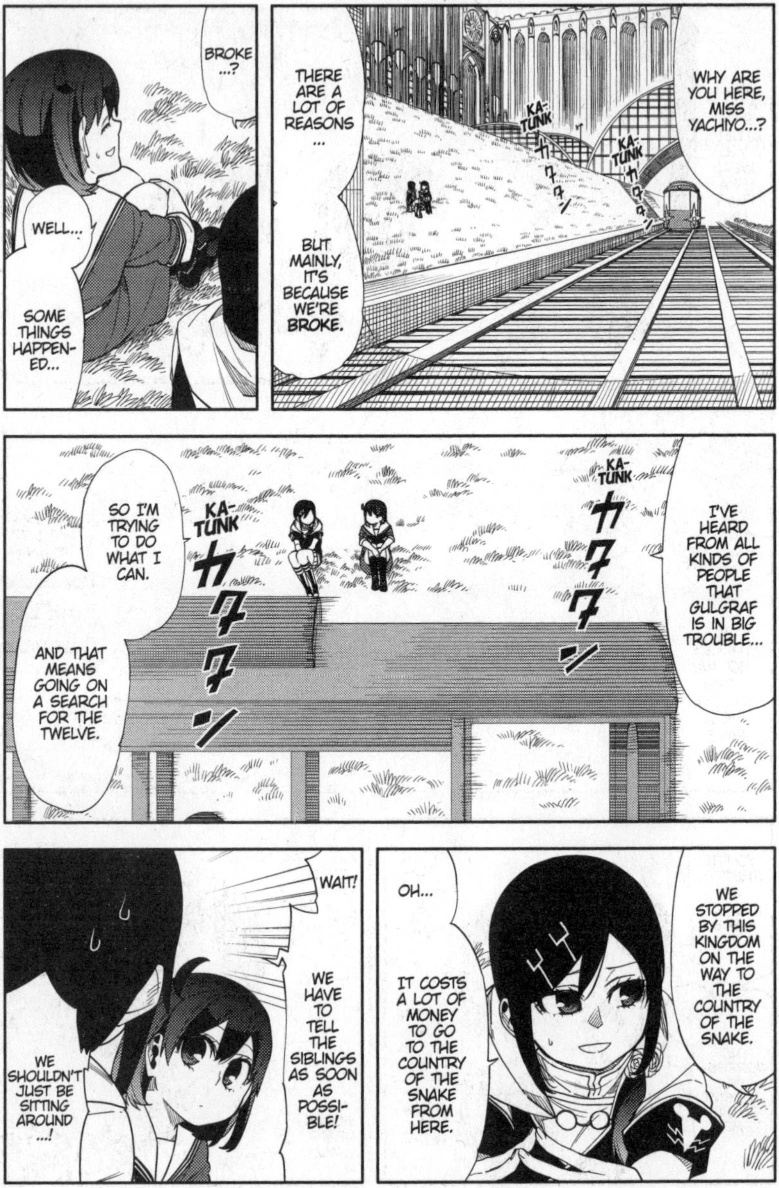
WHY ARE YOU HERE, MISS YACHIYO...?
KA-TUNK
KA-TUNK
THERE ARE A LOT OF REASONS ...
BUT MAINLY, IT'S BECAUSE WE'RE BROKE.
BROKE ...?
WELL...
SOME THINGS HAPPEN-ED...
KA-TUNK
I'VE HEARD FROM ALL KINDS OF PEOPLE THAT GULGRAF IS IN BIG TROUBLE...
KA-TUNK
SO I'M TRYING TO DO WHAT I CAN.
AND THAT MEANS GOING ON A SEARCH FOR THE TWELVE.
WE STOPPED BY THIS KINGDOM ON THE WAY TO THE COUNTRY OF THE SNAKE.
OH...
IT COSTS A LOT OF MONEY TO GO TO THE COUNTRY OF THE SNAKE FROM HERE.
WAIT!
WE HAVE TO TELL THE SIBLINGS AS SOON AS POSSI-BLE!
WE SHOULDN'T JUST BE SITTING AROUND ...!

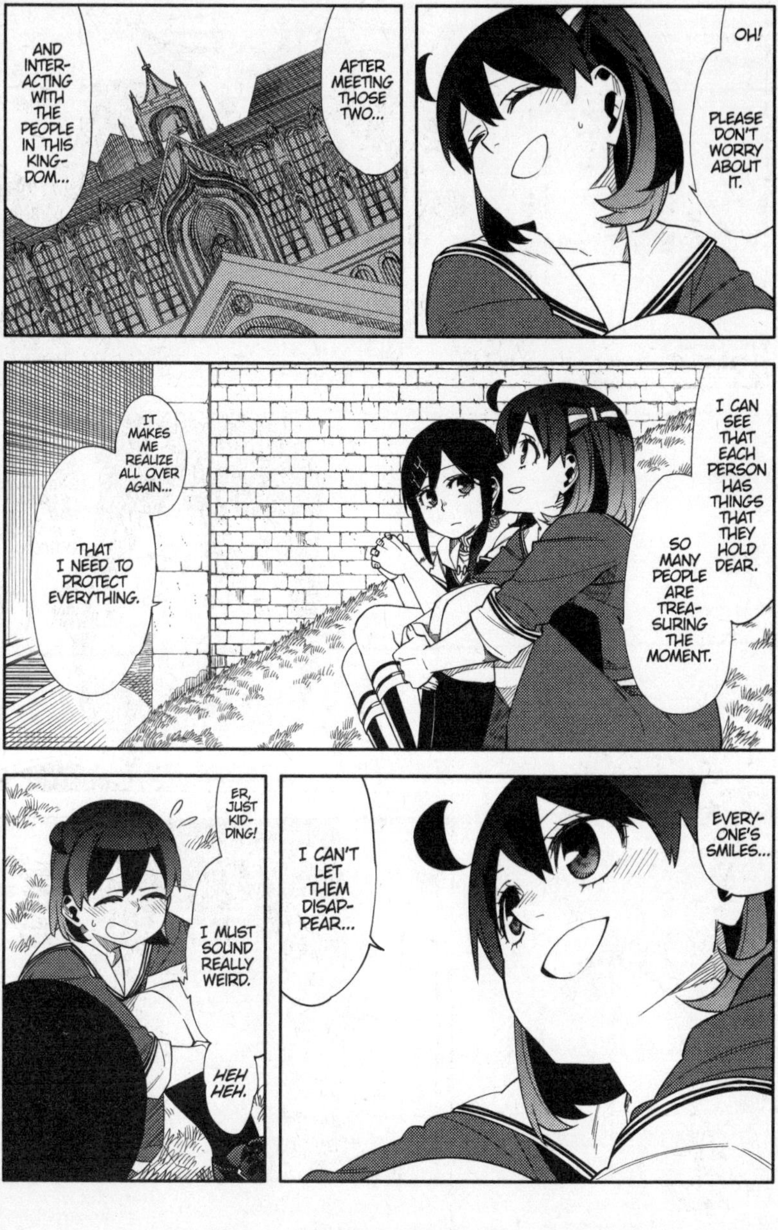
OH!
PLEASE DON'T WORRY ABOUT IT.
AFTER MEETING THOSE TWO...
AND INTERACTING WITH THE PEOPLE IN THIS KINGDOM...
I CAN SEE THAT EACH PERSON HAS THINGS THAT THEY HOLD DEAR.
SO MANY PEOPLE ARE TREASURING THE MOMENT.
IT MAKES ME REALIZE ALL OVER AGAIN...
THAT I NEED TO PROTECT EVERYTHING.
EVERYONE'S SMILES...
I CAN'T LET THEM DISAPPEAR...
ER, JUST KIDDING!
I MUST SOUND REALLY WEIRD.
HEH HEH.

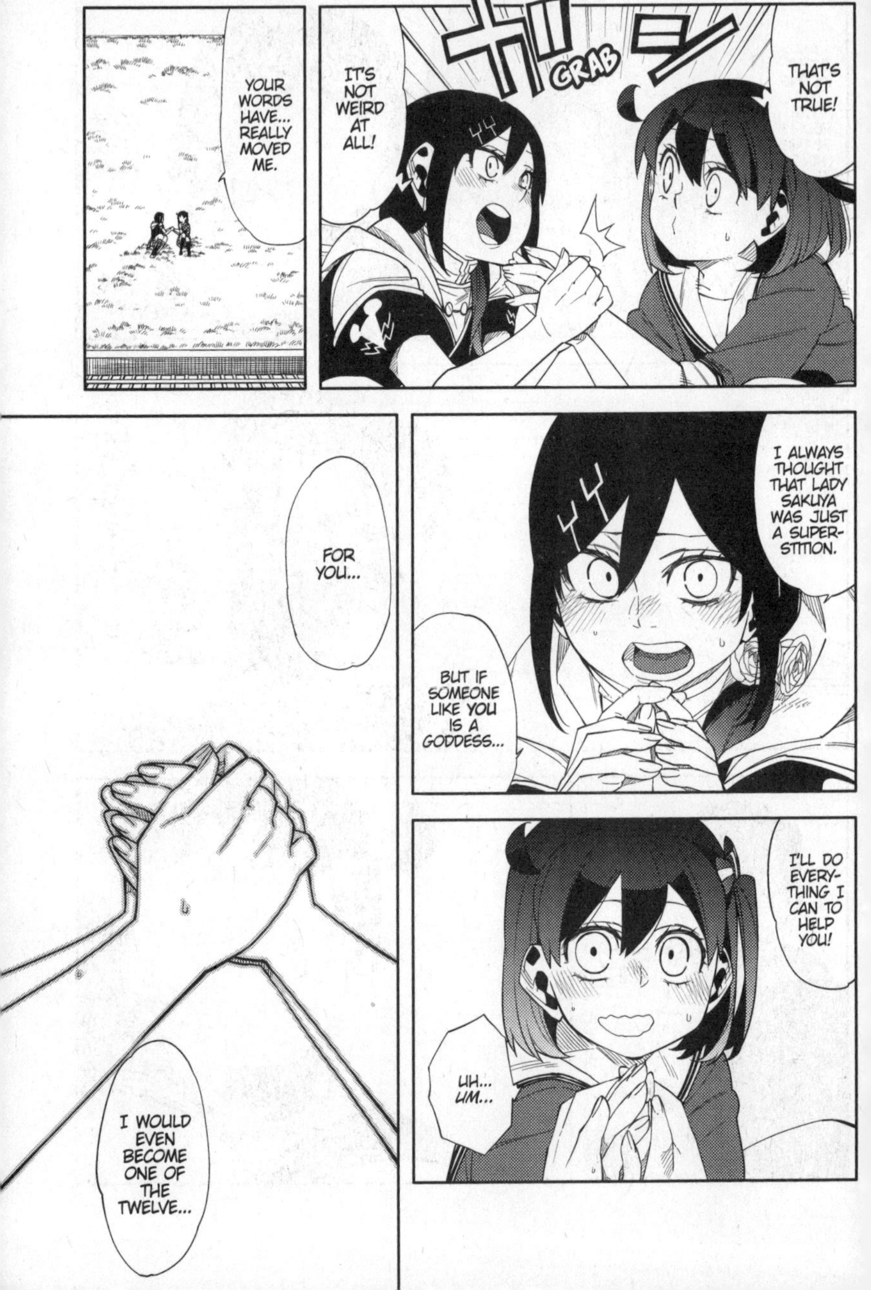
THAT'S NOT TRUE!
GRAB
IT'S NOT WEIRD AT ALL!
YOUR WORDS HAVE... REALLY MOVED ME.
I ALWAYS THOUGHT THAT LADY SAKUYA WAS JUST A SUPER-STITION.
BUT IF SOMEONE LIKE YOU IS A GODDESS...
I'LL DO EVERY-THING I CAN TO HELP YOU!
UH... UM...
FOR YOU...
I WOULD EVEN BECOME ONE OF THE TWELVE...

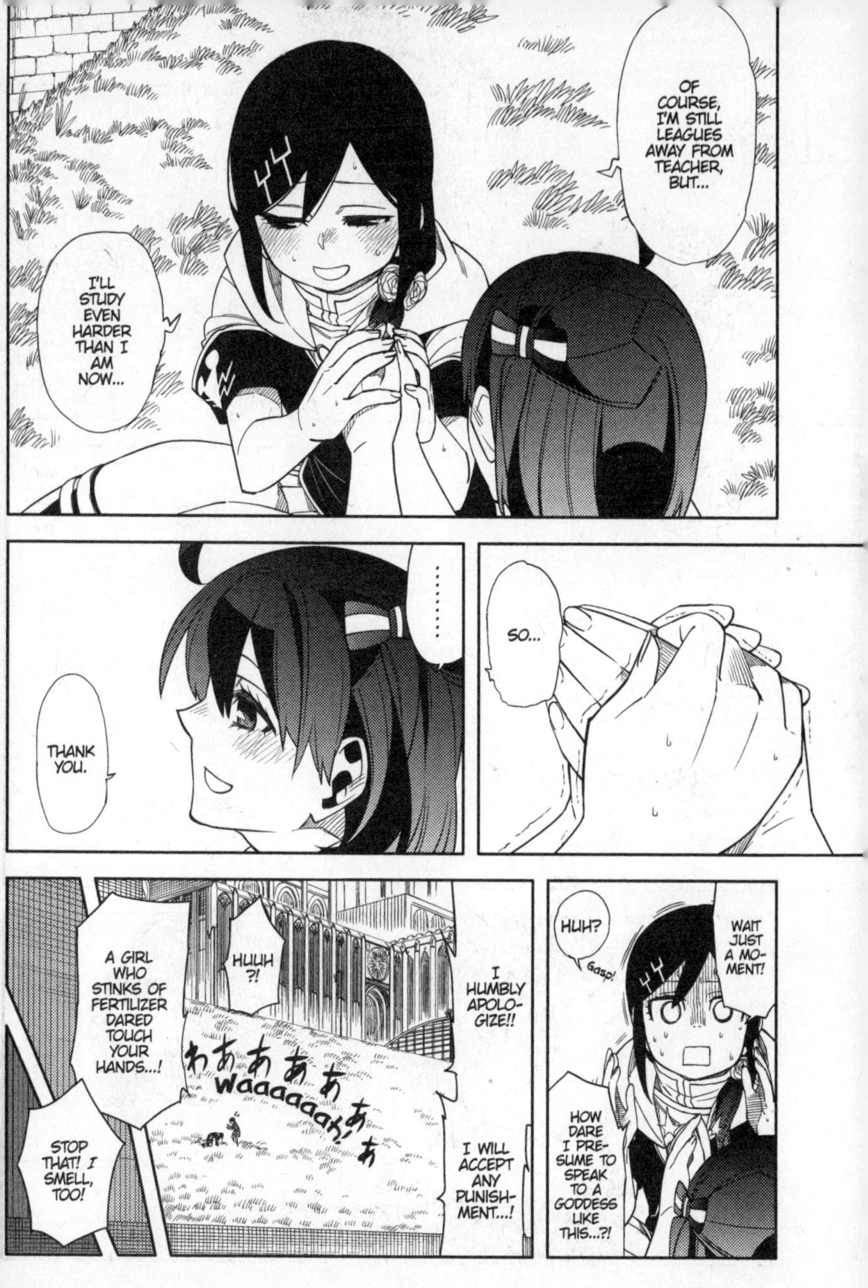
OF COURSE, I'M STILL LEAGUES AWAY FROM TEACHER, BUT...
I'LL STUDY EVEN HARDER THAN I AM NOW...
SO...
......
THANK YOU.
WAIT JUST A MOMENT!
HUH?
Gasp!
HOW DARE I PRESUME TO SPEAK TO A GODDESS LIKE THIS...?!
I HUMBLY APOLOGIZE!!
HUUH ?!
A GIRL WHO STINKS OF FERTILIZER DARED TOUCH YOUR HANDS...!
わあああああ
Waaaaaaah!
I WILL ACCEPT ANY PUNISHMENT...!
STOP THAT! I SMELL, TOO!

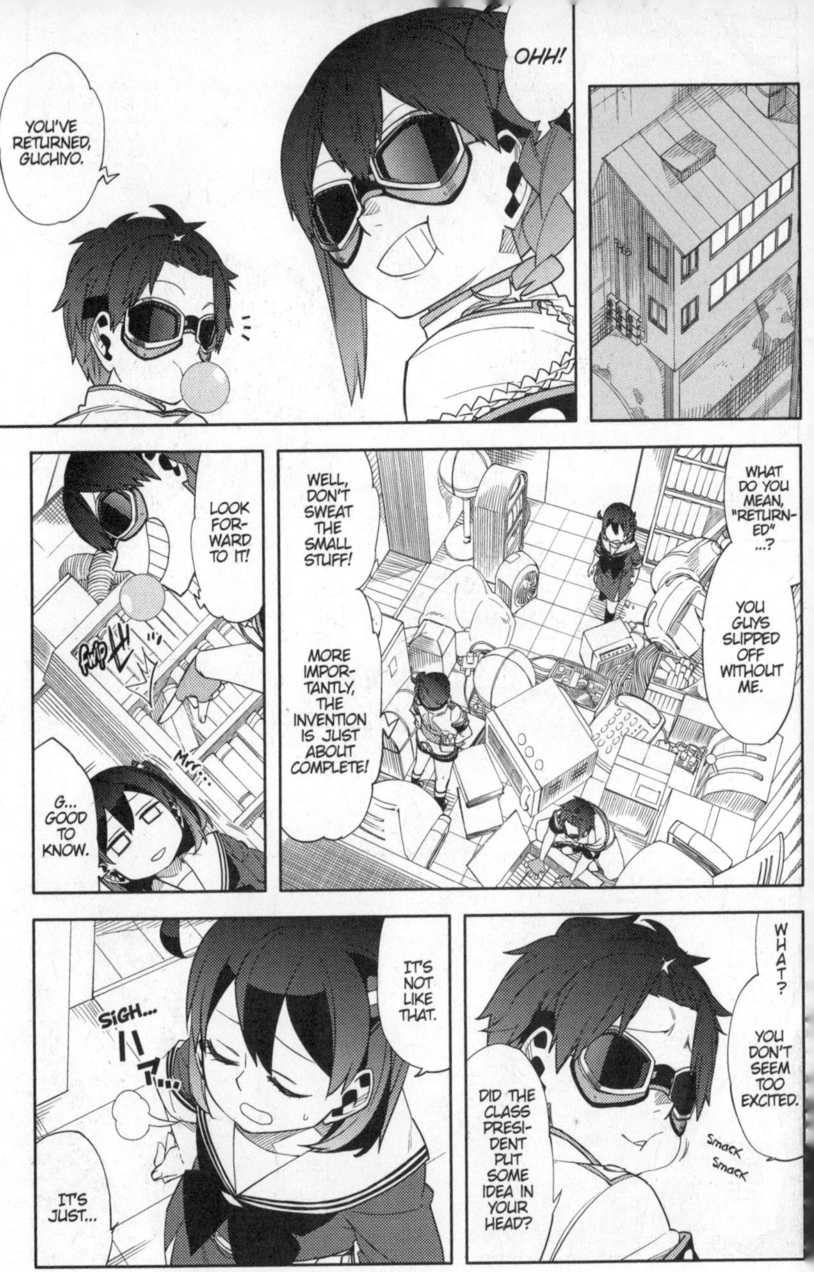
OHH!
YOU'VE RETURNED, GUCHIYO.
WHAT DO YOU MEAN, "RETURNED" ...?
YOU GUYS SLIPPED OFF WITHOUT ME.
WELL, DON'T SWEAT THE SMALL STUFF!
MORE IMPORTANTLY, THE INVENTION IS JUST ABOUT COMPLETE!
LOOK FORWARD TO IT!
Fwip
Mrr...
G... GOOD TO KNOW.
WHAT?
YOU DON'T SEEM TOO EXCITED.
Smack Smack
DID THE CLASS PRESIDENT PUT SOME IDEA IN YOUR HEAD?
IT'S NOT LIKE THAT.
SIGH...
IT'S JUST...

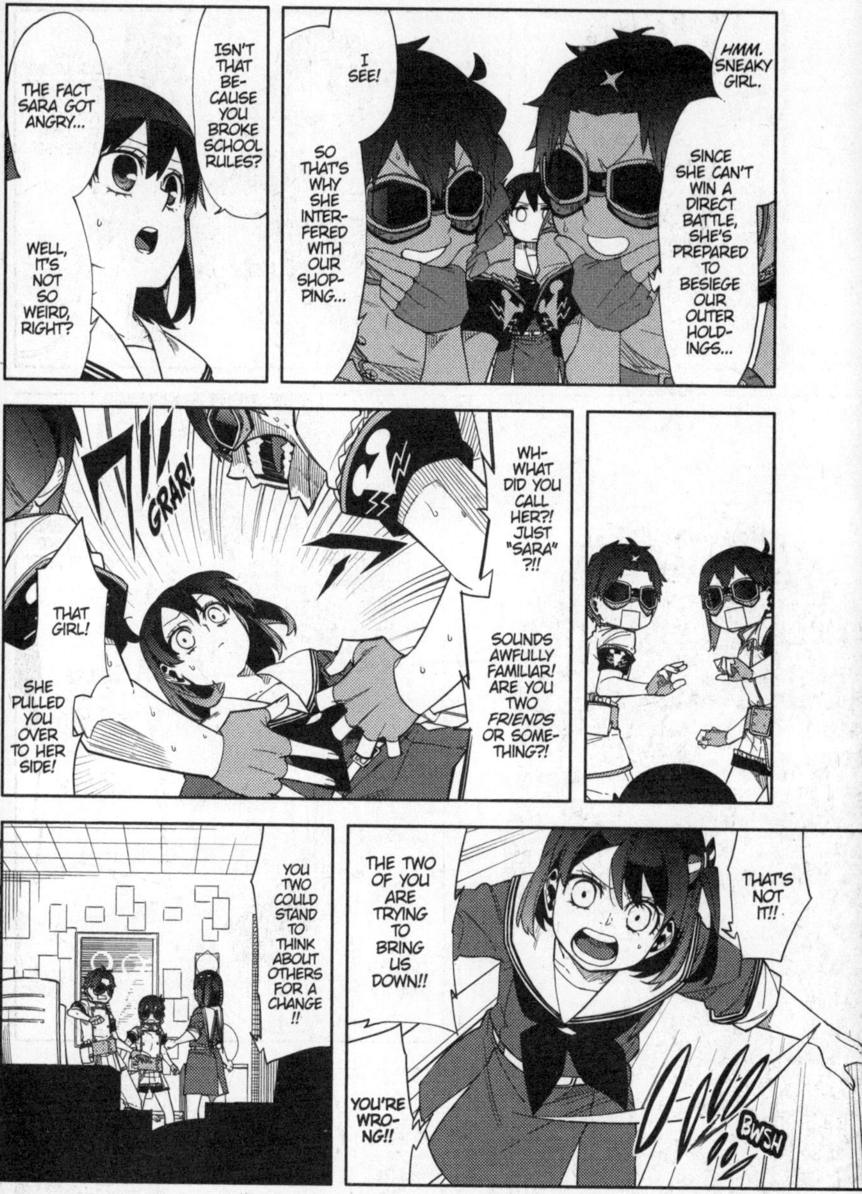
HMM. SNEAKY GIRL.
SINCE SHE CAN'T WIN A DIRECT BATTLE, SHE'S PREPARED TO BESIEGE OUR OUTER HOLDINGS...
I SEE!
SO THAT'S WHY SHE INTERFERED WITH OUR SHOPPING...
ISN'T THAT BECAUSE YOU BROKE SCHOOL RULES?
THE FACT SARA GOT ANGRY...
WELL, IT'S NOT SO WEIRD, RIGHT?
GRAR!
WH-WHAT DID YOU CALL HER?! JUST "SARA"?!!
SOUNDS AWFULLY FAMILIAR! ARE YOU TWO *FRIENDS* OR SOMETHING?!
THAT GIRL!
SHE PULLED YOU OVER TO HER SIDE!
THAT'S NOT IT!!
THE TWO OF YOU ARE TRYING TO BRING US DOWN!!
BWSH
YOU'RE WRONG!!
YOU TWO COULD STAND TO THINK ABOUT OTHERS FOR A CHANGE!!

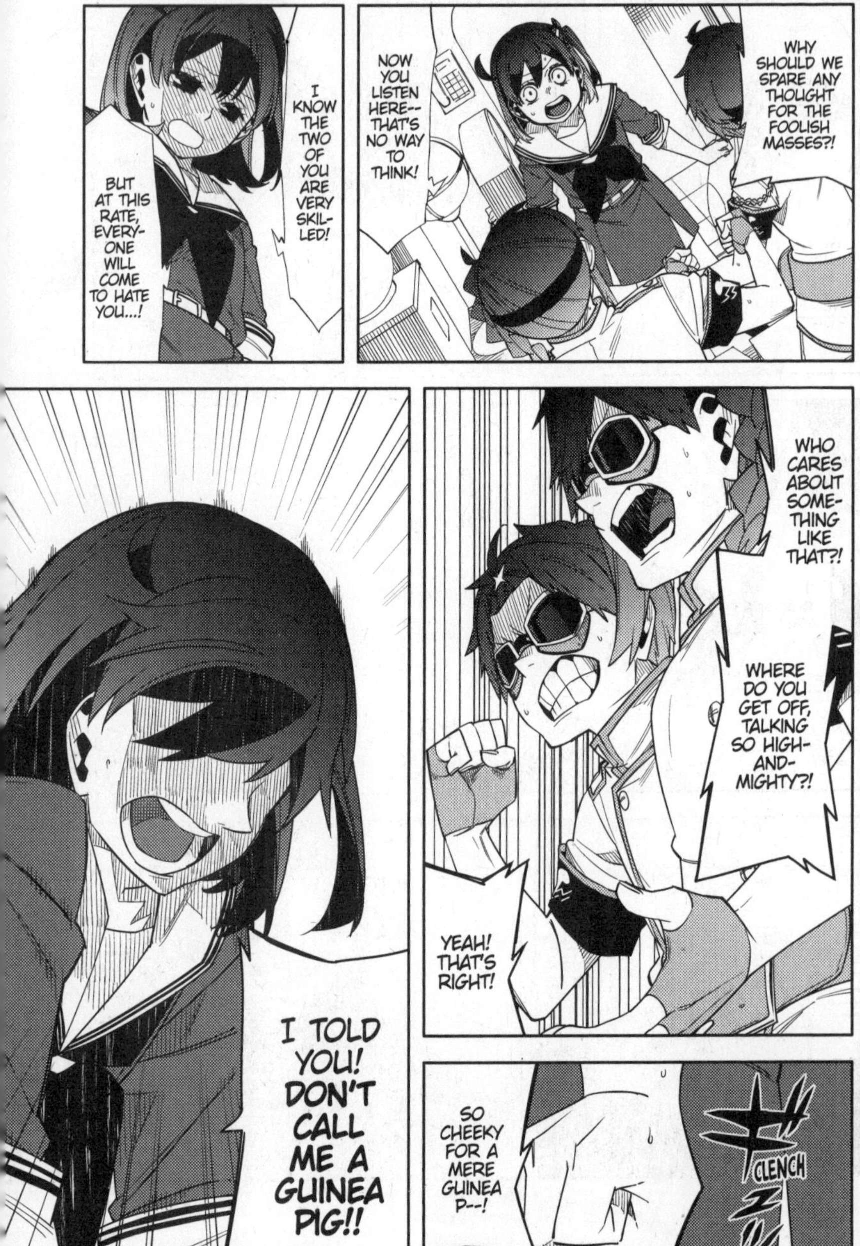
WHY SHOULD WE SPARE ANY THOUGHT FOR THE FOOLISH MASSES?!
NOW YOU LISTEN HERE-- THAT'S NO WAY TO THINK!
I KNOW THE TWO OF YOU ARE VERY SKIL-LED!
BUT AT THIS RATE, EVERY-ONE WILL COME TO HATE YOU...!
WHO CARES ABOUT SOME-THING LIKE THAT?!
WHERE DO YOU GET OFF, TALKING SO HIGH-AND-MIGHTY?!
YEAH! THAT'S RIGHT!
CLENCH
SO CHEEKY FOR A MERE GUINEA P--!
I TOLD YOU! DON'T CALL ME A GUINEA PIG!!

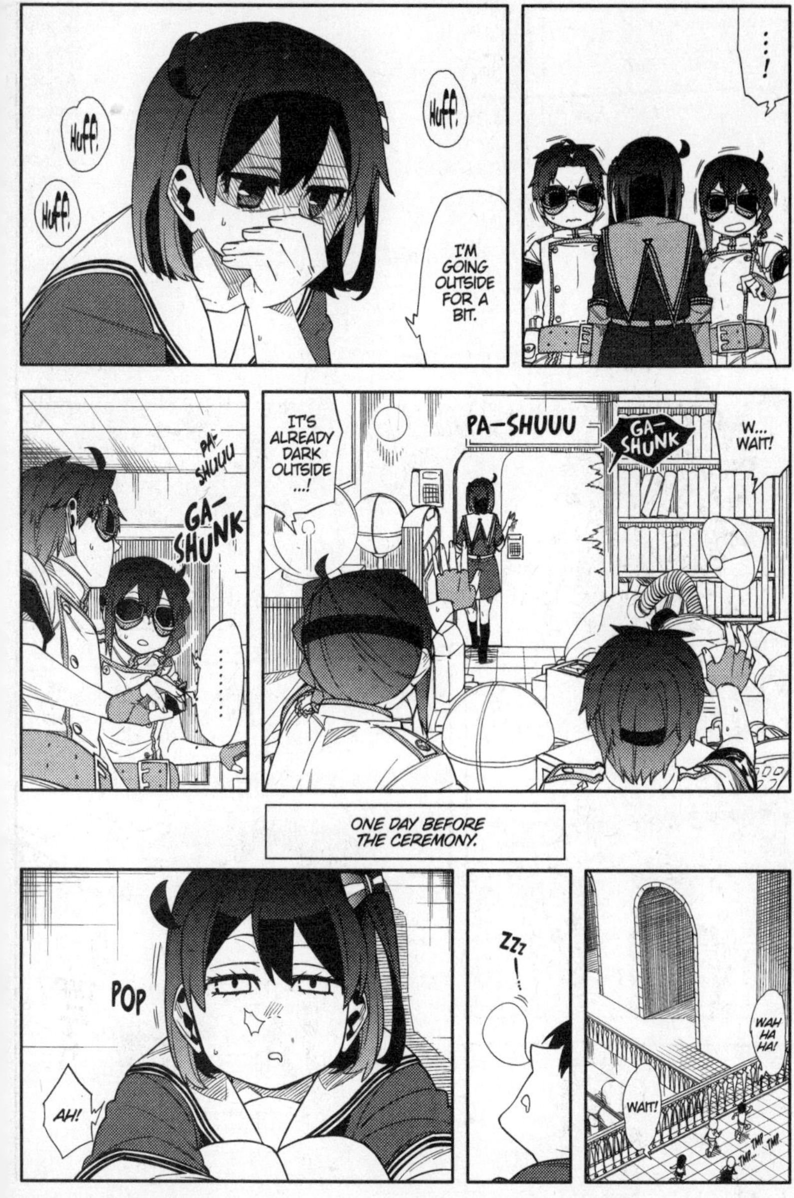
...!
HUFF!
HUFF!
HUFF!
I'M GOING OUTSIDE FOR A BIT.
W... WAIT!
GA-SHUNK
PA-SHUUU
IT'S ALREADY DARK OUTSIDE ...!
PA-SHUUU
GA-SHUNK
......
ONE DAY BEFORE THE CEREMONY.
WAH HA HA!
WAIT!
TMP... TMP TMP
ZZZ
!...
POP
AH!

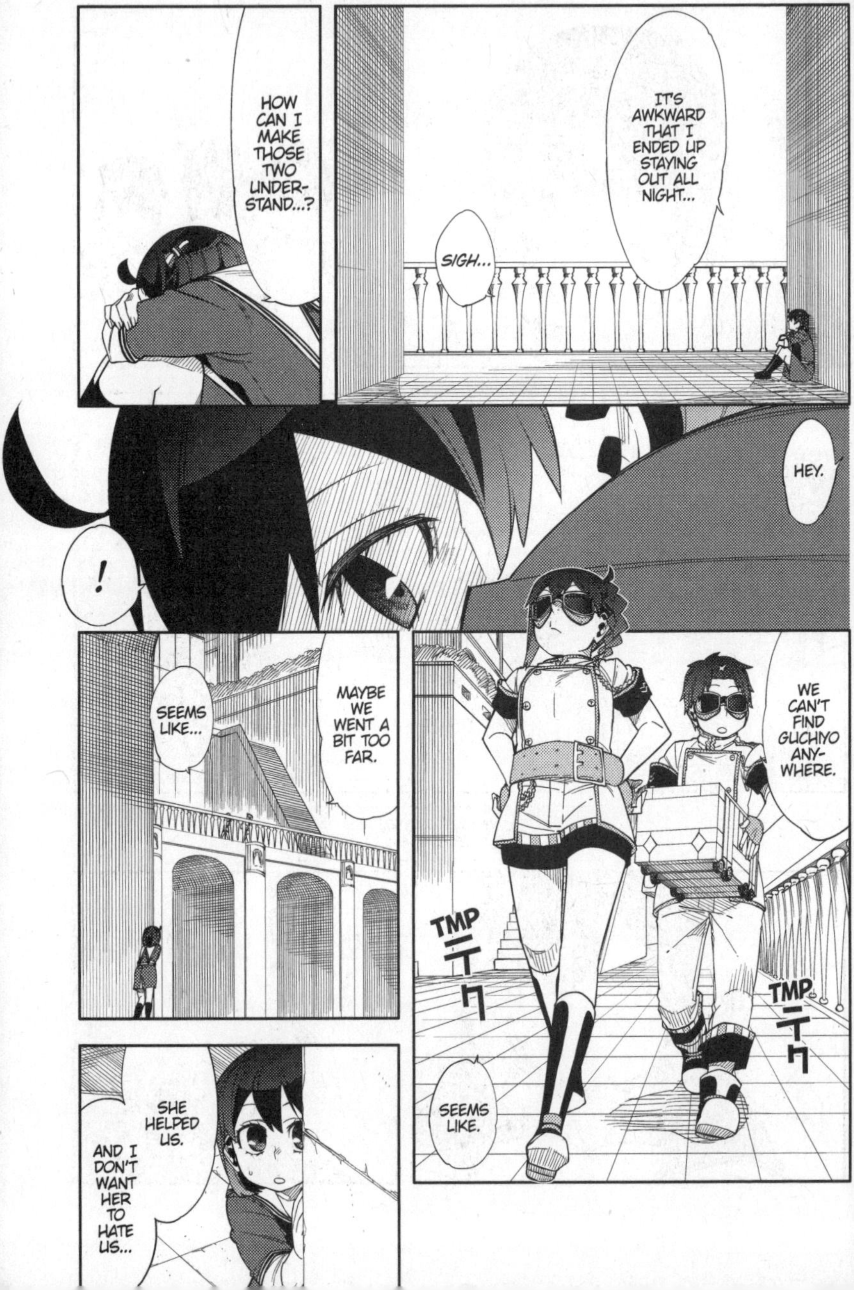
IT'S AWKWARD THAT I ENDED UP STAYING OUT ALL NIGHT...
SIGH...
HOW CAN I MAKE THOSE TWO UNDER-STAND...?
HEY.
!
WE CAN'T FIND GUCHIYO ANY-WHERE.
TMP テク
TMP テク
SEEMS LIKE.
MAYBE WE WENT A BIT TOO FAR.
SEEMS LIKE...
SHE HELPED US.
AND I DON'T WANT HER TO HATE US...

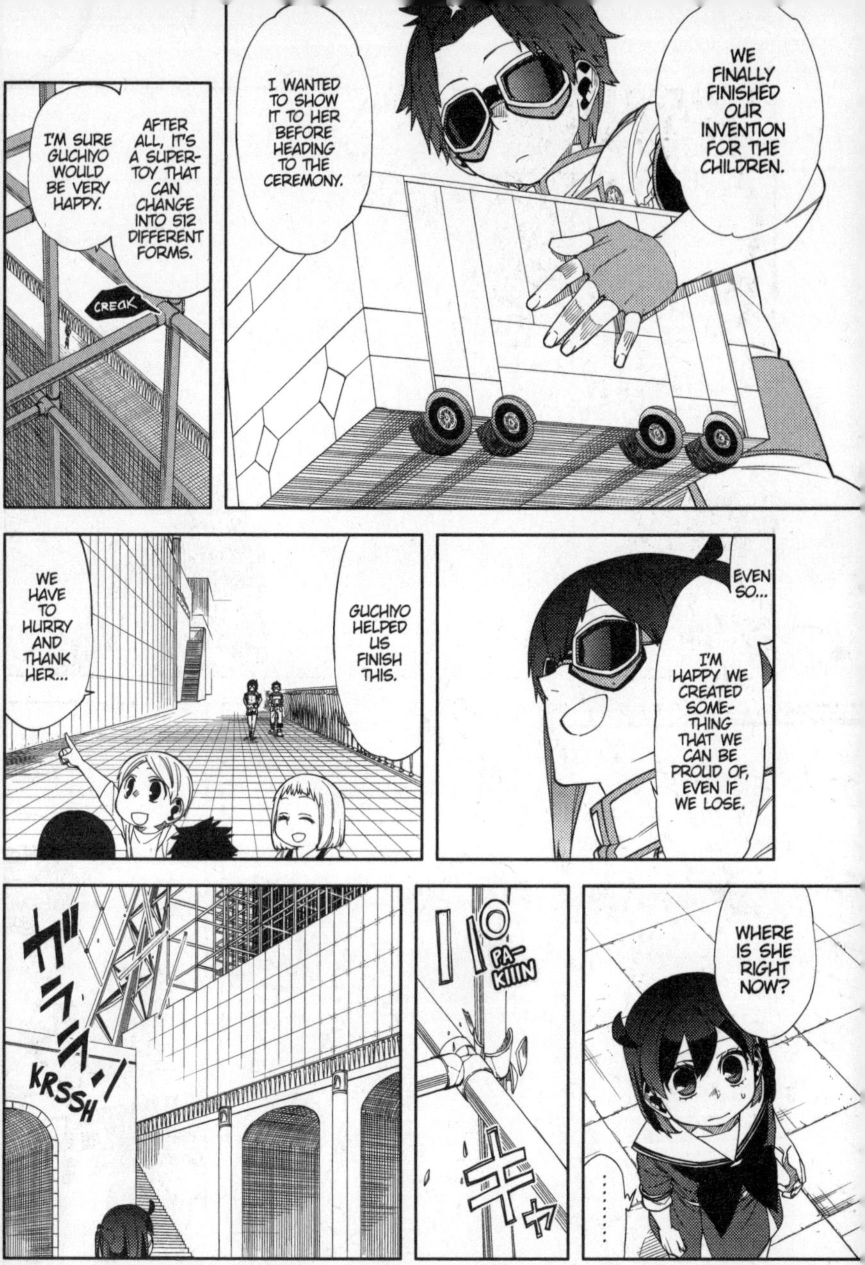
WE FINALLY FINISHED OUR INVENTION FOR THE CHILDREN.
I WANTED TO SHOW IT TO HER BEFORE HEADING TO THE CEREMONY.
AFTER ALL, IT'S A SUPER-TOY THAT CAN CHANGE INTO 512 DIFFERENT FORMS.
I'M SURE GUCHIYO WOULD BE VERY HAPPY.
CREAK
EVEN SO...
I'M HAPPY WE CREATED SOME-THING THAT WE CAN BE PROUD OF, EVEN IF WE LOSE.
GUCHIYO HELPED US FINISH THIS.
WE HAVE TO HURRY AND THANK HER...
WHERE IS SHE RIGHT NOW?
......
PA-KIIIN
KRSSH

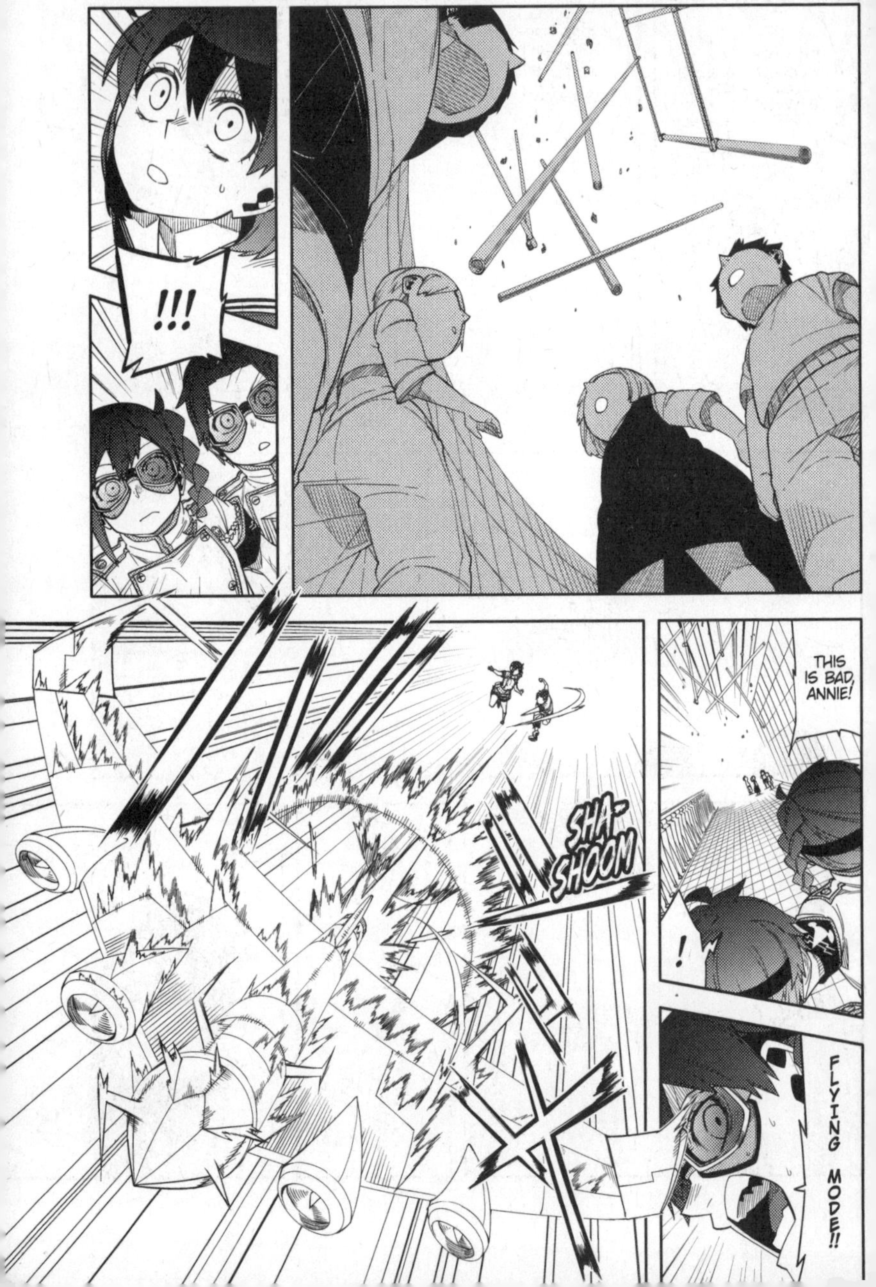
!!!
THIS IS BAD, ANNIE!
!
FLYING MODE!!
SHA-SHOOM

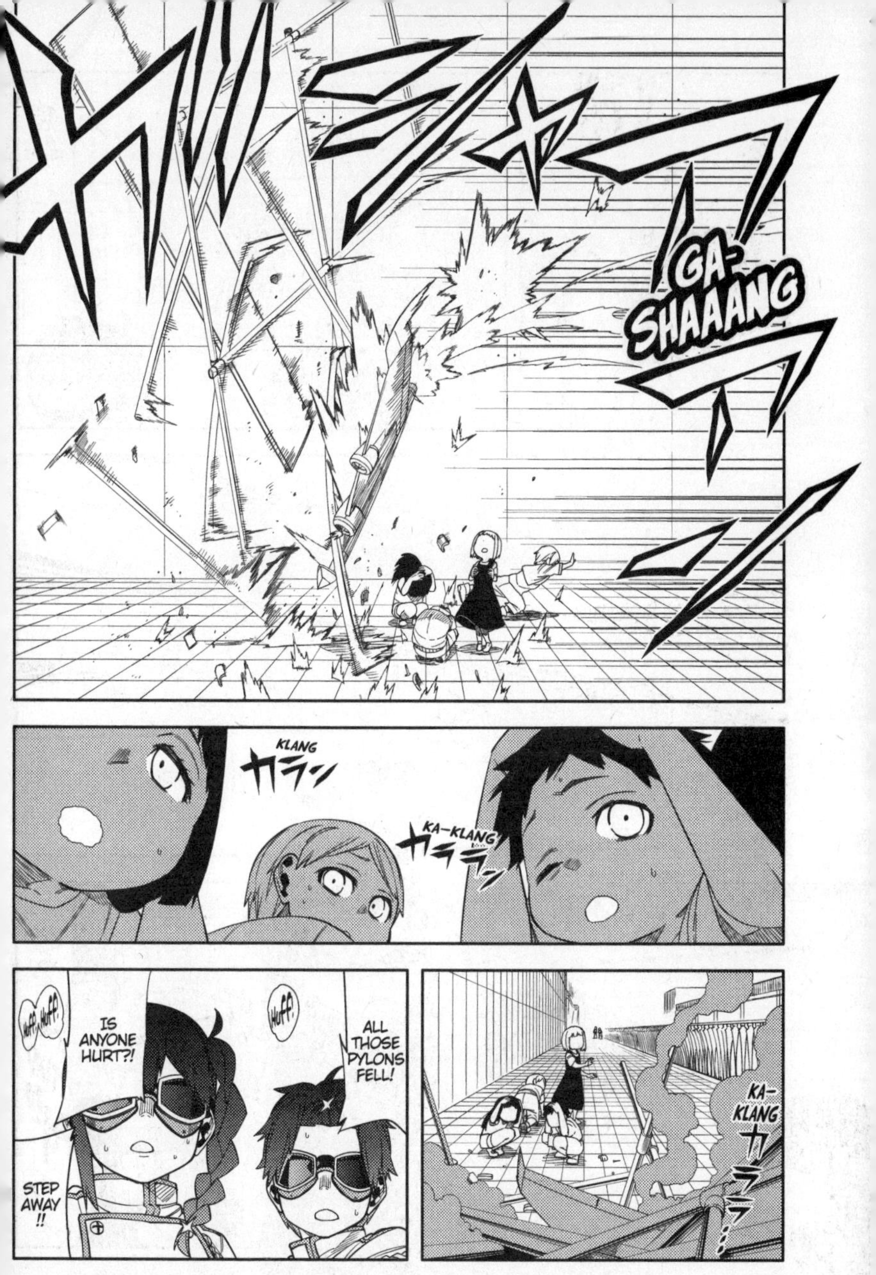
GA-SHAAANG
KLANG
KA-KLANG
KA-KLANG
ALL THOSE PYLONS FELL!
HUFF!
IS ANYONE HURT?!
HUFF, HUFF
STEP AWAY!!

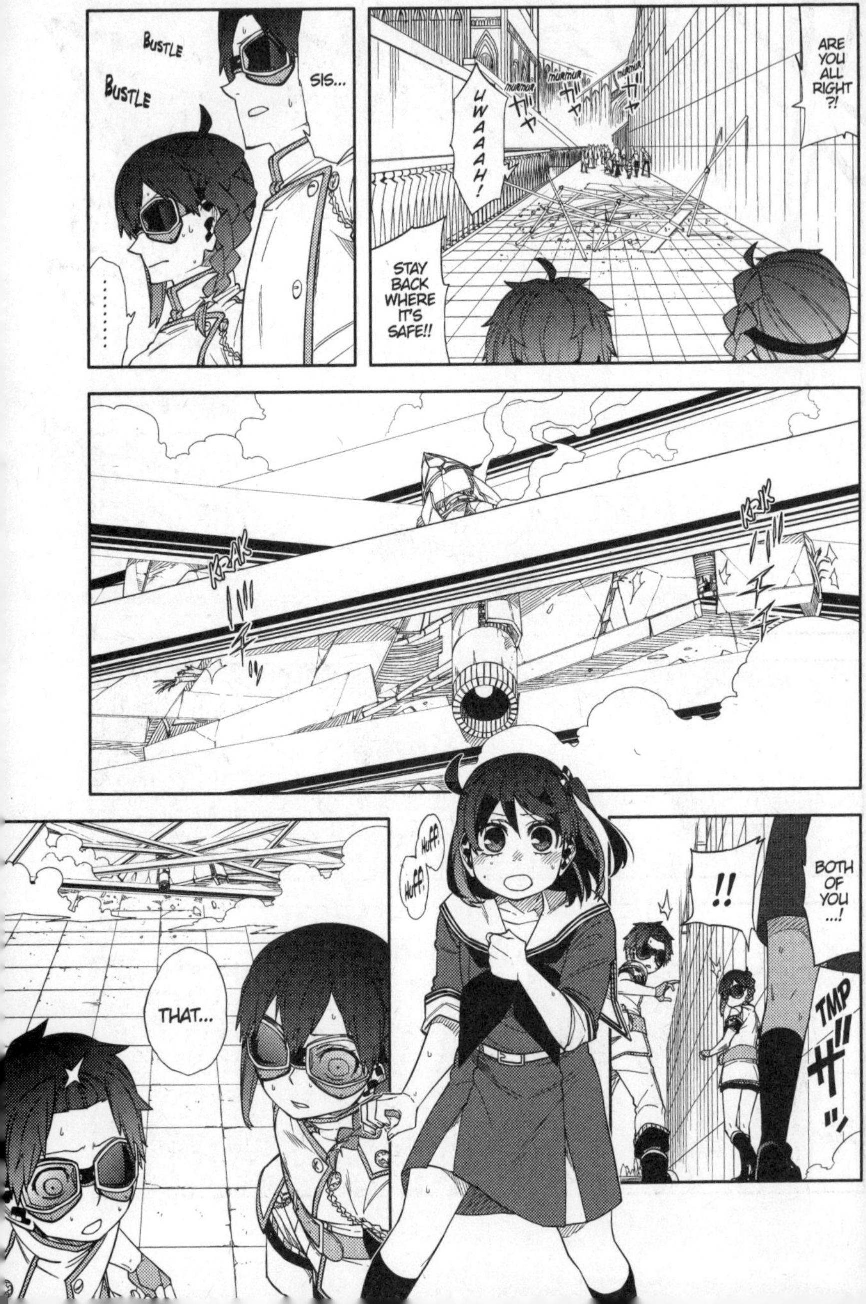
ARE YOU ALL RIGHT?!
MURMUR ガヤ
MURMUR ガヤ
MURMUR ガヤ
UWAAAAH!
STAY BACK WHERE IT'S SAFE!!
BUSTLE
BUSTLE
SIS...
......
KRIK
KRAK
BOTH OF YOU ...!
!!
TMP ザッ
HUFF.
HUFF.
THAT...

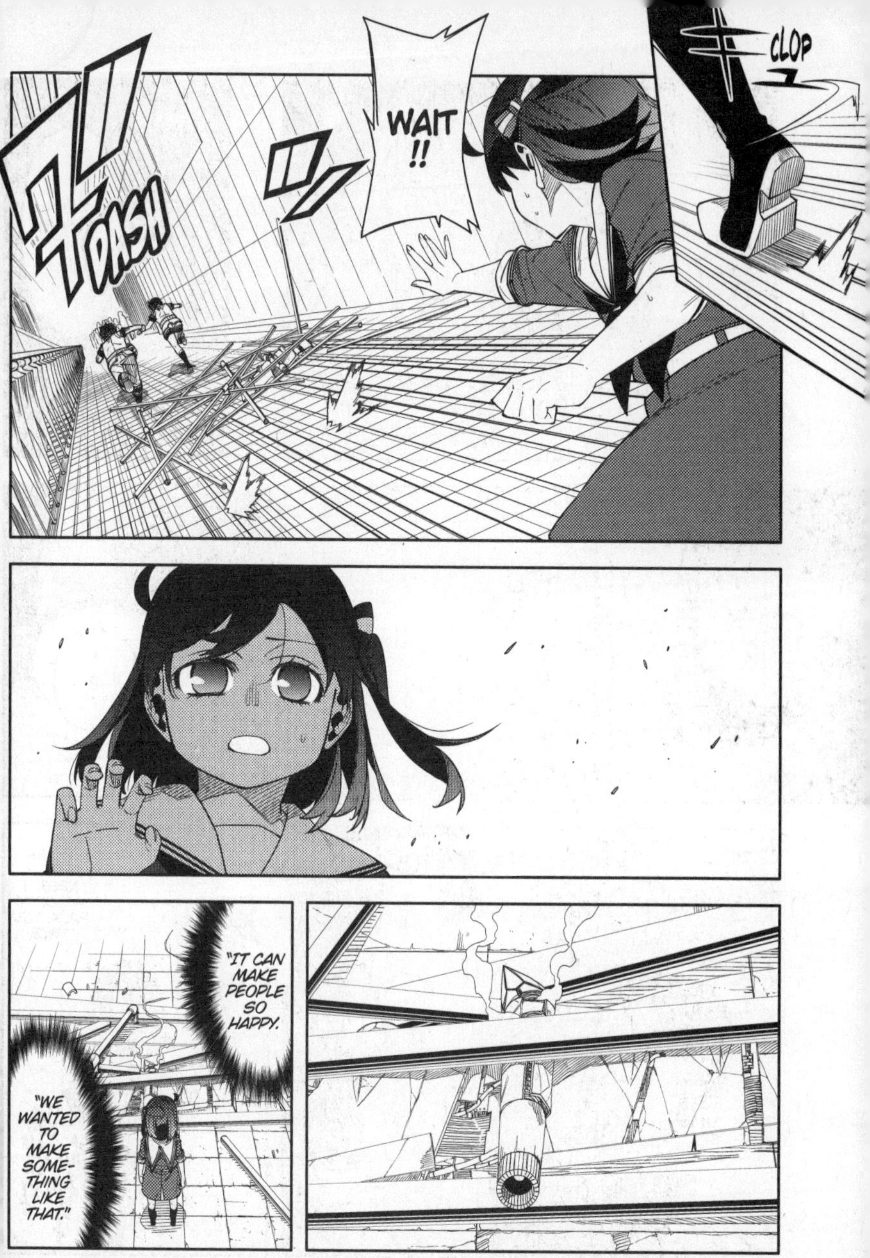
CLOP
WAIT !!
DASH
"IT CAN MAKE PEOPLE SO HAPPY.
"WE WANTED TO MAKE SOME-THING LIKE THAT."

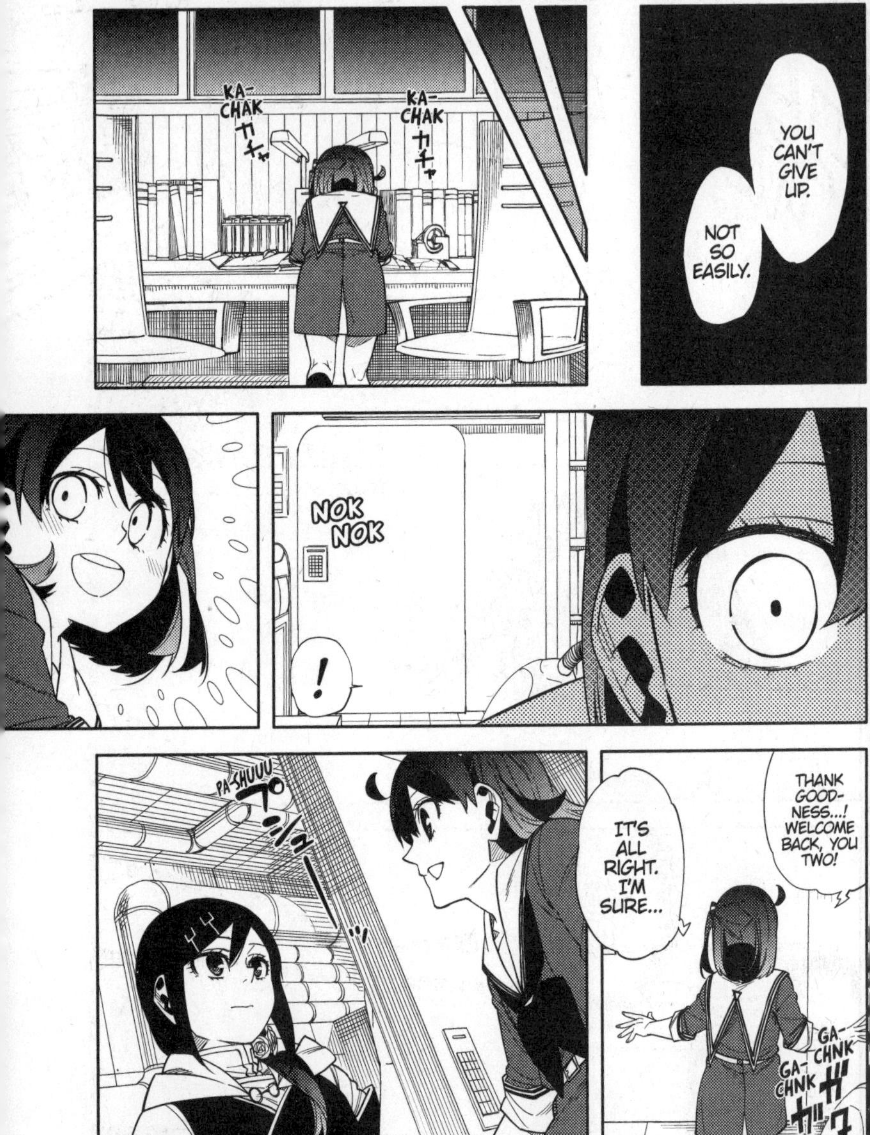
YOU CAN'T GIVE UP.
NOT SO EASILY.
KA-CHAK
KA-CHAK
NOK NOK
!
THANK GOODNESS...! WELCOME BACK, YOU TWO!
GA-CHNK
GA-CHNK
IT'S ALL RIGHT. I'M SURE...
PA-SHUUU

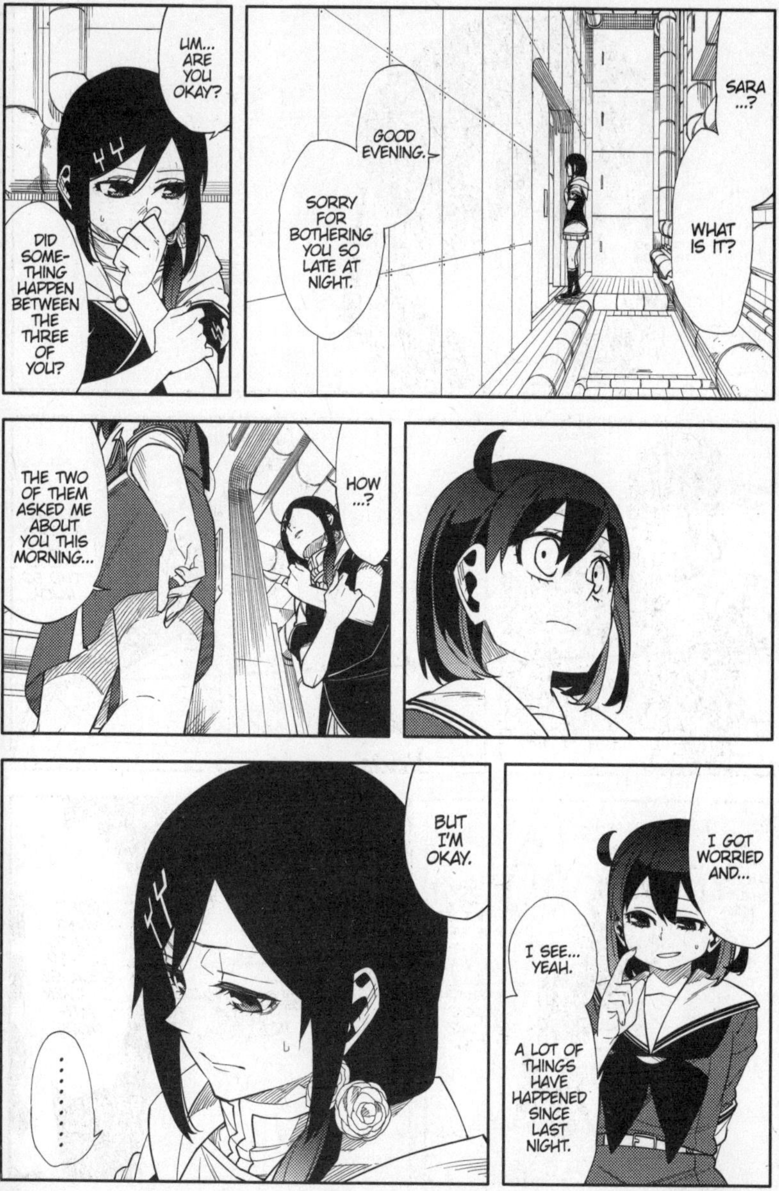
SARA ...?
WHAT IS IT?
GOOD EVENING.
SORRY FOR BOTHERING YOU SO LATE AT NIGHT.
UM... ARE YOU OKAY?
DID SOME-THING HAPPEN BETWEEN THE THREE OF YOU?
HOW ...?
THE TWO OF THEM ASKED ME ABOUT YOU THIS MORNING...
I GOT WORRIED AND...
I SEE... YEAH.
A LOT OF THINGS HAVE HAPPENED SINCE LAST NIGHT.
BUT I'M OKAY.
....

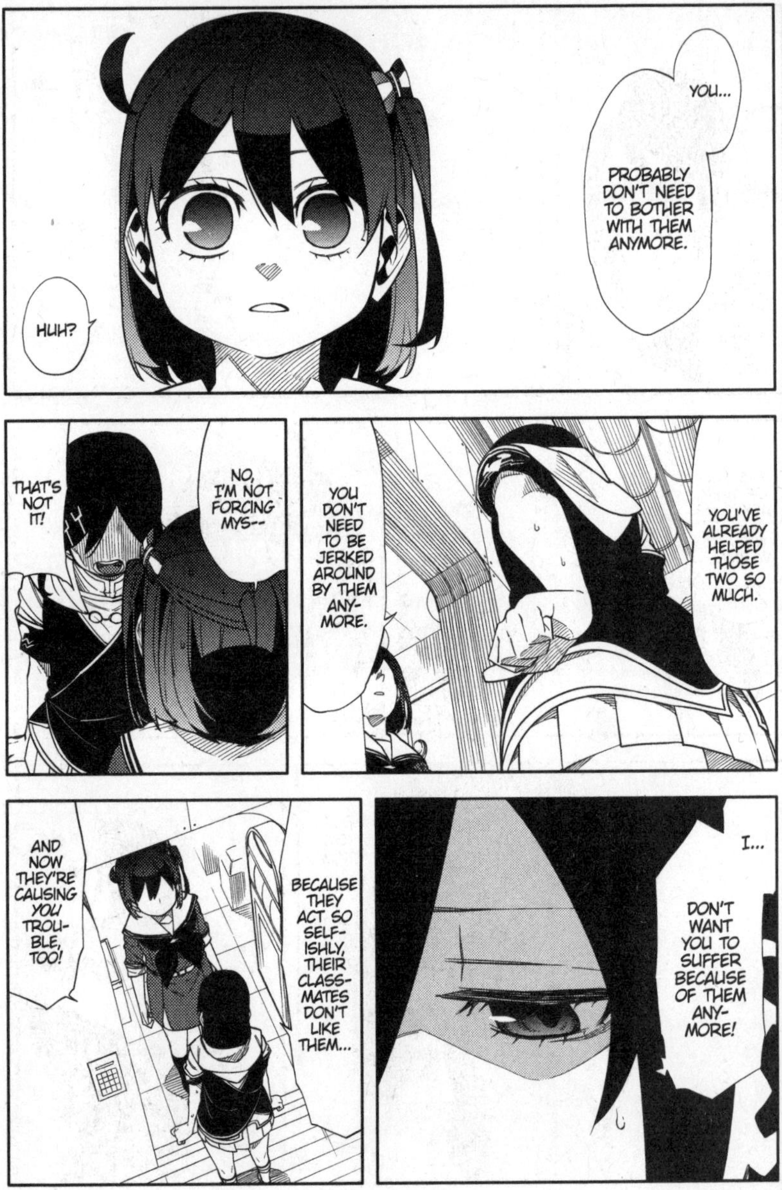

YOU...
PROBABLY DON'T NEED TO BOTHER WITH THEM ANYMORE.
HUH?
YOU'VE ALREADY HELPED THOSE TWO SO MUCH.
YOU DON'T NEED TO BE JERKED AROUND BY THEM ANYMORE.
NO, I'M NOT FORCING MYS--
THAT'S NOT IT!
I...
DON'T WANT YOU TO SUFFER BECAUSE OF THEM ANYMORE!
BECAUSE THEY ACT SO SELFISHLY, THEIR CLASSMATES DON'T LIKE THEM...
AND NOW THEY'RE CAUSING *YOU* TROUBLE, TOO!

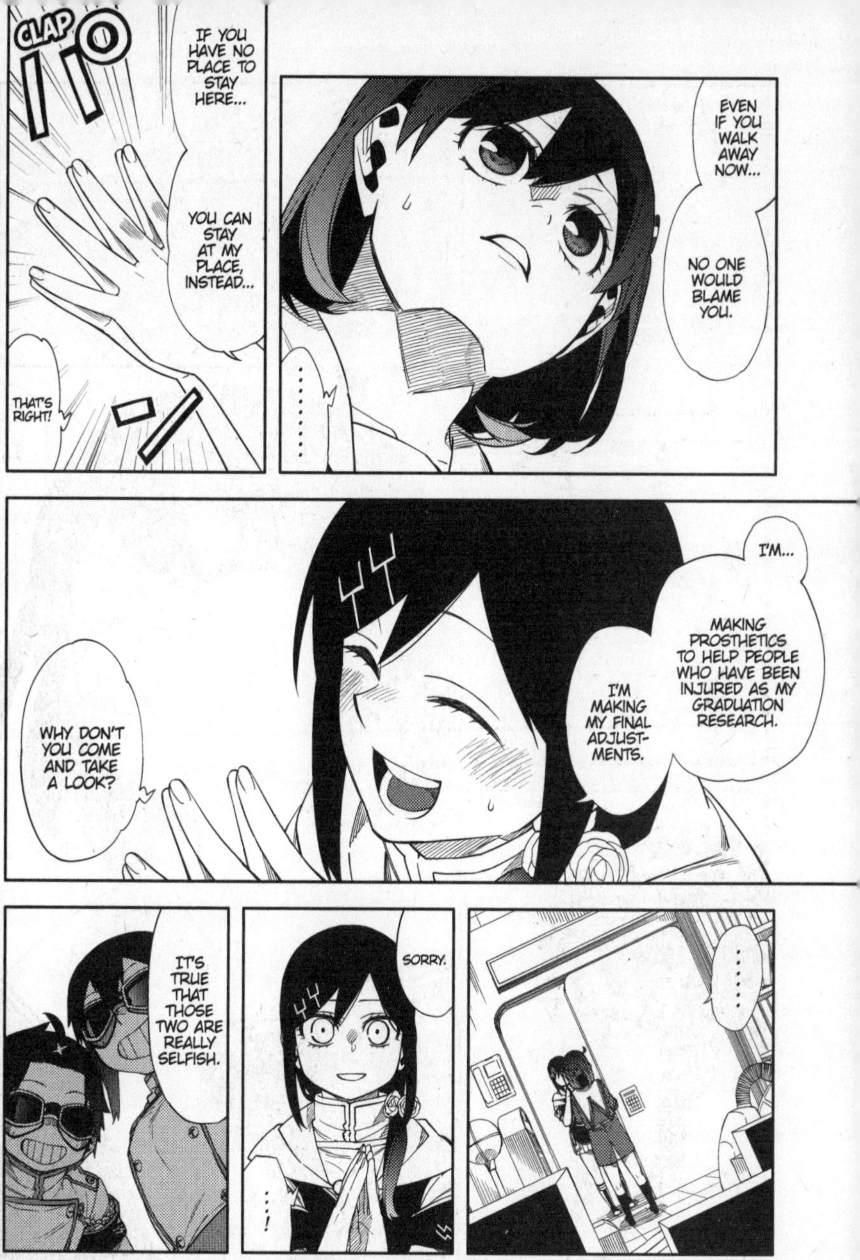
EVEN IF YOU WALK AWAY NOW...
NO ONE WOULD BLAME YOU.
......
CLAP
IF YOU HAVE NO PLACE TO STAY HERE...
YOU CAN STAY AT MY PLACE, INSTEAD...
THAT'S RIGHT!
I'M...
MAKING PROSTHETICS TO HELP PEOPLE WHO HAVE BEEN INJURED AS MY GRADUATION RESEARCH.
I'M MAKING MY FINAL ADJUSTMENTS.
WHY DON'T YOU COME AND TAKE A LOOK?
......
SORRY.
...!
IT'S TRUE THAT THOSE TWO ARE REALLY SELFISH.

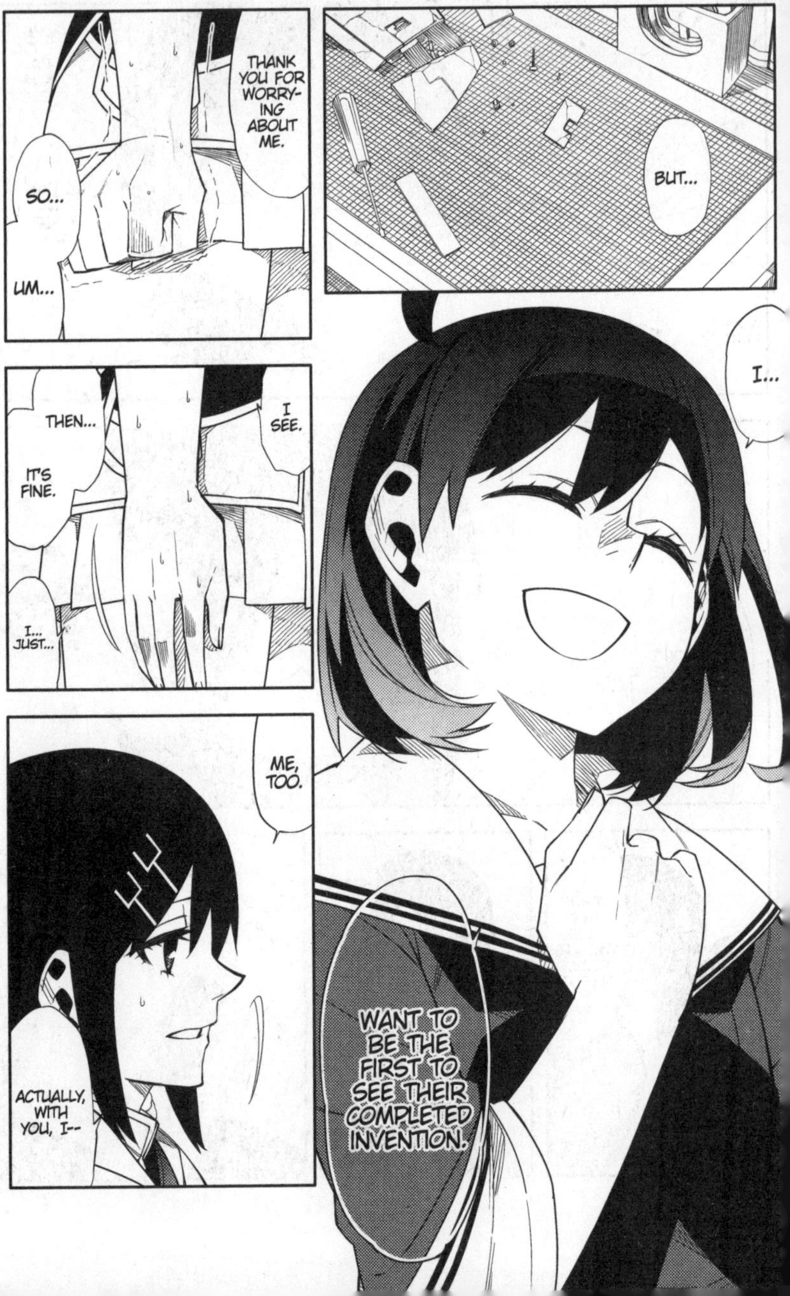
BUT...
THANK YOU FOR WORRYING ABOUT ME.
SO...
UM...
I...
WANT TO BE THE FIRST TO SEE THEIR COMPLETED INVENTION.
I SEE.
THEN...
IT'S FINE.
I... JUST...
ME, TOO.
ACTUALLY, WITH YOU, I--

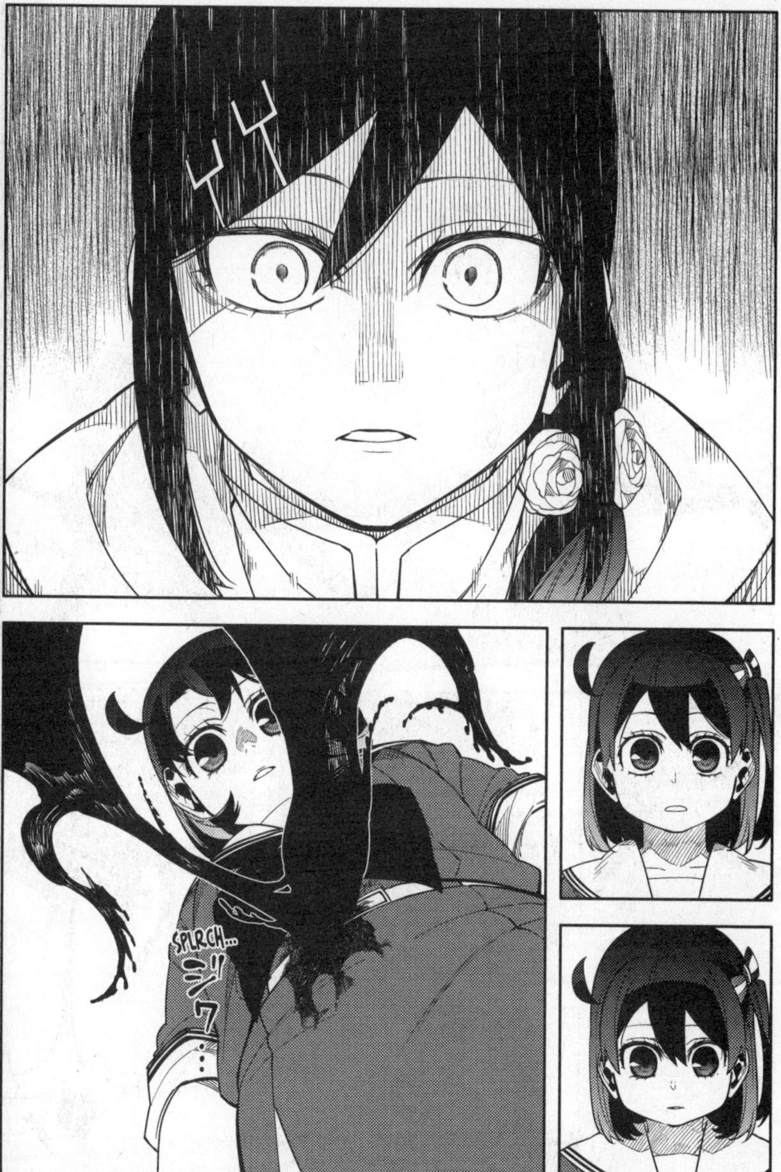
SPLRCH...
ジワ…

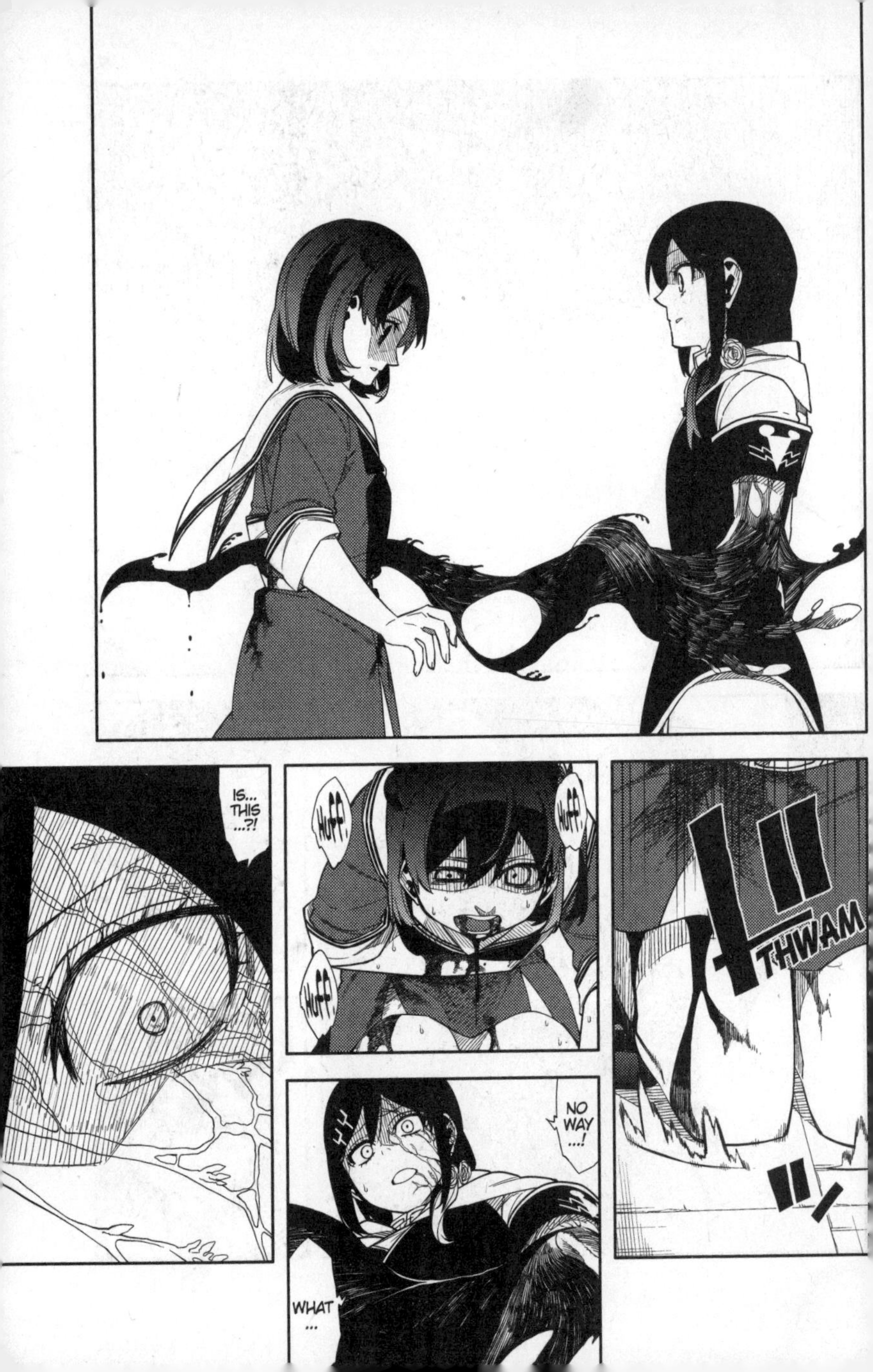
THWAM
HUFF,
HUFF,
HUFF,
NO WAY ...!
WHAT ...
IS... THIS ...?!

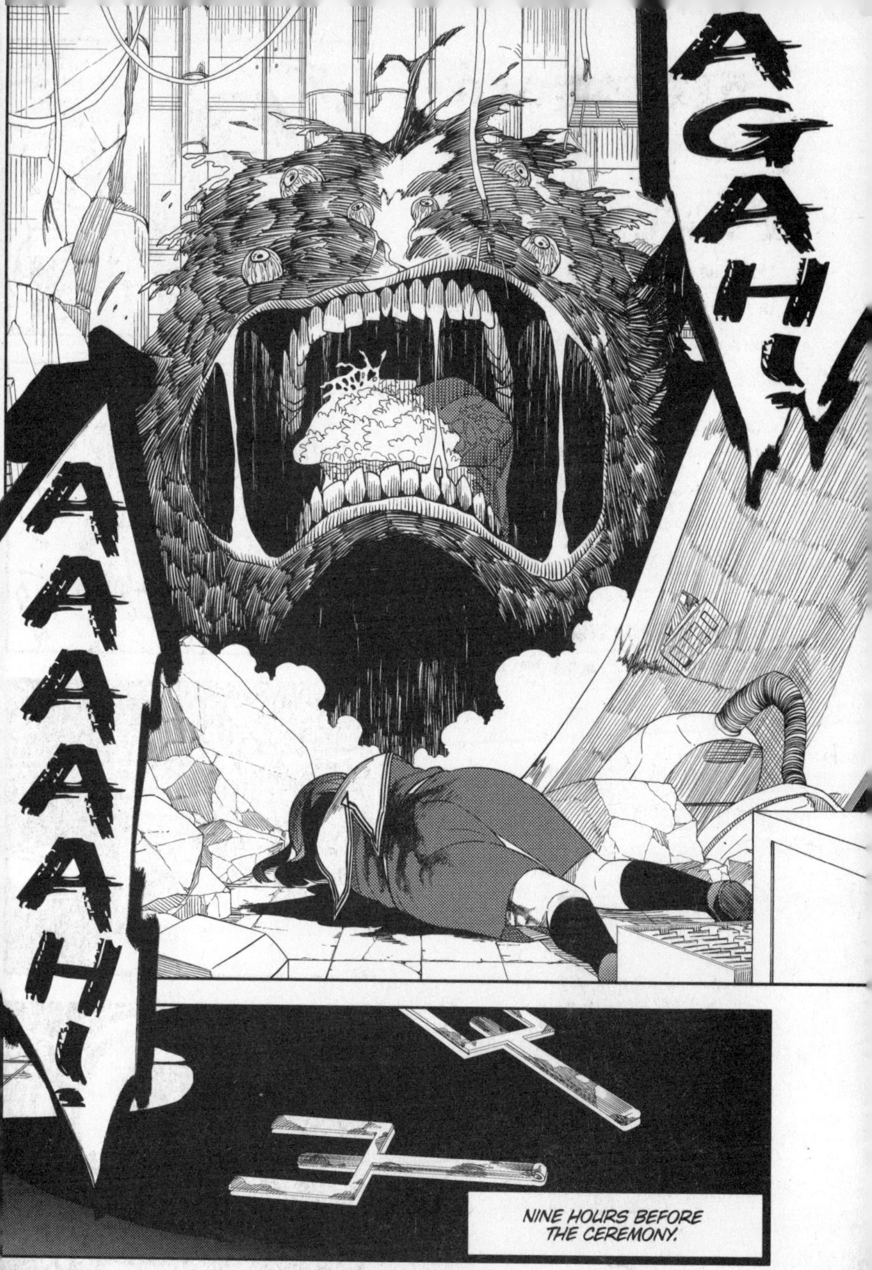
AGAHN
AAAAAH!
NINE HOURS BEFORE THE CEREMONY.

To be continued...